Music as Social Text

Music as Social Text

John Shepherd

Polity Press

First published 1991 by Polity Press
in association with Basil Blackwell

Editorial office:
Polity Press, 65 Bridge Street,
Cambridge CB2 1UR, UK

Marketing and production:
Basil Blackwell Ltd
108 Cowley Road, Oxford OX4 1JF, UK

Basil Blackwell Inc., 3 Cambridge Center,
Cambridge, MA 02142, USA

ISBN 0 7456 0825 6
ISBN 0 7456 0826 4 (pbk)

British Library Cataloguing in Publication Data

A CIP catalogue record for this book is available
from the British Library.

Library of Congress Cataloging in Publication Data

A CIP catalogue record for this book is available
from the Library of Congress.

Typeset in 10 on 12 pt Sabon
by Wearside Tradespools, Fulwell, Sunderland
Printed in Great Britain by Billing and Sons Ltd.,
Worcester

Contents

Preface

The work in this book dates back some sixteen years to my time as a graduate student at the University of York. The thinking it represents has benefited from exchanges and conversations with individuals too numerous to mention. I would, however, like to thank in a collective manner all my friends and colleagues in the International Association for the Study of Popular Music. The criticisms to which my work has been subjected in this forum since 1983 have been of enormous benefit to me. I would also like to mention five people by name: Trevor Wishart, who supervised my doctoral thesis and without whose support, encouragement and constant and constructive criticism I would never have become launched on the path of which this book is a temporary summation; Graham Vulliamy, with whom I have enjoyed many years of collaboration in the field of music education; Charlie Keil, my musical and social conscience, who never lets tortuous theory stand in the way of true insight; Simon Frith, who has done so much for popular music studies, and has on many occasions been a gracious and thoughtful discussant of my work; and Alan Gillmor, my erstwhile teacher, my friend and now a most valued colleague.

I would also like to thank Jenny Giles-Davis for allowing me to use her material in chapter 9. The fieldwork reported in this chapter was carried out by Jenny, and many of the concepts to do with the relation of sound to subjectivity as reported in this chapter originated with her. Thanks are also due to Jean Brearley, the editorial assistant of Carleton University's Centre for Research on Culture and Society, who word-processed the text.

Almost all the work in this book has previously been published elsewhere. I would like to thank Transaction Books for permission to use material in chapters 1, 2, 3, 5 and 6 which first appeared in *Whose Music? A Sociology of Musical Languages* (New Brunswick: 1980); *Catalyst: Social Science Controversy* for permission to use material in chapter 4 which first appeared in 'Music and Social Control: An Essay on the Sociology of Musical Knowledge' (no. 13, 1979); the *Canadian*

University Music Review for permission to use material in chapter 1 which first appeared in 'Towards a Sociology of Musical Styles' (no. 2, 1982); the Cambridge University Press for permission to use material in chapter 7 which first appeared in 'A Theoretical Model for the Socio-musicological Analysis of Popular Musics' in *Popular Music* (no. 2, 1982), and for permission to use material in chapter 8 which first appeared in 'Music and Male Hegemony', in Richard Leppert and Susan McClary (eds), *Music and Society: The Politics of Composition, Performance and Reception* (1987); the *Canadian Journal of Communication* for permission to use material in chapter 10 which first appeared in 'Prolegomena for the Critical Study of Popular Music' (vol. 11, no. 1, 1985); Sage Publications for permission to use material in chapter 5 which first appeared in 'Music Consumption and Cultural Self-Identities: Some Theoretical and Methodological Reflections', *Media, Culture and Society* (vol. 8, no. 3, 1986); *Arena* for permission to use material in chapter 9 which first appeared in 'Theorizing Music's Affective Power', (no. 85, 1988 – co-authored with Jennifer Giles-Davis); and Professor Margaret J. Kartomi (General Editor, SIMS '88 Publications) for permission to use material in chapter 11 that is to appear in 'Towards a Socially Grounded Criticism of Music', *Trends in Music Since 1960* (Proceedings of the 1988 Symposium of the International Musicological Society, Melbourne, Australia). Material which appears in chapters 1, 2, 3, 4, 5, 6, 7 and 10 has previously been published in Italian translation. I am grateful to Professor Luigi Pestalozza, Le Sfere, and Ricordi and Unicopli of Milan for permission to use material in chapters 1–7 which appeared in *La Musica come sapere sociale* (Milan, 1988). I am also grateful to Professor Luigi Pestalozza, *Musica/Realta*, and Unicopli of Milan for permission to use material in chapter 10 which appeared in 'Prolegomeni allo studio critico della popular music' (no. 17, 1985).

As I look over the text which follows I am invaded with a sense of the exertions of past research, the excitement of past revelations, as well as the sting of past criticisms. The journey has been an exciting one for me, and I would like to thank all those who have helped to make it possible, especially Margaret, Julie and Ian Shepherd.

Carleton University, Ottawa
February 1990

Introduction

In her eloquent criticism of British subcultural analyses, Angela McRobbie makes the following observation:

> One of the central tenets of the women's movement has been that the personal is political. . . . Although few radical (male) sociologists would deny the importance of the personal in precipitating social and political awareness, to admit how their own experience has influenced their choice of subject-matter (the politics of selection) seems more or less taboo. (McRobbie, 1980, pp. 38–9)

McRobbie's statement could stand as a leitmotif for this book in two ways. Firstly, this book is personal. I cannot explain why I have been interested in music, except, perhaps, that my interest was a statement about identity as I grew up in a family of scientists. But the interest has always been there. I started on the ubiquitous recorder at a young age, graduating to the flute, and also served for a short while as a cathedral chorister until my voice started to do the predictable unpredictable things. Music has always been a part of me, and I have always felt – in a way that I suspect is common to many musicians – a responsibility towards it. I can remember, at the age of ten, standing at a bus stop with a school friend, and being asked by this friend, with some incredulity, why I spent so much time on music. 'After all,' my friend observed, 'what's the use of music?' I was dumbfounded. At the time, I thought my shock was caused by what I rationalized as my friend's unintelligent question. If music was all around us, surely it must be of some use. It did not take me long to realize, however, that I was the cause of my own disquiet. I had not a clue as to how to answer this most simple of questions.

But while music has always been a part of me, the study of music has not. I was one of the first people at my secondary school to study music academically as a graduating subject. This, at a British public school in the early 1960s, was liable to mark one out as a certain kind of person. I did not fit the mould. For a start, I played rugby. My experience of studying something that was an important part of me, therefore, has always involved a tension between living in the 'real' world, and inhabiting a world that seemed marginal, peripheral and cloistered. That sense of tension was heightened dramatically in the mid and late 1960s with the advent of British rhythm-and-blues. On the one hand, there was the 'official' music that I studied. On the other, there was the music that constituted a large measure of the commonsense reality of myself and my peers. Those who taught the former either ignored or denigrated the latter.

A large part of my working life has been concerned with making sense of and working through the implications of this tension. It is for this reason that I have always had a love-hate relationship with the study of music. I have always wanted to be able to answer my schoolfriend's question, yet the professional world that I inhabit seems ill equipped, as it always has, to help me answer it. As a student of 'classical' music, I found it particularly curious, for example, that the majority of music historians seldom connected the music about which they were writing to the social and cultural circumstances of its creation and consumption in any more than a superficial manner. Social and cultural 'background' was seldom related explicitly to the technical characteristics of the music in question. The cultural experiences of the 1960s, mediated as powerfully as they were through 'popular' music, led me to the belief that while music spoke perhaps more concretely and immediately than many other media to the world of personal experience, it was also intensely political in the way in which it mediated that world. As a consequence, my own motivation as a student experiencing the world of music *from the inside* became that of deconstructing the traditional problematics of musicology as a prelude to developing an understanding of how music, *from within its own internal processes*, could articulate social and cultural messages that were intensely personal.

Help in this undertaking came not, in fact, from the world of musicology, but from another discipline. When I went to the University of York to start work on my doctorate, I was lucky enough to live in the college that housed the Department of Sociology and Anthropology. I did not know it at the time, but I could hardly have arrived in a more propitious intellectual and cultural environment. The early 1970s were the heady days of the National Deviancy Conferences, the new sociology of education and the rise to pre-eminence of the Centre for Contemporary Cultural Studies at the University of Birmingham. I spent more time talking to graduate sociology students and reading books on sociology and anthropology than I did in the Department of Music or reading books on music. I shall always be grateful to Wilfrid Mellers for allowing me to follow my nose, leave behind the life and work of Frederick Delius and concentrate instead on the sociology and aesthetics of music.

This book represents the development of the work that began at York. The work was not conceived originally as a book. Most of it has appeared previously as independent articles and chapters in books. However, the work is linked for me by one common theme, a theme that speaks to the second way in which McRobbie's statement stands as a leitmotif. This theme, simply put, is about connectedness: connectedness to our biographies, our cultures, our societies and our environments. It is about getting behind the way in which, at least since the Renaissance, male-directed forms of hegemonic thought and social organization have attempted to downplay and control unilaterally – if not hide from view – many of the consequences of human relatedness. Simply put, it is about the use of music in telling us about the nature of our relatedness to ourselves, other people and the environment, *and*, in the context of the societies in which most of us presently live, about the fundamental and inescapable fact of that relatedness.

Arguments about the special qualities of music in confronting us globally, concretely and immediately with the conditions of our own sociality are hardly new. They have been put forcefully and persuasively by progressive ethnomusicologists such as John Blacking, Charles Keil, Steven Feld and Catherine Ellis. They are even echoed, perhaps, in Simon Frith's statement that 'the intensity of [the] relationship between taste and self-definition seems peculiar to popular music – it is 'possessable' in ways that other cultural forms . . . are not' (Frith, 1987, p. 144). Yet they have not been put in specific relation to the total musical field of *everyday* realities in modern industrial societies (which I take to exclude the world of modernist and avant-garde composition). Neither have they been put in relation to the disciplines of historical musicology, music theory and conventional ethnomusicology.

I am acutely aware of the criticisms that can be levelled against the arguments presented in this book. At one level, the book could be read as the attempt of a white, middle-class male to uncover the conditions of his own musical pleasures. That level is undoubtedly there. However, I make no apology for it. On the one hand, it seems to do no harm to analyse the conditions of one's own existence. On the other, I would not wish to claim any privileged position for the nature of this analysis. While the analysis may well be privileged in terms of my own position in the academic world and of the dominance of male discourses within that world, I am not convinced that the analysis *as such* precludes different arguments originating from other social locations.

The arguments presented here resonate strongly with issues prevalent in the 1960s and early 1970s. The political and intellectual terrain has changed dramatically since then, and some readers may feel that these changes are not adequately represented in this book. However, I remain unconvinced that the professional world I inhabit has been significantly affected by these changes. Indeed, I remain unconvinced that this world was *significantly* affected by the moral, cultural and intellectual issues which characterized the 1960s and early 1970s. In this respect, the following remarks may seem ungracious and harsh, but I believe them to be true. A majority of my musicological colleagues seem to have learnt that it is not intellectually fashionable to 'put down' popular music, to argue that it is inferior and not worthy of study in the academic world. Many of them have learnt that it is fashionable to pay lip service to the 'sociality of music'. Yet, faced with challenges to the conservative nature of curricula within the majority of university music departments, a majority of my colleagues also seem to have learnt that the best line of defence is simply not to engage, to remain silent, to pretend that the challenge is not there, or, if it has to be recognized, to argue that it has been realistically met, or that, within the administrative and financial constraints of the university, it cannot be met.

In this sense, the book is directed more at my musicological colleagues than it is at my colleagues in the world of critical communications and cultural studies. There are, to be sure, many more courses in university music departments on ethnomusicology, popular music and the sociology of music than there used to be. However, these courses are usually marginal and peripheral to the mainstream of musicological studies. In some instances, the courses cannot count as a credit towards a degree in music; they can only count as an 'elective' or 'option'. The effect, therefore, is to ghettoize these areas of intellectual inquiry while claiming, if only implicitly, that they have their proper and appropriate place within the curriculum. It is the rare department of music that includes these areas as an integral and fundamental part of its curriculum.

Many of the arguments presented in this book therefore remain apposite to the world of musicology. Musicology as a discipline continues to turn its back towards the future, acting in a majority of instances as little more than a museum or haven for forms of music which now only constitute a very small proportion of the music practised on the surface of the planet. The same criticism is only slightly less true of mainstream, conventional ethnomusicology. Within ethnomusicology, studies of the political and economic situation of urban popular musics in the Third World are rare. The point here is not that 'classical', 'serious' and 'traditional' musics should not be studied and preserved. Succeeding generations should continue to have knowledge of the many different ways there have been and continue to be of being musical in this world. The point is that this work should not be carried out in such a way as to exclude almost completely any understanding of the contemporary situation of music on a world basis. The sad truth is that institutionalized musicology as a discipline is almost completely ignorant of the current circumstances of the majority of the world's music. It attempts to preserve certain musics against forces which it assumes to be there, but of which it has almost no understanding, while at the same time turning its back on the majority of the world's musics: musics which are used by people in the context of their everyday lives, and which have the most intimate of relationships with the forces that musicology does not wish to confront. In this sense, it could be argued that musicology as a discipline has entered into the most abject abdication of professional responsibility.

The debates of the 1960s and early 1970s remain of relevance in the sense that musicology as a discipline will not be able to enter the territory it has for so long ignored without following through thoroughly on the proposition that music is, indeed, pervasively social. Some musicologists may wish to argue that this territory is more legitimately the preserve of sociologists, communications scholars and cultural theorists. To make this argument is, however, to draw an implicit line between the study of musical life and the study of music – to assume that the social nature of music has only to do with the circumstances of its creation and consumption, not with the way it sounds. Sociologists, communications scholars and cultural theorists do have a legitimate interest in music, and it is only through a continual and permanent dialogue with the intellectual areas they represent that musicology will be able to expand its horizons convincingly. However, to turn the study of the majority of contemporary musics over to such intellectual areas (as musicology presently does through omission) will probably result in this music continuing to be studied with scant reference to its sonic qualities. Musicology (and, indeed, ethnomusicology) will continue to imply that this music is not worth studying *as music*, and so will continue increasingly to isolate themselves from the mainstream of contemporary intellectual life. However, it is not impossible that the terrain of contemporary political and intellectual life will impinge on musicology in one way or another. Either musicology will face the future, and come to terms with the implications of international capital and 'postmodernism'; or it will continue to back away and discover, perhaps, that a museum without tourists may not be able to continue as a viable proposition.

To stress the study of all music *as music* (which should be the business of musicology) – to stress the centrality of sound to music as a social phenomenon – is to invite criticism from some sociologists, communications scholars and cultural theorists. The temptation for some non-musicologists who study music is to assume that the relationship of sound to music is not unlike that of sound to language. That is, if one does not have any professional expertise in music, it at the least becomes convenient to assume that signification and sound are as arbitrary in their relationship as they are taken to be in language: that, in other words, there is no element of necessity in the relationship between 'signified' and 'signifier'. This is clearly not the position adopted in this book. The position adopted in this book is that the sound of music is heavily implicated in processes of meaning construction, although *not* in a determining fashion. The consequences of assuming that the materiality of a medium is significantly implicated in processes of meaning construction leads in a direction that does not sit too easily with some current thinking within cultural theory. It raises the spectre of Marshall McLuhan, who, as a Canadian and a Catholic, had a healthier perspective than many on the consequences of twentieth-century verbal rationality. It raises the possibility that, although language, through its arbitrary processes of signification, is fundamental to the symbolic character of human worlds, and fundamental, perhaps, to imparting this potential for symbolism to other modes of human expression and communication, it could not impart *in its entirety* this crucial quality of arbitrariness to these other modes. Thus arises the possibility of many modes of signification the materiality of whose 'signifiers' are fundamentally implicated in process of meaning construction to an extent that does not, however, detract from the symbolic and therefore *partially* arbitrary character of those modes. If human language is important to facilitating a clear distinction between thought and the world on which thought operates, then other modes of communication, in making their materiality felt, remind us of our connectedness to the materiality of the world as signified. Music, for reasons to be discussed in the book, is most notable among these other modes of communication.

One of the arguments to be presented in the book is that post-Renaissance, 'educated' men became so aware of the potential for separating the meaning of a word from its referent, and so seduced by the intellectual power this represented in terms of manipulating and controlling the world, that they had difficulty seeing beyond the immediate implications of their own cleverness. In acting as an antidote to this tendency, the very fact of music as a social medium *in sound* reminds us, not so much of what has been lost, but of that of which we have ceased to be publicly enough aware. It is in this sense that the work of scholars such as McLuhan and Ong, and their bringing into play of an awareness of cultures of other times and other places, is relevant, not only for an understanding of music, but for an understanding of what music can represent in terms of grasping the conditions of our own socialities. It is part of the argument of this book that music is fully implicated in the social conditions of its production and consumption. However, implicit equally in this book is a valorization of music as a social medium whose sonic materiality is especially welcome in a 'postmodern' world where a surface facade of exploded visual fragmentation detracts from an awareness of objective material conditions. It is in terms of music's possible specificities as a social form that the book is directed more at sociologists, communications scholars and cultural theorists.

It is important to stress, however, that this book seeks only to establish that it is theoretically *feasible* to conceive of music as articulating from within the inherent characteristics of its sonic channel socially mediated messages. It does not seek to *establish* the theoretical legitimacy of this conception in all its aspects. The notion of the structural homology has been important to developing this *prima facie* case, not so much in terms of thinking about music as expressing, in a homologous fashion, social meanings extrinsic to itself, but rather in terms of thinking about music as expressing iconically, from within itself, meanings which will likely resonate powerfully in other areas of non-musical social process. This discussion does, as a consequence, leave open the presently contentious question of how, precisely, music's meanings are related to music's sounds – of how, that is, music signifies. That, however, is the subject for another book.

Part I

Music as Social Knowledge

1 Basic Premises

The Inherent Sociality of Music

The idea that different groups and societies create and appreciate their own stylistically distinguishable kinds of music is not one that would be likely to invite dissent from musicologists or sociologists. Neither, on the face of it, is the assumption that the stylistic characteristics of these different kinds of music might have some connection with what may be loosely termed the 'cultural background' of their creation. As Lévi-Strauss has argued with respect to language:

> Between culture and language there cannot be no relations at all.
> ... If there were no relations at all that would lead us to assume that the human mind is a kind of jumble – that there is no connection at all between what the mind is doing on one level, and what the mind is doing on another level. (Lévi-Strauss, 1968, p. 79)

That there are connections between 'what the mind is doing on one level, and what the mind is doing on another level' is not difficult to illustrate on a *prima facie* basis where music is concerned. Is it a complete coincidence, for example, that functional tonality arose from the fervour of an intellectual and artistic movement (the Renaissance) which arguably laid the foundations for modern capitalist society? Is it a complete coincidence that alternatives to that musical 'language' began to develop at a time when the 'reality' of three-dimensional perspective in painting was under attack, and when classical physics was facing a very considerable crisis? Is it completely without foundation that many people have seen in the rise of the Afro-American-influenced popular musics of this century social implications of great importance?

It is, of course, possible to argue that the cultural and social implications of different music styles are completely associative or arbitrary in nature. That is, that although there are connections between what the mind is doing on different levels, a particular musical style carries the cultural and social implications it does only because the group or society in question externally imposes a set of meanings or significance on the music in a manner completely arbitrary to the music's basic qualities. The argument is that any kind of music will serve a group or society provided the music is stylistically distinguishable from all others; there is nothing internal to the music, in other words, which predisposes it to impart one kind of significance above all others.

In contrast, it is also possible to argue that the internal qualities of a musical style are of themselves significant. This is not necessarily to assume that the significance of music is located in some form of 'asocial', 'ultimate' reality, however. It can be asserted that because *people* create music, they reproduce in the basic qualities of their music the basic qualities of their own thought processes. If it is accepted that people's thought processes are socially mediated, then it could be said that the basic qualities of different styles of music are likewise socially mediated and so socially significant.

It is in the light of this second possibility that a sociology of musical styles becomes a viable proposition, at least in theory. If musical styles have an inherent social significance, then it should be possible to demonstrate that significance by carrying out musical analysis in terms of the social reality which gave birth to and is articulated by a particular musical style.

Such analyses are notably absent from both the musicological and sociological worlds. Surface reasons for the scant attention given to the sociology of music (as opposed to the sociology of musical life) are not difficult to find. Few sociologists feel themselves to be competent in a discipline which requires a significant degree of technical knowledge as well as, preferably, some first-hand experience as a practitioner. Most musicologists and music theorists, on the other hand, repelled by what they see as unending waves of pseudo-scientific jargon, have apparently decided that the area should be left well alone. The art of musical analysis is well established, and most musicologists and music theorists see in sociology no good reason for changing their methods or approaches where traditional analysis is concerned. The problems that have, for example, arisen in popular music studies through the coming together of sociologically and musicologically oriented approaches to the analysis of music as a cultural form are discussed in part III.

Reasons for the neglect of a sociology of musical styles go deeper, however, than sociologists' lack of musical knowledge, or musicologists' perhaps healthy scepticism about social 'science'. Part I of this book seeks to outline the major and more substantial difficulties which have stood in the way of the development of a sociology of musical styles.

The Aesthetic Perspective

Implicit in the central assumption of this book is the view that the meaning of music is somehow located in its function as a social symbol. It is the word 'meaning' which creates the greatest problem in this context. For most people a symbol has meaning because it refers to something outside itself. Pictures have meaning because they refer to something in physical reality, and words have meaning because they refer to concepts and ideas. But to suggest that a piece of music has meaning because of extra-musical reference is, at the least, highly contentious. The alternative has been to look for the meaning of music within the structure of individual pieces, an alternative whose strictest formulation, as Leonard B. Meyer indicates, is to be found in the attitude of the absolutists:

> The absolutists have contended that the meaning of music lies specifically, and some would assert exclusively, in the musical processes themselves. For them musical meaning is non-designative. But in what sense these processes are meaningful . . . they have been unable to state with either clarity or precision. . . . This failure has led some critics to assert that musical meaning is a thing apart, different in some unexplained way from all other kinds of meaning. This is simply an evasion of the real issue. (Meyer, 1956, p. 33)

The real issue can be stated in terms of the following comparison. Because their meaning is 'located outside them', words and pictures may be thought of as 'carrying' their meaning and 'giving' it to the recipient. The symbol, in other words, survives the divulgence of its message. If, on the other hand, musical meaning is acknowledged to lie within the musical process itself, then in 'giving way' that meaning, a piece seemingly compromises the very being or essence responsible for the meaning in the first place. As Susanne Langer (1942, p. 236) has put it, the absolutists 'seem to feel that if musical structures should really be found to have significance, to relate to anything beyond themselves, those structures would forthwith cease to be musical.'

This difficulty results from confusing a symbol which has no referent in the world of objects and ideas with one which is informationally a closed system. Music certainly falls within the former but not, as the absolutists imply, the latter category. It is this distinction which facilitates the theories of Meyer and Langer. Broadly, both authors locate musical significance in 'psychological constants' (Meyer, 1973, p. 14) or 'psychological laws of "rightness"' (Langer, 1942, p. 240). That is, since all music originates in the minds of individual people, and since all minds are assumed to possess similar psychological characteristics, it is taken that there will be a certain conformity of patterning or structure between all music and all minds. Consequently, all minds are presumed to be suitably predisposed for the superimposition of the particular structure that constitutes a piece, and there is no longer any need to have recourse to the notion of symbols which divest themselves of externally referential meanings. 'Information' is conveyed by another method.

On the surface, this might seem to be a suitable and adequate explanation of musical process. It is ultimately compromised, however, by resulting from a mode of thought similar to that responsible for the original difficulty. In order to understand this anomaly and the failure of aestheticians and music theorists to circumvent it by invoking a social theory of music, it is necessary to make two basic assumptions. The first is that the collective reality of any society is mutually constructed by its members rather than being externally given, and the second that the form the reality of any particular society takes is significantly influenced by the medium of communication prevalent in that society.

The Social Construction of Reality

An approach to the understanding of the social construction of reality may best be made through a consideration of the role played in that process by symbols. A symbol may be thought of as any occurrence in the world, whether or not produced by people, which carries a *generally* agreed meaning for the members of a particular group or society.

Societies can only arise and continue to exist through communication, that is, the creation and exchange of symbols. Symbols are not self-contained phenomena. They are not 'God-given', but created by people to cope with the many varied situations in which they find themselves. The meanings of symbols and sets of symbols are originally derived from *specific* and *real* situations. But there is another side to the coin. Once a symbol or set of symbols have been created in response to a new situation these symbols, in retrospect, colour that situation. When people look back at a series of events they do so by means of and *through* the symbols created to define it. Furthermore, the new symbols may be used in other situations. Since the symbols are not specifically created for these other situations they bring to them meanings which although not necessarily irrelevant or wrong, are obviously coloured by previous usage. The reverse, of course, is equally true, for new situations modify the meanings of the already existing symbols used to denote such situations. In other words, situations and symbols have a mutually interdependent, but not determinant, relationship crucial to the constantly changing dynamics of the social process.

This relationship is most easily understood with regard to words, which constitute people's most important – but certainly not exclusive – symbolic mode. Not only do the meanings which arise in social situations give rise to words and continually modify the meanings of pre-existing words, but words and complete symbolic languages bring pre-conceived meanings to bear on our everyday sense of the world. Indeed, any new situation and/or symbol is mediated to an extent by pre-existing adjacent meanings. The world we live in has meaning for us only because we symbolically mediate the events that take place in it with other people, and we do this primarily with words. Reality – often conceived as an objective fact which cannot be changed, but only misconstrued – is thus *constructed* by people through the mutual *agreement by words and other symbols* on experiences undergone by individual people, as Walter Ong describes:

> 'World-view' is an elusive term, but when we speak of someone's world view in any sense, we do not mean simply the world impressing itself upon his passive receptors, sensory or intellectual. A person does not receive a world view, but rather takes or adopts one. A world view is not a datum, a *donné*, but something the individual himself, and the culture he shares partly constructs; it is the person's way of organising from within himself the data of actuality coming from without and within. (Ong, 1969, p. 634)

Society is thus quintessentially symbolic. That is to say, world senses – the meanings of society – are created and maintained in and through people's collective externalizations. To put it another way, people's consciousness both of themselves and the world they live in is mediated by and through an all-encompassing and symbolic people-made filter whose influence is utterly inescapable.

The Importance of Media

The principal line of argument in the three succeeding chapters is that the assumptions underlying the hegemonic and therefore dominant world sense of industrial capitalist societies (and their industrial, but non-capitalist alternatives) are ultimately responsible for some major difficulties within the field of music aesthetics. The form the assumptions or world sense of a particular society takes would seem to depend on the way the symbols of that society depict, denote and categorize what might be *imagined* as a previously 'unformed' world. Many people have had the experience of trying to understand, even in closely related European languages, words for which there are no direct equivalents in English. A true understanding of these words involves a change in their outlook on the world, however slight. What is about to be suggested here, on the other hand, is rather different. That is, that *the way* people communicate in constructing their reality (whether the face-to-face oral-aural situation of spoken discourse, the visuality of handwriting and printing or the aural-visual immediacy of electronic forms of communication) affects their outlook on the world in a fundamental fashion. It is not so much what is conveyed that is important, but how it is conveyed.

The view that media are highly influential in the structuring both of individual psyches and entire civilizations has most notably been put forward by Marshall McLuhan (1962 and 1964). While McLuhan's arguments received a great deal of attention during the late 1960s, they have, since then, fallen out of fashion, particularly in the academic world. A scholar who has put forward a rather more considered view than McLuhan on the role of media in structuring consciousnesses and social realities is Kathleen Gough. The following is her view on the influence of writing on complex societies:

> Writing, like other communication media, is problematic because it forms part of both the technological and ideological heritage of complex societies, as well as being intricately involved with their social structures. Difficulties arise because it is hard to disentangle the implications of literacy from those of other techniques (for example, plough agriculture, settled cultivation, rapid transport or power industry), or of other institutions (for example, specialized priesthoods or powerful governments) commonly found in advanced societies. Literacy appears to be, above all, an *enabling* factor, permitting large-scale organization, the critical accumulation, storage and retrieval of knowledge, the systematic use of logic, the pursuit of science and elaboration of the arts. Whether, and with what emphases, these developments will occur seems to depend less on the intrinsic knowledge of writing than on the overall development of the society's technology and social structure, and perhaps, also, on the character of its relation to other societies. *If* they occur, however, there seems little doubt or contention that the use of writing as a dominant communication medium will impose certain broad forms on their emergence, of

which syllogistic reasoning and linear codifications of reality may
be examples. (Gough, 1968, p. 84)

Most media philosophers would seem to assume, as Gough does here,
that the creation and influence of media constitute integral aspects of any
society's development. Yet it has perhaps been a central weakness of
media philosophy that the implications of this assumption have never
been fully explored in any theoretical fashion. Indeed, it was not until
1967 that the clear connection between the sociology of knowledge and
media philosophy as areas of academic inquiry was made by Ong (1967
and 1969). In Gough's case, for example, a lack of this kind of theoretical
connection appears to result in a paradox. For although, at the beginning
of her statement, Gough seems to acknowledge the dialectic relationship
of media to all other aspects of the social process, she later implies
something quite different, namely, that if a social structure is predisposed
to develop in a certain way, then the presence of the appropriate media
will permit or facilitate that development. Only then can media shape
social organization and dominant modes of thought. In this sense, the
influence of media can be said to be largely passive or negative, this latter
if the appropriate media are not in existence. There is little question of
media having a fundamentally dialectic and therefore active influence on
the future development of a society.

The position adopted here is that different media not only facilitate but
may actively encourage the development of certain modes of cognition,
thought and social organization in a society, especially if it is in the
interests of a particular class in that society to make use of a specific
medium or set of media to further their own political ends. The
legitimacy of this position would seem to be borne out by the substantive
discussions of succeeding chapters. However, this neither means, as
McLuhan often infers, that there is an inevitable relationship between
media and certain modes of cognition, thought and social organization,
nor that the influence of media is exclusive. It is important to realize that
a particular medium or set of media may only have an active influence on
the structuring of consciousness and realities within a society if they are
permitted or encouraged to by groups with sufficient political power. A
theme developed in chapter 8, for example, is that the influence of
analytic phonetic literacy and movable type printing on the development
and entrenching of certain, dominant epistemologies within the 'modern'
industrial world (described in chapter 3) has been an influence exercised
essentially by 'educated' men as a means of entrenching and furthering
their own political power as the dominant class in this world.

Conclusion

Before proceeding to a discussion of the way writing and typography have engendered certain categories of analysis in industrial societies incompatible with an adequate understanding of the musical process, it is necessary to indicate why such a discussion should involve a consideration of 'pre-literate' societies.

It is only through a discussion of the ideal-typical world senses of 'pre-literate' and 'industrial' cultures respectively that it can be argued that world senses mediated overwhelmingly *visually* give rise to categories of understanding inherently unsuited to revealing the full significance of music, while world senses mediated overwhelmingly in an *oral-aural* fashion give rise to categories of understanding that have much to tell us about grasping the full impact of music as a form of human cultural expression.

Because the focus of attention in the following two chapters is that of music aesthetics and not media philosophy, the discussion of the influence of different media in specific societies will be restricted in the main to an *ideal-typical* scheme involving 'pre-literate' and phonetically literate societies. It must not be thought that this distinction is as clear cut as the contents of the succeeding chapters might imply. There are many types of literacy which are not fully phonetic or even phonetic at all. Furthermore, societies which are either completely pre-literate or which tend strongly towards universal literacy are rare. Finally, it should be understood that the discussion of the 'pre-literate' world sense which follows is not intended to valorize it as something inherently superior to that dominant in industrial societies, or as something to which we might usefully 'return'. History does, indeed, march forward with inevitability. This inevitability does not, however, exclude the possibility that in affecting and influencing our own situation, we cannot learn from those of other peoples and other times.

2 The Inadequacy of Psychologistic Theories

Introduction

There are two parallel dichotomies around which discussions concerned with the significance of music usually revolve. As we shall see, both these dichotomies form integral aspects of the modes of thought prevalent in industrial societies. On the one hand, the contention that the significance of music cannot and does not rely on symbolic reference to specific objects and ideas is predicated on a basic distinction between the physical and the mental, the outer and the inner, the non-human and the human. Because the significance of music cannot and does not reside in the materiality of objects or the full objectivation of ideas, it must, according to Langer and Meyer, reside in the total fluidity of the inner life, in that which is mental and quintessentially human. On the other hand, the idea that music might be an informationally closed system is predicated on a fundamental distinction between symbol and meaning, form and content. In the opinion of the absolutists, if music cannot and does not refer outside itself to objects and ideas, then, within the commonly accepted meaning of the word, music can have no 'meaning'. The symbol is its own meaning, and the content of music is taken to be its form. Langer and Meyer have seemingly overcome this tautology by claiming that the meaning or content of music, in deriving from the *structural conformity* of music and psychological processes, resides 'outside' music 'in' the mental lives of individual people. This chapter argues, by way of a comparison of 'oral-aural' and 'visual' world senses, that the seeming transcendence by Langer and Meyer of the form and content, symbol and meaning dichotomy is, in fact, only a partial transcendence because it fails, at the same time, to transcend the structurally related dichotomy of physical and mental, outer and inner.

The Oral-Aural World of Pre-literate People

Practically all communication in pre-literate societies takes place in face-to-face situations. It is because sound takes on a great importance in pre-literate people's world that, in order to understand the way this world is structured, it is necessary to understand some of the inherent qualities of sound *as a perceived phenomenon.* Sound has certain qualities not generally associated with the other phenomenona that impinge on our senses. Sound is evanescent. It can only exist as it is going out of existence. It is never static and can only be considered sequential by the application of discontinuous analytic thought to its existence. A sight, on the other hand, can generally be more easily isolated in its effect and examined without destroying the inherent quality of the experience. The only way a sound can be so examined is by repeating it in its entirety if, indeed, the circumstances of its creation allow this.

Sound is more symptomatic of the flow of time than any other phenomena impinging on our senses. Although all other phenomena occur within a stream of time, the fact that they may be generally isolated and examined at leisure demonstrates that, *as far as their influence on the arrangement of people's sensoria is concerned,* they are not so inexorably tied to that stream as sound is.

Sound evokes a sense of space very different from that evoked by other phenomena. A person can only look in one direction at a time, and can easily rid themselves of an unpleasant sight by closing their eyes or turning away. Taste is very much a sense of acceptance and rejection, and the power to escape a tactile stimulus is clear. Smell, although possessing something of sound's all-encompassing quality, may still be avoided by holding one's nose or moving away. In all these cases avoidance involves the parameter of visual space. The sound of the world, on the other hand, impinges on our ears from all directions and all distances at once, and the ability to totally cut out or ignore sound is severely limited, as Carpenter and McLuhan argue:

Auditory space has no point of favoured focus. It's a sphere without fixed boundaries, space made by the thing itself, not space containing the thing. It is not pictorial space, boxed in, but dynamic, always in flux, creating its own dimensions moment by moment. It has no fixed boundaries; it is indifferent to background. The eye focuses, pinpoints, abstracts, locating each object in physical space, against a background; the ear however, favours sound from any direction. We hear equally well from right or left, front or back, above or below. If we lie down, it makes no difference, whereas in visual space the entire spectacle is altered. We can shut out the visual field by simply closing our eyes, but we are always triggered to respond to sound. (Carpenter and McLuhan, 1970a, p. 67)

Sound is symptomatic of energy. Something has to be going on for sound to be generated, and with sound that is not electronically generated or conveyed, the source usually occurs within a geographical range that means it can have an immediate effect upon the listener. Total staticity and the generation of sound is rare. An example of this quality of sound is given by Ong (1967, p. 112) when he points out that 'a primitive hunter can see, feel, smell and taste an elephant when the animal is quite dead.' When, however, 'he hears an elephant trumpeting or merely shuffling its feet, he had better watch out. Something is going on. Force is operating.' Sound is dynamic. It requires a more immediate response, and does not allow so much time or the space necessary for initial avoidance, subsequent, cooler exposure and considered rationalization.

Pre-literate people seem to sense themselves as being at the centre of a sound universe, which is dynamic and bounding with energy. Furthermore, since the paradigm of sound for people is the human voice, they seem to impute power and influence to the physical phenomena that surround their existence as they would impute it to the human voice. This orientation of pre-literate people to their world is noted by Mary Douglas:

> ... the lot of individual humans is thought to be affected by power inhering in themselves or in other humans. The cosmos is turned in, as it were, on man. Its transforming energy is threaded on to the lives of individuals so that nothing happens in the way of storms, sickness, blights or droughts except in virtue of these personal links. So the universe is man-centred in the sense that it must be interpreted by reference to humans. (Douglas, 1970, pp. 103–4)

The world of pre-literate people is a revelationary and, in our terms, relatively unpredictable world. This difference in relationship to the environment is reflected in, and partly caused by, a slipperiness of knowledge, which again relates back to pre-literate people's orality. There is thus much impetus for the creation of firm and comparatively unyielding legitimating structures.

> Man knows what he can recall – all else is so ephemeral as to be negligible. In an oral culture this means he knows what is cast in

fixed thematic formulatory patterns. Anything else will seem un-real, nonknowledge, reprehensible and dangerous. This is the noetic foundation for the traditionalism stemming from oral cultures. What is non-traditional . . . is dangerous because it is slippery and unmanageable. Oral-aural man does not like the non-traditional because, beyond his limited means of control, it advertises the tenuousness of his hold on rationality. (Ong, 1969, p. 640)

The hermetic and revelationary world of oral-aural people, with its tight grip on supporting mythological structures, leads to a certain conservatism where knowledge is concerned. Freshly perceived phenomena tend to be mediated through the rock certainty of orally accretive legitimations. This does not mean that legitimating structures in pre-literate societies do not change in a manner that would prove historically contradictory, merely that pre-literate people, because of their orality, seem not to be overly conscious of the contradictory nature of successive legitimations, something illustrated by Goody and Watt in reference to the Tiv of Nigeria:

Early British administrators among the Tiv of Nigeria were aware of the great importance attached to . . . genealogies which were continually discussed in court cases where the rights and duties of one man towards another were in dispute. Consequently they took the trouble to write down the long list of names and preserve them for posterity, so that future administrators might refer to them in giving judgment. Forty years later, when the Bohannans carried out anthropological field work in the area, their successors were still using the same genealogies. . . . However, these written pedigrees now gave rise to many disagreements, the Tiv maintained that they were incorrect, while the officials regarded them as statements of fact, a record of what had actually happened, and could not agree that the unlettered indigines could be better informed about the past than their literate predecessors. What neither party recognised was that in any society of this kind changes take place which require a constant readjustment in the genealogies if they are to continue to carry out their functions as mnemonics of social relationships. (Goody and Watt, 1963, p. 309)

Change in pre-literate societies, then, tends to be continual and gradual rather than infrequent and radical, and something of which pre-literate people are not obviously conscious.

Pre-literate people's relationship to change is symptomatic of their sense of time. As they exist in a people-centred world where events in space are threaded onto their lives, so events in the past and potential occurrences in the future are mediated in terms of the present. This is evidenced by Goody and Watt's story concerning the Tiv of Nigeria. In this sense pre-literate people live within time. And against the background of industrial societies' spatialized and objectified concept of time, with its sense of the pastness of the past, and the futurity of the future, it is not being merely redundant to say that, for pre-literate people, all past and potential events are irrevocably tied to the present.

Living within time and having little consciousness of time as we conceive it, pre-literate people may be said to have little abstract temporal sense. Time unfolds and is revealed through specific events which recur, and which are of great importance for the ordering of existence (Hallowell, 1937). Such events, as Edmund Leach has pointed out (Leach, 1954), are likely to be seasonal changes of some sort. It must be emphasized, however, that these recurring events are *not* used as a means of dividing up abstract continuous time into a mechanical succession of separate instants (see, for example, Whorf, 1971, pp. 142–3). As A. I. Hallowell puts it (1937, p. 660) in discussing the time concept of the Saulteaux Indians, 'the "moon" is not a division of continuous time, it *is* a recurrent event.'

Experiencing time in a concrete and cyclical fashion, pre-literate people do not conceive it as regressing or progressing into the vanishing points of past or future infinity. Although pre-literate people have a sense of the past, it is seldom linear and quickly melts into the contemporary simultaneity of mythology.

> On the whole, then, events that are believed to have taken place 'long ago' are not systematically correlated with each other in any well-defined temporal schemata. There are discrete happenings, often unconnected and sometimes contradictory. Yet the past and present are part of a whole because they are bound together by the persistence and contemporary reality of mythological characters not even grown old. (Hallowell, 1937, p. 668)

Corroboration for this feature of pre-literate time is to be found in Dorothy Lee's (1970) description of Trobriand time concepts.

All these aspects of pre-literate time are interrelated, and are summarized by Edmund Leach:

> Primitive time can be regarded as a recurring cycle. Certain events repeat themselves in definite sequence. This sequence is a continuity

without beginning or end, and thus without any clear distinction between past and present. The most important time-sequences are seasonal activities and the passage of human life. Both these cycles are conceived as of the same kind. For such thinking there is no chronology, and time is not measurable. (Leach, 1954, p. 114)

For pre-literate people time is a revelationary circumjacence of concretely recurring events, which is constantly in flux, and over which, *in Western terms*, there is relatively little control.

This 'lack of control' is evidenced in pre-literate people's concept of space. Their ordering of space results from the particular and immediate configuration of objects and not from a preconceived framework. For the majority of Western people, space is an empty hopper made up of horizontal and vertical dimensions into which objects are placed with direct relevance to the visual relationship that an observer has with these objects. This is reflected in art during and after the Renaissance. In this art, 'everything is dominated by the eye of the beholder.' There is 'a space conception that is graphically depicted by the perspective projection of long level vistas upon a plane surface' (Giedion, 1970, p. 74). Within this unified and centrally oriented perspective there is a *linear* ordering of objects which presupposes and reinforces sequentially segmented time. Pre-literate art completely denies any such abstraction however: 'It is this manner of seeing things without any "relation to myself" that distinguishes primeval art from all later art. It is not disorder but a different order that is being followed – an order to which we, in our sophistication, have lost the key,' (Giedion, 1970, p. 78).

Not surprisingly, a characteristic of this different order is a lack of emphasis on a vertical-horizontal framework or background:

The distinguishing mark of the space conception of primeval art is the complete independence and freedom of its vision, which has never again been attained in later periods. In our sense there is no above and no below, no clear distinction of separateness from an intermingling, and also, certainly, no rules of proportional size. . . . Primeval art never places objects in an immediate surrounding. Primeval art has no background. . . . This is inherent in the prehistoric conception of space: all linear directions have equal right and likewise all surfaces, whether they be regular or irregular. They can be tilted at any angle with the horizontal throughout the entire 360 degree range. To the eye of primeval man, animals that to us appear to be standing on their heads, do not appear inverted to them because they exist, as it were, in space free from the forces of gravity. Primeval art has no background. (Giedion, 1970, pp. 85–7)

With its concrete situation in specific objects, its lack of concern with fixed boundaries and backgrounds, its easy acceptance of intermingling and consequent lack of concern with separateness, pre-literate space is auditory in nature. And as the visual bias of industrial societies links people's temporal and spatial orientations, so are those of pre-literate people linked through their oral-aural bias. This is demonstrated with regard to the lack of concern for spatial separateness:

> All is within the continual present, the perpetual flow of today, yesterday and tomorrow. . . . Whenever possible previous lines are not destroyed, but the lines of both earlier and later works intermingle till they sometimes – but only to our eyes – appear inextricable. It was recognised quite early that this superimposition was not due to idle chance but to a deliberate reluctance to destroy the past. (Giedion, 1970, pp. 85–6)

The juxtaposition of past and imminent events in the present requires a spatial sense that transcends the mutual separation of all objects in visual space. As industrial societies have tended to spatialize time, it could be said that pre-literate societies temporalize space.

From whichever angle it is approached the pre-literate world displays an instancy and immediacy which most people in industrial societies – given those societies' degree of 'rational control' over the events of the world – would find it difficult to relate to. It is dynamic, in a constant state of flux, and at all times pregnant with happenings. It is a world whose encroaching massivity is constantly requiring response.

The Form/Content Dichotomy

Literate people possess the ability of storing information. This information attains a permanency and safety not before possible. Within this innovation lies the potential for preserving as inviolate discrepancies between succeeding legitimations, and so for the emergence of an historically based dialectic and the concomitant growth of a comparatively based rather than mythologically mediated critical method. The keeping of records makes possible a sense of the pastness of the past, of historical perspective, and so lays the foundation for the separation of 'history' from 'myth'.

As well as encouraging an historical and analytic perspective, literacy emphasizes the visual at the expense of the auditory. Whereas sound underlines *the dynamic immediacy of the environment*, visual stimuli underline the *distancing and separateness of events and objects from each other and individual people*. As sound underlines immediacy in time, so vision underlines distancing in space. Further, since literacy facilitates the safe and permanent storage of information *apart from people's consciousness*, it also induces a psychic distancing. This psychic distancing is related to the physical distancing just indicated.

Literacy may be divided into two categories: ideographic and phonetic. Whereas phonetic literacy encodes the sounds people make in speaking, ideograms encode directly the objects and concepts about which people speak. Ideograms require a knowledge/acceptance of the ideas they ideally represent, because, in terms of the already existing set of ideograms, there is little way in which the ideas may be discussed critically. The world sense of an ideographic culture can only be transcended with difficulty, because the ideograms are only capable of encoding that world sense, and not what people say in it, or about it. Since orally mediated knowledge is slippery, its power to avoid assimilation of important aspects of ideas encoded ideographically (which thus become more manageable, permanent, and influential) is limited. The power of literacy to alter orally mediated knowledge is so massive compared with the ability of oral people to influence knowledge encoded literately, that, when a literate and an oral society come into contact, the thought patterns of the former tend to be superimposed on those of the latter. Any meaningful questioning of ideographic intellection is thus severely circumscribed, and since ideograms *are* very much the ideas they 'represent', the potential for a fundamental distinction between symbol and meaning or form and content is strictly limited.

When the *sounds* of *words* are encoded in writing, oral questioning of the visual code may be encoded visually *in terms of already existing symbols*. Criticism which was oral may more easily influence knowledge which was literately encoded at the time the original criticism was made. However, in the case of those forms of phonetic literacy which are mnemonic, such questioning usually concerns itself with establishing exactly what sounds have been notated. Because the higher reality is still located in the spoken word the questioning of *ideas* encoded in mnemonic phonetic literacy usually occurs only after the visual code has been translated back into the full semantic potency of the spoken word. There is a predominantly oral questioning of knowledge mediated in a predominantly oral fashion. Since a mnemonically phonetic world sense is predominantly oral in its mediation, there is little potential for the emergence of the dichotomies of form and content, mental and physical in a manner of fundamental importance.

With the advent of a full phonetic alphabet, the mnemonic dependency of phonetic writing is broken. Because a fully phonetic alphabet is analytic rather than mnemonic of the sounds essential to meaning, and because it comes to possess the potential for prescriptive manipulation (that is, new words and ideas can be created through the manipulation of visual symbols without any initial reference to spoken words), it becomes capable of facilitating the creation and mediation of thoughts in isolation from any spoken word. These thoughts can then be translated back into the world of spoken discourse. In the case of an analytic, prescriptive and *self-sufficient* phonetic literacy, the problem ceases to be that of establishing what sounds have been encoded. Attention may focus instead on a direct oral questioning of visually encoded ideas – ideas which might well have been conceived and presented independently of any spoken word. Because of this easy and safe interchange between spoken and written words the different symbolic media of sound and sight can act as mutual yardsticks of comparison and criticism. Not only may the written word be effectively questioned in terms of the spoken word, but the efficacy of the spoken word (now used in an increasingly 'literate' fashion) becomes such that questioning it in terms of the written word becomes a continuing necessity. As well as questioning what people meant in contradistinction to what they 'actually' wrote, one may also question what people meant in contradistinction to what they 'actually' said. The word is no longer restricted to face-to-face communication, and the idea may be prized out of its pictorial prison.

In facilitating a divorce between meaning and symbol, phonetic literacy is instrumental in creating an epistemological dichotomy, that between content and form, which has been pervasive in the dominant modes of thought of modern industrial societies, and which is of importance to any discussion of music aesthetics. Of more importance to the present line of thought, however, is the manner in which the divorce between meaning and symbol encourages a comparative and analytic, rather than mythological dialectic, and so aids the growth of historical dialecticism implicit in any literate society. One concomitant of this growing historical-analytic approach is the ability a *phonetically* literate person may develop to put a *much* greater temporal-spatial distance between themselves and the phenomena or knowledge they are examining. Initially, this ability derives from the permanent storage of information in a place removed from human consciousness. Gradually, however, the possibility of critically examining spoken words in a manner similar to written words *leads to the distancing principle being applied to face-to-face communication*. The distinction between meaning and symbol, content and form, and the distancing involved have become so pervasive in the cognitive and intellectual orientation of most people in industrial societies, that it becomes difficult to understand the immediate power words possess for pre-literate people. Indeed, without a conscious realization of how this distinction and distancing arose, any meaningful insight into the role played by language in pre-literate societies becomes extremely difficult.

Because spoken words in pre-literate societies cannot be divorced from everyday use in face-to-face communication, and because of the indissoluble links that exist in those societies between people, the universe and sound, words come to have an immediacy and power little known in industrial societies. And *because of the imposing immediacy of pre-literate people's world*, there is little way in which this immediacy and power can be diluted or questioned. Words and referents are inextricably intertwined, a phenomenon illustrated by Carothers through reference to his non-literate son:

> Some years ago my little son said: 'Is there a word "pirates",
> Daddy?' When I replied in the affirmative, he asked 'Are there
> pirates?' I said, 'No, not now, there used to be'. He asked, 'Is there
> a word "pirates" *now*?' When I said, 'Yes', he replied, 'Then there
> must be pirates now'. This conversation . . . is a reminder that, for a
> child, a thing exists by virtue of its name; that the spoken or even
> imagined word must connote something in the outer world.
> (Carothers, 1959, p. 309)

As Carey (1967, p. 10) has put it, words in pre-literate societies 'become icons, they do not represent things, they are themselves things'. They are instrumental in *all* their aspects, efficacious over and above any hard information that we, as people in industrial societies, might distill from them. There is little attempt by pre-literate people to separate meaning from symbol, content from form, and to relegate symbol or form to a position of neutral insignificance. As *sound* the word is dynamic and pregnant with consequence. The following passage from a Papago Indian's autobiography provides an illustration:

> Many, many songs the men sang but I, a woman, cannot tell you
> all. I know that they made the enemy blind and dizzy with their
> singing and that they told the gopher to gnaw their arrows. And I
> know that they called on our dead warriors who have turned into
> owls and live in Apache country to come and tell them where the
> enemy were. (quoted, Riesman, 1970, pp. 109–10)

From such accounts Riesman concludes that

> We become aware of the emotional force that can be harnessed by

the spoken or sung word in such a group – so powerful here that it can shatter the moral of a distant enemy and can bring alive the desert with its small creatures slipping like spies through the bush. (Riesman, 1970, p. 110)

The Inner/Outer Dichotomy

In view of this comparison of the significance assigned to words in pre-literate and industrial societies it may be concluded that, firstly, the distinction between content and form that we take so much for granted is likely specific to phonetically literate societies and that, secondly, the conundrum the absolutists find themselves in is inextricably linked to that distinction. That is, if the form of music is its content, how can it have any content (or significance) at all?

There is, however, a second distinction, *inter*dependent with that just indicated, on which the theories of Langer and Meyer are predicated. Because this second distinction *is* interdependent with the first, the significance assigned to music by Langer and Meyer becomes questionable. The positions they adopt seem not very far removed from that of the absolutists. This distinction, its interdependency and the consequences that interdependency have for the theories of Langer and Meyer will now be described.

The distancing inherent in the meaning/symbol dichotomy of phonetic literacy greatly reinforces the emphasis on visual space that results with any form of literacy. This reinforcement has consequences for people's relationship to themselves, to others, and to the physical environment. The inter-subjective designation of self no longer requires the presence of the 'significant other', since socially efficacious information may be received in writing. If one thinks of consciousness, which is mediated through communication with others, as communication with self, then it follows that the reception of written information, which originates with others, but whose perusal (silent or oral) is essentially communication with self, induces a shift of emphasis to self. Literate people can put others at a distance and become conscious of self in a manner not easily possible for pre-literate people.

Literate people may put others at a distance in the same way that they put the environment at a distance. The analytic method inherent in phonetic literacy changes the nature of pre-literate people's relationship to their people-centred universe (see Ong, 1967, p. 45). Literacy enables comparisons through time of environmental events. In enabling people to be more intensely conscious and analytic of self and others as *individual* subjects, it also permits the energy and events of the environment to be unravelled from the lives of people. As phonetically literate people can distinguish symbol from meaning, they may draw a line between themselves (the words they utter) and the external world (the *things* to which the words referred). *A distinction between the physical and the mental develops* in contrast to oral societies, where the difference between physical and mental, non-human and human, 'outer' and 'inner', although realized and understood, is not of fundamental significance.

The spatiality and distancing of literacy provides the link between a more intense consciousness of self as an individual subject and 'objectivity'. Through the provision of a surrogate other, literate people may become more aware of their own, individual consciousness, and of their position in the universe – of partially stepping outside themselves and, in a move formalized by Copernicus, of vacating their central, orally enveloped position in the cosmos. As Ong argues, this is something difficult for pre-literate people: 'for early man, the world was something he only participated in, not an object to be manipulated in his consciousness' (Ong, 1969, p. 635).

This objectivity is linked with the time-sense predominant in industrial societies. The historical perspective possible with literacy leads to a straight-line sense of time, as Lee suggests:

> In our culture, the line is so basic that we take it for granted, as given in reality. We see it in visible nature, between material points, and we see it between metaphorical points such as days or acts. It underlies not only our thinking, but also our aesthetic apprehension of the given; it is basic to the emotional climax, which has so much value for us, and, in fact to the meaning of life itself. In our thinking about personality and character, we have assumed the line as axiomatic. (Lee, 1970, p. 142)

Through their ability to record events and through their sense of the pastness of the past, literate people can halt the events of time in their ongoing flow and so, in effect, halt time. Coupled with the development of their analytic ability, literate people thus developed a tendency to examine time from the outside, a tendency reaching full fruition with the Renaissance.

With the end of the Renaissance the feeling of spontaneous inter-communication in all individual activity within the cosmic *becoming* has also disappeared. Human thought no longer feels itself a part of things. It distinguishes itself from them in order to reflect upon them, and is thus no longer upheld by their own power of enduring. From the motion of bodies which inexplicably and incessantly modified it, human thought feels itself to be disengaged by the very act of thinking, for in this act it places itself outside the motion which is its object. (Poulet, 1956, p. 13)

Literate people can exist 'outside' time in the same way as they can partially exist apart from themselves, and their society, and in the same way as their more intense sense of an isolated consciousness and their sense of objectivity allow them to unravel the events of the environment from a human-like volition. In becoming more aware of their own consciousness, literate people become as conscious of their own temporal flow from which they cannot *totally* escape, as they do of the events of the environment which they can fix in a linear order. There thus rises up in Western thought a distinction between time concepts as relating to the physical world and to the mental, as Capek argues:

When Hermann Weyl claims that the objective world *is* and does not become, he has to admit that at least our 'blindfolded consciousness' *creeps* along the world line of its own body into the area of the universe called 'future', or when it is said that we meet the pre-existing future events *on our way to the future*, we concede that even if the future is completed, our way to the future is still going on. . . . Thus arises an absurd dualism of the timeless physical world and temporal consciousness, that is, a dualism of two altogether disparate realms whose correlation becomes completely unintelligible. (Capek, 1961, p. 165)

This 'absurd dualism' underpins the human/non-human, mental/physical, inner/outer, subjective/objective epistemological split already noted.

Psychologistic Theories Reconsidered

It is now possible to understand why neither Meyer nor Langer transcend the limitations of their own intellectual tradition. By restricting musical significance to the inner, emotional and subjective side of this split, they have failed to transcend the first, *interdependent* form and content dichotomy. By restricting music to the inner and mental worlds, they deny music *substantial* significance beyond its 'mere existence' as form. Indeed, a *purely* psychological significance can only be assigned to music

– and the difficulty of the absolutists' position overcome – by denying the interdependency of the two dichotomies.

This criticism implies that the significance attached to music by these two authors is questionable. Symptomatically, Langer, in referring to the work of Wagner, claims music to express *'the Unspeakable'* (1942, p. 235), and goes on to assign such significance a low rational priority:

> Music is a limited idiom, like an artificial language, only even less successflul; *for music at its highest, though clearly a symbolic form, is an unconsummated symbol*. Articulation is its life, but not assertion; expressiveness, not expression. The actual function of meaning, which calls for permanent contents, is not fulfilled. (Langer, 1942, p. 240)

Because she assigns a low rational priority to musical significance, Langer's stance comes close to that of the absolutists. Meyer, however, allows for a more explicit significance through his emphasis on analysis. Yet it is again symptomatic that this analysis, by Meyer's own admission, fails as a method of elucidating that significance.

This admission comes in Meyer's book, *Explaining Music*. At the beginning, Meyer states: 'As I intend the term, criticism seeks to explain how the structure and process of a particular composition are related to the competent listener's comprehension of it' (Meyer, 1973, p. ix). This comprehension is elaborated on toward the end of the book:

> A competent listener perceives and responds to music with his total being. . . . Through such empathetic identification, music is quite literally *felt*, and it can be felt without the mediation of extramusical concepts or images. Such kinesthetic sensing of the ethos or character of a music event is what the term *ethetic* refers to. (Meyer, 1973, p. 242)

It is this ethetic relationship, which stands at the heart of musical apprehension, that is problematic for Meyer: 'Ethetic relationships are unquestionably important . . . [but] are hard to analyse with rigour and precision. . . . [There is an] absence of an adequate theory of ethetic change and transformation' (Meyer, 1973, pp. 245–6). Again: 'The analysis must end here . . . [because] the rigorous analysis of ethetic relationships is beyond my knowledge and skill' (Meyer, 1973, p. 267).

It might be that Meyer's difficulties can be traced to music's encoding of that which is *genuinely* 'unspeakable' or unutterable. It might be thought that, because music refers outside itself to psychological constants, the inner-outer distinction has been truly transcended. But as a symbol may only have meaning in relation to something outside itself, so a thought or feeling might only exist because it too relates to something in the outside world. More specifically, there exists an equivalence between the inner-outer distinction as it applies to both symbols and consciousness: a symbol may only refer outside itself to something because a thought (itself having the same external referent) gave that symbol its meaning; conversely, a thought may only exist because it possesses an external referent implanted by a symbol (itself having the same external referent). 'Outerness' in the world of symbols necessitates a similar 'outerness' in the world of thought and feeling (and vice versa).

Although people may possess desires which are genetically programmed, there seems little doubt that a high proportion of the way we relate to the world results from symbolic interaction with other people. As far as we are concerned, these other people exist 'out there' in 'objective reality'. If it is maintained that there is no need to transcend the inner-outer distinction as it applies to the mind (because all psychological constants or psychological laws of rightness are presumed to be genetically programmed, thereby making reference to the outside world unnecessary), then that is something which needs to be argued. Symptomatically, neither Langer nor Meyer undertakes this argument.

The remedy to Meyer's difficulties lies in his own hands. In his opening chapter, Meyer draws a distinction between critical analysis and style analysis. Whereas critical analysis is concerned with the singular and idiosyncratic, style analysis 'is concerned with discovering and describing those attributes of a composition which are common to a group of works' (Meyer, 1973, p. 7). Theory, moreover, 'endeavours ... to discover the principles governing the formation of the typical procedures and schemata described in style analysis' (Meyer, 1973, pp. 7–8). To complete the relationship: 'Critical analysis uses the laws formulated by music theory ... in order to explain how and why the particular events within a composition are related to one another' (Meyer, 1973, p. 9).

It could be assumed that the principles and laws of music theory are important to the development of a critical method. Apparently, this is not so. In being required to explain why the melodies of Palestrina display a certain structural feature, Meyer suggests one answer 'with a general law of some sort' (Meyer, 1973, p. 8). This law might be 'the Gestalt law of completeness, which asserts that the human mind, searching for stable shapes, wants patterns to be as complete as possible' (Meyer, 1973, p. 8). Beyond this Meyer does not think it necessary to go. There is no need to explore the processes inherent in the search for stable shapes: 'I doubt that the explanation of musical practice needs to be pushed back this far.

As a rule we are, I think, satisfied with the least inclusive law which will account for the events described' (Meyer, 1973, p. 8).

But Meyer does not attain satisfaction. In one breath he tells us that 'the rigorous analysis of ethetic relationships is beyond my knowledge and skill,' and in another argues that the psychological processes basic to those ethetic relationships do not require that same 'rigorous analysis'.

It is possible to trace this conundrum to the central difficulty in music aesthetics. Unlike words and pictures, the significance of music cannot be approached through 'the mediation of extra-musical concepts or images'. If music can be said to have 'meaning' (given the usual referential significance of that term) then, in the minds of most musicians and musicologists, it is *undoubtedly* to be located within the internal structuring of each particular composition. Since music both originates and is efficacious within the minds of people, it can be assumed (a) that there must be a congruence between musical structures and the structure of the human mind, and consequently (b) that this structure can be revealed through the analysis of any musical idiom. Both these assumptions are implicit in Meyer's thought:

> In music, psychological constants such as the principles of pattern organization, the syntax of particular styles, and typical schemata ... constitute the rules of the game. ... For any given musical repertory, the 'rules' determine the kinds of pattern that can be employed in a composition. (Meyer, 1973, p. 14)

It follows that music can satisfactorily be explained in terms of itself, and it is symptomatic that, in supporting his idea of the 'least inclusive law', Meyer incorporates Mario Bunge's view that 'every system and every event can be accounted for ... primarily in terms of its own level and adjoining levels' (quoted, Meyer, 1973, p. 8).

Since there would appear to be nothing fallacious in this line of argument, Meyer looks elsewhere for the cause of his difficulties with ethetic relationships. He concludes that the cause is to be found in the impossibility of distinguishing between psychological constants and the conventions of particular musical idioms.

> In theory, it is possible to distinguish between archetypal patterns and schemata. The former would be those patterns which arise as the result of physiological and psychological constants presumed innate in human behaviour. The latter would be those norms which were the result of learning. But the distinction breaks down in practice. For most traditionally established norms have some basis

in innate constants, and, on the other hand, patterns derived from innate constants become parts of tradition. This being the case the terms will be used more or less interchangeably. (Meyer, 1973, p. 14)

It is not to be disputed that psychological or physiological constants *might* be incorporated in all forms of musical expression. But since, on Meyer's admission, the constants are assimilated in, and become indistinguishable from, the norms of specific musical idioms, would it not be more fruitful to seek the basis of ethetic relationships in these different identifiable norms? To pose a parallel question, if Langer can reach the conclusion that *'what music . . . actually reflects is only the morphology of feeling'* (1942, p. 238) why does she not inquire into the origins of that morphology? Why does she implicitly doubt, with Meyer, 'that the explanation of musical practice needs to be pushed back this far', and thereby ignore the entire sociological tradition?

It would be wrong to imply that psychologistic theories go *absolutely* no way towards transcending the form and content dichotomy. In maintaining a structural conformity between music and mind such theories lay the ground for an understanding of the transfer of 'musical information'. The superimposition of the structure of a particular piece onto a suitably predisposed mind is indeed essential to all musical communication. But equally essential is the social interaction responsible for the 'structural' disposition of that mind.

It may be concluded that while Langer and Meyer transcend the form and content dichotomy as it applies to the manner in which 'musical information' is transferred, they fail to transcend it in terms of the substance of that transfer (this because the inner-outer dichotomy is not transcended). Formulated in these terms, psychologistic theories do not guarantee music an 'outerness' *where significance is concerned*. They guarantee it only in *the sense that music communicates beyond itself to people.*

3 The Post-Renaissance, Industrial World

Introduction

Answers to the question of why it is that music aestheticians and music theorists tend to ignore the social as the fundamental and ultimate site for musical significance can only emerge through an understanding both of the dominant world sense of industrial societies, and of the highly pervasive social structures which are a dialectic correlate of that world sense. These two aspects of the industrial world are discussed respectively in the two sections of this chapter. Against this background, chapter 4 will set out answers to the question just identified.

A Structural Ambiguity

Literate people's ability to view time as a sequence of instants fed back upon their understanding of language until all language, whether spoken or written, was conceived in terms of the segmented nature of the written word. One discrete word was thought of as following another to give a specific meaning. Pre-literate people, by contrast, tended not to think in terms of the discrete word, but in terms of utterances relevant to the face-to-face situations in which meanings were conveyed, as Albert B. Lord illustrates:

> Man without writing thinks in terms of sound groups and not in words, and the two do not necessarily coincide. When asked what a word is, he will reply that he does not know, or he will give a sound group which may vary in length from what we call a word to an entire line of poetry, or even an entire song. The word for 'word' means an 'utterance'. (Lord, 1964, p. 25)

It was the concepts of sequentiality and arrested time that facilitated the invention of movable type printing: the visuality of handwriting acted back upon itself and created the potential for mentally arresting and splitting up the action of scribing. Furthermore, the difference inherent in phonetic literacy between word and meaning, form and content, enabled people to conceive of the blank page as a container into which could be poured meaning in the shape of interchangeable bits of type, linearly arranged. Finally, an awareness of linear processes itself facilitated the invention of the process of movable type printing, which involves a number of steps, sequentially arranged (see Ong, 1967, p. 48).

The invention of movable type printing both facilitated and encouraged the formulation of a dominant 'Western' epistemology in its most crystalline form. Although manuscript literacy permitted the rise of all the visual concepts so far mentioned, it could not allow for the rise of uniformity and repeatability to the extent possible in post-Renaissance societies. Manuscripts of the same 'article' or 'book' were copied at different times by different people with different handwriting. A copy made by one person would *look* quite different to a copy made by another, and there was no guarantee that the wording of one copy would be identical with the next (see Chaytor, 1970, pp. 177ff, and Ong, 1967, pp. 21ff). Furthermore, the number of copies that could be made by this method was limited. Movable type printing, on the other hand, facilitated the production of numerous identical copies.

This development of a uniform outlook has two aspects, one physical, one mental. Firstly, the visuality and segmentation encouraged by printing, together with the regularity and repeatability of the printed page, instigated the concept of a unified pictorial space. The encroaching immediacy and tangibility of pre-literate people's environment, their disunified, multidimensional but 'uniquely structured spaces and times' (McLuhan, 1962, p. 178) were eventually syncretized into the depth of a single three-dimensional space. The visual stress of printing gave a focal point to the distancing and spatiality of phonetic literacy.

But this development of a single, physical point of view has an intellectual analogue, as Goldschmidt indicates:

> It cannot be doubted that for many medieval writers the exact point at which they ceased to be 'scribes' and became 'authors' is not at all clear. . . . We are guilty of an anachronism if we imagine that the medieval student regarded the contents of the books he read as the expression of another man's personality and opinion. He looked upon them as part of that great and total body of knowledge, the *scientia de omnia scibili*, which had once been the property of the ancient sages. (Goldschmidt, 1943, p. 113)

Organic knowledge is split into *segmented* and *individual* points of view, a development that Marshall McLuhan (1962, p. 125) links to the advent of silent reading: 'The reader of print', he says, '. . . stands in an utterly different relation to the writer from the reader of manuscript. Print gradually made reading aloud pointless and accelerated the act of reading till the reader could feel "in the hands of" his author.' But it was not only the reader who reacted to this desire for uniformity of feeling.

> Individual writers throughout the sixteenth century varied tone sentence by sentence, even phrase by phrase, with all the oral freedom and flexibility of preprint days. Not until the seventeenth century did it become apparent that print called for a stylistic revolution. The speeding eye of the new reader favoured not shifting tones but steadily maintained tone, page by page, through-out the volume. . . . By the eighteenth century the reader could depend on a writer controlling the purr of his sentences and giving him a swift smooth ride. Prose became urbane, macadamised. The plunging, rearing horses of sixteenth century journalese were more like a rodeo. (McLuhan, 1970, p. 129)

Instead of partaking of the constantly developing *scientia de omnia scibili* therefore, 'educated' people in typographical cultures internalized a permanent, finished and individually propagated piece of knowledge (see McLuhan, 1970, p. 129).

In the same way that historical dialecticism inculcated a linear sense of the past, so the predictable repeatability of the printed page reinforced the linearity of the future. This reinforced sense of linear futurity found its clearest expression in the concept of applied knowledge, as McLuhan suggests: 'The Medieval Book of Nature was for *contemplatio* like the Bible. The Renaissance Book of Nature was for *applicatio* and use like movable type' (McLuhan, 1962, p. 185). The analytic method of phonetic literacy and historical dialecticism coupled with the concept of repeatability gave 'educated' men in typographical societies the idea of projecting the analytically examined causes and effects of past events into the future. 'Science' grew out of this one level (the *single* point of view), linear, cause-and-effect epistemology. The acid test of the accuracy of scientific prediction lies in the *visual* observance of repeatability, an approach unknown before the Renaissance. As McLuhan points out in referring to the work of Nef (1958, p. 27):

> Observation and experiment were not new. What was new was insistence on tangible, repeatable visible proof. Nef writes . . . 'Such

insistence on tangible proof hardly goes back beyond the times of William Gilbert of Colchester, who was born in 1544. In his *De Magnete*, published in 1600, Gilbert wrote that there was no description or explanation in the book that he had not verified "with his own eyes"'. But before printing had a century and more to build up the assumptions of uniformity, continuity and repeatability, such an impulse as Gilbert felt or such a proof as he offers would have attracted little interest. (McLuhan, 1962, p. 184)

Nowhere is the dominant epistemology of modern industrial societies as clearly evidenced as in the Newtonian-Laplacian view of the universe. As words are locked into the homogeneous printed page, so the universe is viewed as homogeneous empty space peopled by discrete and ultimately immutable units of matter. The indestructibility of matter is itself a concept analogous to the idea of permanence engendered by the keeping of written records, while the juxtaposition and motion of matter in space may be predicted by invoking laws derived from the past observation of matter in space. Future events may thus be *determined* and *controlled*, and the increased control of knowledge resulting from the distancing and objectivity of phonetic literacy may be said to have reached its highest pitch.

The Newtonian-Laplacian view of the universe in turn reinforced the dominant epistemology so that modern, 'educated' Western men *failed to differentiate between what was legitimately predictable and controllable in terms of Newtonian mechanics and what lay outside the field of those laws*. The crucial step in formulating this all-inclusive cosmology is the unfounded assumption that all reality consists in the material. This assumption derives from conceiving matter, which is *not* maintained by people, in the image of eternal unchanging type which *is* maintained by people. In this way matter was assigned a spurious eternity and immutability which encouraged people to think of it as fundamental to the universe. The concept of matter tended to obscure all else, as Capek indicates: 'For psychological reasons, the concept of matter sometimes obscured the concept of void or both concepts obscured that of motion; and nearly always the concepts of space, matter and motion tended to obscure that of time' (Capek, 1961, p. 135). It was this assumption that reality was grounded in the material that both facilitated and encouraged the hegemony of scientific thought in modern industrial cultures. This hegemony, as Carey notes, has approached the condition of mythology:

Science is, of course, the unquestioned source of authoritative knowledge in the modern world. Scientific myths enjoy the claim of being factually true even if they are in no way demonstrable, even if they must be taken on faith, even if they attempt to answer what are, after all, unanswerable questions. Scientific myths have the great advantage in this self-conscious society of not appearing as myths at all but as truths, verified or capable of being verified by the inscrutable methods of the scientist. (Carey, 1967, p. 38)

This hegemony was inevitable, because not to support it would have resulted in questioning the unified pictoral space upon which Newtonian physics is predicated, a questioning unlikely to be undertaken in view of the enormous practical benefits derived therefrom. The seduction became complete, and 'educated' men assumed that the behaviour of all phenomena could ultimately be explained and predicted in mechanical terms. As Helmholtz put it: 'To understand a phenomenon means nothing else than to reduce it to the Newtonian laws' (quoted, Hanson, 1965, p. 91). A similar process occurred with the metaphysical aspects of the dominant world sense of industrial societies. As 'educated' men filtered out experiences not conforming to the order of matter in space, so they filtered out the inflectional information of spoken discourse, a phenomenon noted by McLuhan:

Inflectional complexity, in written form, is not only burdensome for the ear; it is also in conflict with the spatial order that the scanning eye finds natural. To the eye, inflections are not part of the simultaneous order of linguistic variations, which they are for the ear. The reader's eye not only prefers one sound, one tone, in isolation; it prefers one meaning at a time. Simultaneities like puns and ambiguities – the life of spoken discourse – became, in writing, affronts to taste, floutings of efficacy. (McLuhan, 1970, p. 125)

From the point of view of the analysis of the 'industrial world sense', the Newtonian-Laplacian world view remains a particularly lucid expression of that world sense. The world sense also finds expression in the analysis of other spheres of activity which have little to do with classical physics. But so seductive is the Newtonian-Laplacian world view, and so strong is scientific mythology that some people, such as Helmholtz, believe that every phenomenon can be reduced to its constituent material parts and satisfactorily explained through classical physical theories. All that such people will admit is that in many cases this procedure is prohibitively complex and detailed. This constitutes the strictest formulation of the dominant industrial world sense. A further, less strict, formulation remains possible without resurrecting those aspects of experience filtered out as 'non-knowledge'. Although all phenomena may be reducible to their material parts, an adequate explanation of these phenomena according to material-factual modes of thought does not require this. This latter position is one adopted commonsensically by many people in European civilizations since the Renaissance. For them, everything is explicable when *reduced* to the appropriate analytic constituents. Anything which cannot be so reduced and which therefore cannot be made *visually explicit*, becomes non-knowledge, as McLuhan argues:

> The inflectional suggests, rather than expresses or spells out, relations. Technology is explicitness. Writing was a huge technological advance in this respect. It expressed, it made explicit, many relations that were implicit, suggested in inflectional language structures. And what writing couldn't make explicit quickly got lost. Far more than writing, printing was a technological means of explicitness and explanation. But those auditory inflections and relations which could not be made visually explicit by print were soon lost to the language. (McLuhan, 1970, p. 132)

The power of this mode of thought has varied considerably over the last five hundred years. At no time, however, was it as pervasive as during the Enlightenment.

> Seeing the beautiful demonstrations of Descartes and Newton as they explained the heavens with their co-ordinates, the great classical minds sought to rival this perfection and simplicity on earth. Philosophers used the geometric method to arrive at moral and religious truth; social scientists reduced government to mechanics; the tragic muse imitated the tight deductive gate of Euclid; and I am not merely playing with words when I say that poetry itself adopted one common meter as if scientific accuracy depended on it. In all the imponderables of life, conduct, and art, the test was no longer the flexible, 'Is it good, true or beautiful for such and such a purpose?' but 'Is it correct?' (Barzun, 1943, p. 40)

The epistemological dichotomy of industrial societies is capable of acting back on itself at more than one level. The tendency for 'educated' men to suppress the inner, mental, subjective and emotional side of the dichotomy and emphasize the outer, physical, objective and intellectual, operates in *both* the physical and metaphysical aspects of their world sense. This paradox points up the central ambiguity of the world sense, an ambiguity already indicated in respect of the hegemonic and dominant temporal sense of industrial societies. For although a majority of people in industrial societies tend to think that all phenomena are susceptible to material-factual modes of thought, they cannot, if pressed, deny the temporal flow of their own consciousness. Unfortunately, because world senses are processual phenomena to be lived within rather than examined, people in industrial societies are seldom pressed. The consequent inability of 'educated' men to differentiate between what is genuinely material-factual in the universe and what is not has led to an unfounded assumption of *total* objectivity. 'Educated' men in particular have tended to slide into the position of thinking themselves to be *totally* outside time and ultimately, *totally* capable of knowing about everything, including themselves.

This approach to reality does only constitute a tendency, albeit a strong one. If the above exposition of the dominant industrial world sense is strictly interpreted, two mutually exclusive epistemologies emerge. These epistemologies may be labelled the 'universal' and the 'dichotomous'. The dichotomous asserts that any particular phenomenon may be understood *either* in terms of the physical, outer, objective world, *or* in terms of the inner, mental, subjective world. This is the epistemology that most musicians implicitly support. The universal, in representing this latter side of the dichotomy, asserts that *all* phenomena are explicable in terms of the physical, outer and objective world.

This rigorous formulation is only possible in the light of one possible understanding of how the world sense came into being. For people who do not question the assumptions upon which their sense of the world is founded and who live largely within this dominant world sense, the categories of understanding derived therefrom do not appear as clearly formulated. Rather, there is an uneasy vacillation 'around' and 'between' the two epistemologies that passes for one homogeneous epistemology appropriate to the common understanding of the world.

This third, vaguer, epistemology is the 'epiphenomenal'. According to its precepts, if it were shown that a phenomenon is not an integral aspect of the material or objective world, it would be possible to avoid assigning it exclusively to the world of subjective emotion by asserting that it was 'epiphenomenal' to the objective world. The phenomenon could be conceived as being beyond the realms of purely material-factual activity, yet remaining no more than a secondary symptom or manifestation of some material-factual process. For reasons to be made apparent in the next chapter, this is the epistemology to which some sociologists and music theorists have been driven when considering explicitly the relationship between music and society.

Media and Social Structures

This section seeks to situate the social structures of modern industrial societies both historically and across the boundaries of the *class* stratifications which are symptomatic of them. The historical perspective serves to emphasize the culture-specific nature of any structuring, while the concern with anti-classical movements serves to demonstrate that, despite shifts in power between social classes, and despite 'an increasing degree of democracy', the overall structures remain essentially the same. Anti-classical movements, in other words, *tend to be articulated in terms of classical structures.* In the same way that 'educated' men have been ultimately responsible for the development of the hegemonic and dominant world sense of industrial societies, they have likewise been responsible for developing the structures and rules within which political opposition and tension can be worked through.

The process of legitimation – whether achieved by the members of a society acting together, or by specific members appointed by society – involves a suspension of the automatic acceptability of everyday reality. Legitimators voluntarily place themselves in a position where they are more exposed to the impact and implications of fresh phenomena and events. This recession from everyday reality results in an intensification of individual awareness, the nature and degree of this awareness being prorogated ultimately by the means of communication and media available within a society.

So, for reasons already discussed (see also Carothers, 1959, p. 308, and Ong, 1967, pp. 132–3), increased awareness in a pre-literate society cannot help but be re-integrated or sublimated into a collective process during the ritual that symbolizes legitimation. The potential for divergent opinions impinging closely on the assumptions of these societies seems to be low precisely because of the face-to-face and oral-aural mediation of power.

Ideographic literacy, however, encourages the formation of a distinct group of legitimators who align themselves with the ruling elite in a society. Ideographic languages entail a large number of signs (some 50,000 in Chinese, of which 3000 are necessary for a reasonable degree of literacy – see Goody and Watt, 1963, p. 313) which can only be learnt and manipulated by a small group of specialists, a phenomenon which in itself brings about an emergent division of labour. Because of the potential in any form of literacy for the improvement of the administrative and commercial activities of a society, these specialists were important to rulers. There existed a propensity for scribe and ruler to act in common purpose. Because of this propensity, and because ideograms do not code sounds, the information coded tends to be that relevant to the ruling elite (see Goody and Watt, 1963, p. 313); to become literate is to acquire the outlook and ideas of the ruling class, ideas which are of little use or relevance to the ruled oral classes. Goody and Watt have noted the emergence of these characteristics in ancient Oriental civilizations:

> ... it is a striking fact that ... in Egypt and Mesopotamia, as in China, a literate elite of religious, administrative and commercial experts emerged and maintained itself as a centralised governing bureaucracy. ... Their various social and intellectual achievements were, of course, enormous, but as regards the participation of the society as a whole in the written culture, a wide gap existed between the esoteric literate culture and the exoteric oral one, a gap which the literate were interested in maintaining. Among the Sumerians and Akkadians, writing was the pursuit of scribes and preserved as a 'mystery', a 'secret treasure'. (Goody and Watt, 1963, p. 314)

Unlike hieroglyphic literacy, phonetic literacy is relatively easy to learn, the number of symbols varying between twenty and forty. Also, as phonetic literacy can encode the spoken language of the *entire* society, it does not inherently militate against the interests of any particular group in that society. In this sense, phonetic literacy is a potential democratizing influence on previously autocratic regimes.

However, phonetic literacy also aided the incipient division of labour facilitated by ideographic literacy (that is, a basic split between mental and physical tasks). As the concepts of spatialism, segmentation, sequentiality and control developed from the influence of phonetic literacy, so literate elites became increasingly able to think of fragmenting the individual processes of a physical task, and assigning them to different persons. It was then possible to conceive of tasks which could not be completed by one person (or by a very few people working according to the principles of a relatively unsophisticated manufacturing division of labour), but which, for reasons of time or skill, would require the efforts of several people working in succession. This principle can then be applied to broader areas of activity within a society, so that different activities can be achieved with a maximum of skill and efficiency. Consequently, not only is the role of the legitimator entrenched by a developed division of labour, but the division itself, facilitated by the legitimator's intellectual orientation, allows for the growth of class divisions and enables the ruling classes to utilize the services of the legitimator in preserving the *status quo*. As implicated in a developed division of labour, the legitimator tends to have a vested interest in its preservation. Until at least the end of the eighteenth century, it could be argued that literate elites (unexceptionally comprising men) assisted in governmental processes that were autocratic in nature.

Typography is as double-edged as phonetic literacy in encouraging 'democracy'. The typographical process, in which individual bits of type can be changed to form the desired page, engendered the projection of organized mechanization and regimentation throughout society. As uniform printing gave rise to a mechanistic view of space and matter, it gave rise to the idea of using people like the mechanically interacting parts of a machine. People have frequently come to be conceived, in industrial processes, as the interchangeable and atomistic parts of linear, cause-and-effect processes, and, as interchangeable cogs in the nation's machinery, they came to be conceived as increasingly homogeneous. During the nineteenth and twentieth centuries, the division of labour reached a new peak in efficiency.

The increasing homogeneity of post-Renaissance, industrial societies was achieved through the destruction of the 'mutuality' of feudal society. A person no longer played a well-understood and specific role in their local society. Through urbanization they became an increasingly depersonalized source of labour to be accommodated within huge centralized schemes. McLuhan describes this transformation in the following way (1962, p. 162): 'The feudal system was based on oral culture', he says, 'and a self-contained system of centres without margins. ... This structure was translated by visual, quantitative means into great centre-margin systems of a nationalist mercantile kind.' As the simultaneously divergent viewpoints (see McLuhan, 1962, p. 136) and time-spaces (see Poulet, 1956, p. 7) of medieval people slowly came to be snapped into three-dimensional focus, so the disparate functionings of feudal units were gradually unified into single, national points of view. But as European societies changed from ones of centres without margins to ones of centres with margins, so did people. Formerly a 'centre' whose activities were mediated by the oral immediacy of other 'centres', the 'industrial person' may float comparatively rootless in a constantly changing social milieu. No longer is the rationale of existence located in an immediate, self-contained society, but in a remote centre – that of nationalism. This process is described by Ong: 'the development of writing and print ultimately fostered the breakup of feudal societies and the rise of individualism. Writing and print created the isolated thinker, the man with the book, and downgraded the network of personal loyalties which oral cultures favour as matrices of communication and as principles of social unity,' (Ong, 1967, p. 54). Industrial people came to provide their own margins, a process facilitated through the advent of literacy, that surrogate other, as well as, more recently, the advent of electronic media.

Besides being encouraged by a uniformity of function, the growth of nationalism was also aided by the improved control at a distance made possible by the easier production and propagation of knowledge. This control again helped to entrench a highly developed division of labour. Moreover, since the market potential for printed books was greater than could be satisfied by a clerical elite reading in Latin, an increasing number of books were published in the vernacular. Ethnic groups became more aware of their own national identity because they could, in a very literal sense, see themselves.

However, typography may also act as a force for democracy. This possibility exists because of the central ambiguity inherent in the dominant industrial world sense. Nationalism both contains and is predicated upon the suppressed distinction of physical and mental time referred to in the preceding chapter. While homogeneous individuality is a necessary norm for nationalism, in that people with self-contained margins are required to act interdependently for the centrally dictated aims of the nation (or, more recently, international capital), those same people, increasingly literate and critical, came to be more aware of the 'isolated' self and its relationship to others, and so gained an increased possibility for formulating and voicing anti-classical opinions. As McLuhan has so sharply observed: 'individualism, whether in the passive atomistic sense of drilled uniformed soldiery or in the active aggressive sense of private initiative and self-expression, alike assumes a prior technology of homogeneous citizens' (McLuhan, 1962, p. 209). The growth of self-expressive individualism fostered and was in turn reinforced by the emergence of the concept of authorship in post-Renaissance Europe.

The possibility inherent in phonetic literacy for an analytic approach towards the discrepant bodies of knowledge that may be stored in a society was considerably augmented during the Renaissance. The phenomenon of cultural lag consequently becomes of importance in examining *entire* bodies of knowledge within modern societies. The vast dissemination of books and knowledge that resulted from printing encouraged divergent opinions because the body of knowledge a person may be exposed to was probably different in every case. No one person could now know everything. As Goody and Watt pointed out (1963, p. 324): 'the content of the cultural tradition grows continually, and in so far as it affects any particular individual he becomes a palimpsest composed of layers of beliefs and attitudes belonging to different stages in historical time.' In literate societies, where the legitimator constitutes the class of person most intimately exposed to discrepancies and contradictions, there exists the potential for the legitimator's developed degree of self-awareness to be at variance with their role as maintainer of established social norms. Those legitimators who choose to erect new symbolic structures act as catalysts and initiators in the process of change or 'progress', a process which has figured prominently in the consciousness of people in modern industrial societies.

The role of printing in creating the intellectual fervour of the Renaissance need not be recounted. However, it was not until the late eighteenth century that anti-classical movements took on a strong *class* orientation. Williams (1961, p. 50) tells us that 'from the third and fourth decades of the eighteenth century there had been growing up a large new middle-class reading public, the rise in which corresponds very closely with the rise to power and influence of the same class.' Because of this increased market, the author no longer needed to work for a patron but could make his money in the open market-place. As Dr Johnson indicates (writing in 1750), a change of subject matter results:

> The task of our present writers is very different; it requires, together with that learning which is to be gained from books, that experience which can never be attained by solitary diligence, but must arise from general converse and accurate observation of the living world. Their performances have, as Horace expresses it, *plus oneris quantum veniae minus*, little indulgence, and therefore much difficulty. They are engaged in portraits of which everyone knows the original, and can detect any deviation from exactness of Resemblance. Other writings are safe, except from the malice of learning, but these are in danger from every common reader. (quoted, McLuhan, 1962, pp. 273–4)

The result was that, in reading material produced for them and about them, the middle classes began to gain an increased awareness of their political position and its desirability. This kind of awareness spread to the working classes during the nineteenth century (see Williams, 1961, pp. 14–15).

Increasing class consciousness was aided by other developments, such as the mechanization of transport systems and the close proximity of the working classes in the emerging urban areas, both of which are related to the growth of industrial nationalism. Consciousness led to and fed from a demand for increased education, until the foundations were laid for a continuing political and economic dialogue. Legitimators in society, instead of aligning themselves exclusively with a ruling elite possessing a vested interest in class stratification, could now be found as the representatives of practically any class or group. It is not without significance that women remained for the longest time the least visible and least represented class.

Phonetic literacy and typography have thus been heavily instrumental in generating a class dialectic, but *within* the framework of political and economic nationalism as that framework has been largely developed and controlled by men. From the situation where individual feudal units *were* very much the people that constituted them, industrial societies moved to a situation where the nation state became a big hopper in which occupants could be placed and shifted in a highly mobile fashion. Nationalism is founded upon the fallacy of form and content; it is not of the people because it contains them. It is permanent while people are mortal. And as the nation is not constituted of specific individuals it has appeared as a pre-existing and generally unquestioned fact of life, as McLuhan has observed: 'Because the national state does not belong to the citizens of any particular generation,' he says, 'it must not be revolutionised' (McLuhan, 1962, p. 221).

Class dialogue has been overwhelmingly concerned with which men shall wield the centralized power of nationalism and to what effect. In a parallel fashion anti-classical legitimating *structures* have generally been conceived within the intellectual, political and economic frameworks outlined in this chapter, and so grounded very much on the noetic structures induced through phonetic literacy and typography. It is a theme of chapter 8 that the experiences of women and of music alike lead to a questioning of the legitimacy of the ground rules laid down by discourses that are at the same time 'masculine', 'literate' and 'visual'.

4 The Blocks against a Social Theory

Introduction

The purpose of this chapter is to show how the dominant world sense and prevailing social structures of industrial societies have jointly militated against the acceptance of a social theory for the significance of music. The arguments presented in this chapter rely on the background provided in the previous chapter.

Music and Centralized Social Structures

The intellectual correlate of the social structures described in the previous chapter is not difficult to identify. Due to a highly developed division of labour, a hierarchical class structure and the centralism of nationalism, the legitimator has remained in the position of producing and defining knowledge for and on behalf of other people. Academics and artists have on many occasions been associated with those who govern, as this statement by Adam Smith suggests: 'In opulent and commercial societies to think or to reason comes to be, like any other employment, a particular business, which is carried on by a very few people, who furnish the public with all the thought and reason possessed by the vast multitudes that labour' (quoted, Williams, 1961, p. 52).

For the centralized dissemination of knowledge to remain intact in the face of challenge, knowledge is conceived according to the canons of an *absolute* or *objective idealism*. Reality is thought of as 'given' and essentially independent of the vagaries of human volition. However, it is difficult (although not impossible) to think of reality in these terms without the presence of a form of literacy which is fully phonetic. Because spoken words are evanescent, oral-aural cultures are unable to distance their knowledge from the face-to-face social context of its creation and mediation to any great extent. In such cultures, the world and people are assumed to interact in powerful and meaningful ways. Even with earlier, *mnemonic* forms of phonetic literacy, the meaning of writing could only be properly understood by translating the notation back into spoken words, a process involving a certain amount of discussion. The mediation of knowledge remained predominantly oral-aural in character. But with the advent of phonetic literacy there exists the potential for preserving knowledge permanently and independently from the social context of its creation and initial mediation. It was only with the advent of a full phonetic alphabet, therefore, that the potential for idealist thought was fully realized. Not only does a full phonetic alphabet analyse the sounds essential to meaning (rather than acting as an *aide-memoire*). In so doing it becomes prescriptive – that is, it can be meaningfully manipulated independently of the sounds it represents. Once this break between sight and sound is achieved, it is comparatively easy to slip into the position of thinking knowledge and reality as 'given' rather than as socially constructed. The social context of oral-aural discourse is no longer essential to intellection.

The first full phonetic alphabet occurred in ancient Greece. It seems no accident, therefore, that an emphasis on idealist forms of thought occurred in that culture. The supremacy of an independent and objective knowledge over that resulting from social mediation was symbolically asserted through Plato's expulsion of the poets:

> Plato's banishment of the poets and his doctrine of ideas are two sides of the same coin. In banishing the poets from his *Republic*, Plato was telling his compatriots that it was foolish to imagine that the intellectual needs of life in Greek society could still be met by memorizing Homer. Rather than deal in this verbalization, so much of a piece with the non-verbal life-world, one needed to ask more truly abstract questions. (Ong, 1967, p. 33–4)

Experience and intellection were separated so that a considerable amount of importance could be given to the 'cerebrally derived' at the expense of the socially mediated:

> In classic Hegelian thesis-antithesis fashion Plato's ideas, the 'really real', *were polarised at the maximum distance from the old oral-aural human life-world*. Spoken words are events engaged in time and indeed in the present. Plato's ideas were the polar opposite: not *events at all but motionless 'objective' existence, impersonal and out of time*. (Ong, 1967, p. 34)

Meaning is isolated from its social context and grounded in a scheme of absolutes:

> In oral culture words – and especially words like 'God', 'Justice', 'Soul', 'Good', – may hardly be conceived of as separate entities, divorced both from the rest of the sentence and its social context. But once given the physical reality of writing, they take on a life of their own; and much Greek thought was concerned with attempting to explain their meanings satisfactorily, and to relate these meanings to some ultimate principle of rational order in the universe, to the logos. (Goody and Watt, 1963, p. 330)

Art has traditionally concerned itself with this type of absolute and idealist concept since the time of the ancient Greeks. As far as the modern world is concerned we are told by Williams that the argument that 'an artist's precepts were ... the "universals" (in Aristotle's terms) or permanent realities' is one which had been completed in the writings of the Renaissance' (Williams, 1961, p. 56). As Williams points out, it is an argument which united the otherwise disparate creeds of Classicism and Romanticism:

> The tendency of Romanticism is towards a vehement rejection of dogmas of method in art, but it is also very clearly towards a claim which all good classical theory would have recognised: the claim that the artist's business is to 'read the open secrets of the universe'. A 'romantic' critic like Ruskin, for example, bases his whole theory of art on just this 'classicist' doctrine. The artist perceives and represents Essential Reality, and he does so by virtue of his master faculty Imagination. In fact the doctrines of 'the genius' (the autonomous creative artist) and the 'superior reality of art' (penetration to a sphere of universal truth) were in Romantic thinking two sides of the same claim. Both Romanticism and Classicism are in this sense idealist theories of art. (Williams, 1961, p. 56)

This concern with truth has persisted into the twentieth century, albeit in rather less explicit forms. T. S. Eliot argues that diversity of cultural activity is essential to the maintenance of a valid spiritual life. Dialectic is a pre-requisite for truth.

> As in the relation between social classes, and as in the relation of the several regions of a country to each other and to the central power; it would seem that a constant struggle between the

centripetal and centrifugal forces is desirable . . . there should be an endless conflict between ideas – for it is only by the struggle against constantly appearing false ideas that truth is enlarged and clarified, and in the conflict with heresy that orthodoxy is developed to meet the needs of the time. (Eliot, 1948, p. 48)

The complex of arguments associated with an elitist concept of art tends only to be explicitly stated when the concept is faced with a substantial challenge. It could be argued that the first notable challenge to the centralized definition and dissemination of knowledge in post-Renaissance society occurred in the late eighteenth century, with the rise to power and influence of the middle classes. It was then that the notion of art as an approach to essential reality 'received significant additional emphases' (Williams, 1961, pp. 60–1). Faced with a deviant cultural reality, writers and artists were forced back on the notion that culture attains to one, indivisible, essential truth.

But this is only the first step in the line of defence, because it is equally possible for the perpetrators of a deviant cultural reality to claim that they too have access to the essential nature of truth. They may claim that their art forms interpret essential reality more successfully than the traditional art forms with which they vie. Those who produce traditional art forms consequently claim that it is *their* art forms which best reveal essential reality. They then maintain that it is only a limited number of highly tuned minds (such as themselves) who are capable of appreciating this reality in an unaided fashion. F. R. Leavis puts this view explicitly:

In any period it is upon a very small minority that the discerning appreciation of art and literature depends: it is (apart from cases of the simple and familiar) only a few who are capable of unprompted, first-handed judgement. They are still a minority, though a larger one, who are capable of response. The accepted valuations are kind of a paper currency based upon a very small proportion of gold. To the state of such a currency the possibilities of fine living at any time bear a close relation. (Leavis, 1948, p. 143)

The reverse is a disdain for the critical abilities of the 'culturally untutored'. Although such disdain is implicit in the notion of a centrally defined culture, it is again interesting to note the attitude becoming entrenched during the nineteenth century.

Writers had, of course, often expressed, before this time, a feeling of dissatisfaction with the 'public', but in the early nineteenth century this feeling became acute and general. One finds it in Keats: 'I have not slightest feel of humility towards the Public'; in Shelley 'Accept no counsel from the simple-minded. Time reverses the judgement of the foolish crowd. Contemporary criticism is no more than the sum of the folly with which genius has to wrestle.' One finds it, most noticeably and extensively, in Wordsworth. (Williams, 1961, p. 51)

Coupled with the belief that art reveals higher truths fathomable only by a minority of superior minds is the idea that these minds are responsible for preserving the cultural values of a society. The early nineteenth-century writer continued

... to insist, in fact on an Idea, a standard of excellence, the 'embodied spirit' of a People's knowledge, as something superior to the actual run of the market. This insistence, it is worth emphasising, is one of the primary sources of the idea of Culture. Culture, the 'embodied spirit of a People', the true standard of excellence, became available, in the progress of the century, as the court of appeal in which real values were determined. (Williams, 1961, p. 52)

Over a century later Leavis states that:

Upon this minority depends our power of profiting by the finest human experience of the past; they keep alive the subtlest and most perishable parts of tradition. Upon them depend the implicit standards that order the finer living of an age, the sense that this is worth more than that, this rather than that is the direction in which to go, that the centre is here rather than there. (Leavis, 1948, pp. 144–5)

This last line of thought is the one most allied to a centralized dissemination of knowledge. Yet it cannot be maintained without two others. Unless there is a set of objective values and standards against which cultural activity can be judged, and unless it is the case that only a minority are capable of perceiving the essential truth underlying those values, then the legitimacy of the role played by that minority comes into question.

This elitist attitude towards culture is based on the questionable premise that society is divided between those who have inherently superior, and those who have inherently inferior intellects. This premise gives birth to a circular and self-maintaining view of cultural apprehension: it is only those with superior minds who can fathom the ultimate realities of art, yet it is those who can fathom these realities who by definition have superior minds; equally, those with inferior minds cannot fathom the ultimate realities of art, yet it is those who cannot fathom these realities who by definition have inferior minds. This circularity is acknowledged by Eliot when he says that: 'It is an essential condition of the preservation of the quality of the culture of the minority, that it should be a minority culture' (Eliot, 1948, p. 107), and through Arnold Schoenberg's famous aphorism that 'If it is art, it is not for all, and if it is for all, it is not art.'

The attitudes described in this chapter are to be found in the musical as well as the literary worlds. The idea that the composer mediates between 'the open secrets of the universe' and music finds expression in the work of Zuckerkandl. For Zuckerkandl, musical significance is located in laws which may only be discovered in objective reality.

> It is not that the mind of the creative artist expresses itself in tones, words, colours, and forms as its medium; on the contrary, *tone, word, colour, form express themselves through the medium of the creative mind*. The finer that medium the better the tone word, colour, form can express themselves. The greater the genius, the less it speaks *itself*, the more it lends its voice to the tones, the words, the colours, the forms. In this sense, then, music does write itself – neither more nor less, by the way, than physics does. The law of falling bodies is no invention of the genius of Galileo. The work of the genius consists in bringing the mind, through years of practice, so into harmony with things, that things can express their laws through him. (Zuckerkandl, 1956, pp. 222–3)

A similar view is expressed by Ruth Gipps. For her, music is a mystic experience founded on truth:

> I know that from one God comes music and all musical gifts. Some of us were composers from the beginning of our lives; we had no choice in the matter, only a life-long duty to make the most of a given talent. This talent may be large or small, but without it a person is not a composer. . . . My own conception of God is of a limitless contrapuntal mind; perhaps this concept lacks humanity, but that is my own business. From personal experience I know that mysticism is founded on truth. (Gipps, 1975, p. 13)

Consequently, '. . . no human being has ever created anything. The most that a composer can do is to present to other people, in a comprehensible form, music that already existed. Bach wrote 'S.D.G.' at the end of works. None of his music was a product of the cleverness of J. S. Bach' (Gipps, 1975, p. 13).

The idea that a minority of people are imbued with a special gift of musicality which may be cultivated into genius is a commonplace in thinking about music. Such belief in the other-worldly nature of musical inspiration and the ability of only a minority to exploit it in turn leads to the concept of an objective aesthetic. It is assumed that there are fixed criteria against which *all* music can be judged. These criteria tend to be rooted in the musical languages of the ruling classes (see DiMaggio and Useem, 1982, and Haughton, 1983). Meyer, for example, has attempted to extrapolate a universally applicable theory of music from albeit insightful analyses of functional tonality. Pre-literate music does not fair very well.

> The differentia between art music and primitive lies in speed of tendency gratification. The primitive seeks almost immediate gratification of his tendencies whether these be biological or musical. Nor can he tolerate uncertainty. And it is because distant departures from the certainty and repose of the tonic note and lengthy delays in gratification are insufferable to him that the tonal repertory of the primitive is limited, not because he cannot think of the other tones. It is not his mentality that is limited, it is his maturity. (Meyer, 1959, p. 494)

Such opinions are frequently backed up with technical or analytic arguments. Stearns reports the following conversation with a friend about jazz:

> 'Jazz', he told me one evening, 'is unnatural, abnormal and just plain unhealthy'. I know of no effective way to answer this sort of pronouncement on any human activity. When pressed for reasons, however, he fell back on more rational assertions: 'the harmonies of jazz are childish, the melodies are a series of cliches, and the rhythms are monotonously simple'. Here is something technical and specific. What is more these criticisms are reasonably typical and comprehensive. Since my friend (and others like him) occupies an important position in the world of music on the strength of his unquestioned merits, his comments should be taken seriously. (Stearns, 1956, p. 183)

It is not necessary to establish that such criticisms are questionable (although it is the view of this writer that they are), only that they are made in the way in which they are. However, Schuller devotes the first chapter of his book on jazz to spelling out the precise musical differences between early jazz and the 'classical' tradition (Schuller, 1968, pp. 3–62). Further, it is a corollary of the attitude being described that whereas most jazz and rock musicians are happy to concede that 'classical' or 'serious' music operates according to a set of criteria which are irrelevant to their musical requirements, many 'classical' musicians, in their belief that they are in a position to judge other types of music, end up exposing their ignorance to those who create and perform these types. Pete Townshend of 'The Who' has stated that a knowledge of 'classical' music is irrelevant to his needs:

> I'm sure it will surprise a lot of people when I tell you that I can read music and I know how to arrange it; I also know about counterpoint. But as soon as I had learned all the theory, I realised that it was utterly useless to me. All it allowed me to do was to understand what other composers were trying to do, and once you've understood you've got to go and use today's terms to produce new music. (quoted, Palmer, 1970, p. 131)

Conversely, the black jazz musician Cecil Taylor highlights the manner in which jazz (and, *mutatis mutandis*, criticisms of other forms of 'popular' music) are frequently made from a position of ignorance:

> I've spent years in school learning about European music and its traditions, but those cats don't know a thing about Harlem except that it's there. Right away, when they talk about music they talk in terms of what music is to them. They never subject themselves to, like, what are Louis Armstrong's criteria for beauty and until they do that, then I'm simply not interested in what they say. Because they simply don't recognise the criteria. (quoted, Spellman, 1970, p. 34)

The Head of Music in an English technical college has put this point forcefully with regard to 'pop' music. Most teachers' view of 'pop', he maintains

> is simply based on sheer ignorance; they've just got no idea what sort of music today's kids listen to. If I had some of these teachers here for two days playing the records from our collection they would soon have to change their ideas concerning 'pop' music. (reported, Vulliamy, 1972, p. 95)

Since, as Pleasants put it, the musical 'Establishment is concerned with the preservation of what it regards, sincerely, I think, as immutable cultural criteria' (Pleasants, 1969, p. 118), its criticisms of music which does not conform to preordained technical criteria frequently carries an accompanying moralistic component. This tendency in the denunciation of various forms of jazz, rock and 'pop' music is so well known that it hardly requires substantiation. One need only refer to Merriam's cataloguing of the tirade launched against jazz in the United States between the 1920s and 1940s (Merriam, 1964, pp. 241–2). This moralistic attitude carries an opposing perspective. Whereas the music establishment sees it as its task to preserve and maintain standards, those who are in receipt of such criticisms view it as an attempt to destroy their own culture. This opposing perspective is piquantly expressed by Cecil Taylor:

> I've known Negro musicians who've gotten grants but it's very interesting that no Negro jazz musician ever got a grant. If you're a black pianist who wants to learn to play Beethoven, you have a pretty good chance of getting a grant. That's that fucked-up liberal idea of uplifting the black man by destroying his culture. But if you want to enlarge on culture, forget it; your money will have to come from bars and that cut-throat record industry. (quoted, Spellman, 1970, p. 48)

It now becomes apparent why aestheticians and music theorists refrain from assigning music (by which they almost without exception mean 'serious' music) a social significance. If the significance of music is socially located, then it must be understood to form part of the socially constructed reality of the groups or societies responsible for producing and consuming the music in question. The music can only be legitimately understood in terms of categories of analysis which form an aspect of the reality of those groups or societies. There can be little question of recourse to the notion that musical significance is derived from the 'open secrets of the universe' or some other form of mystical, other-worldly truth.

Because the notion that music forms an integral aspect of socially constructed reality is incompatible with the idea that musical significance is derived from the 'open secrets of the universe', there can be no question of a reverse information flow by which society informs the composer. Rather, the mass of people are informed, edified, and improved through the composer's insights into truth. Neither Langer nor Meyer makes any reference to essential truth or a higher reality. But they maintain a unidirectional information flow from a revised form of idealist truth to society by locating the significance of music in the 'psychological constants' (Meyer, 1973, p. 14) or 'psychological laws of rightness' (Langer, 1942, p. 240), which are common to all people, but which only the composer can interpret with any insight. Langer's and Meyer's theories remain implicitly elitist. While they are able to distinguish between a symbol which has no obvious referent in the world of objects and ideas, and one which is 'informationally open', they are constrained to severely restrict the degree of that openness. Although it is admitted that music may refer outside itself to the mental world, it is implicitly denied that it can refer outside to the *external* symbolic interaction which is arguably responsible for a large measure of that world.

It is apparent that once the significance of music is taken to be socially located, the circle of argument predicated on the notion of inherently superior and inferior minds is broken. Differences in cultural values do not flow from differences in levels of intelligence. They flow, rather, from the existence of socially constructed and different cultural criteria which not infrequently display a mutual incompatibility. With this central pillar of the elitist position removed, the right of the institutionalized musician or aesthetician in industrial societies to approach *all* music in terms of certain idealistically conceived categories comes into question. The propensity for such musicians and aestheticians to impose a certain way of thinking about music on the rest of society also comes into question.

The fact that an acceptance of the social mediation of music might result in a weakening of role security is significant, but is not the most telling point against such acceptance. *Any* assertion that the reality or knowledge of a society is socially constructed not only brings into question the notion of absolutely and objectively conceived knowledge. It questions the right of one group in society to use that notion in order to attempt a centralized mediation and control of knowledge and values for other groups. Because centralized social structures depend for their survival on such modes of cognitive mediation and control, questioning of the sort indicated would result in the scrutiny of the entire centralized structure of most industrialized societies.

The connection may seem a distant one, but it is possible that the unwillingness of musicologists and aestheticians to accept the social significance of 'serious' music is due to the fact that acceptance requires a questioning of the social and political structures within which they live. Not only would it mean accepting that the various forms of jazz, rock and 'pop' music are as 'good' as serious forms, it would also mean accepting the music's social and moral relativity. Against these trends, the institutionalized musicologist is led back to a search for objective standards of value, as this statement by Meyer illustrates:

At this point some of our social scientist friends, whose blood pressure has been steadily mounting, will throw up their hands in relativistic horror and cry: 'you can't do this! You can't compare baked alaska with roast beef. Each work is good of its own kind and there's an end of it.' Now granted both that we can enjoy a particular work for a variety of reasons and also that the enjoyment of one kind of music does not preclude the enjoyment of others . . . this does not mean that they are equally good. Nor does it mean that all modes of musical enjoyment are equally valuable. In fact, when you come right down to it, the statement that 'each is good of its kind' is an evasion of the problem, not a solution of it. And so we are driven to ask: are all kinds equally good. (Meyer, 1959, p. 495)

It is a part of the elitist's case that some types of 'non-serious' music *should* be taken to form an integral aspect of the group or society in which they occur. In allowing that these other types of music might be inherently 'asocial', the elitist would open the way for the suggestion that they too have some kind of meaningful relationship to essential reality, and are therefore on an equal footing with 'serious' types of music. It is not essential that *no* relationship be taken to exist between different forms of 'non-serious' music and essential reality, only that these forms are so greatly influenced by the social context of their creation that the revelation of inner truth that might otherwise occur is distorted and blurred beyond recognition. It is often a distinguishing feature of 'non-serious' musics that they are taken to be socially significant, and that such significance is taken to be a mark of disapprobation.

A belief in the social significance of all music not only removes the central pillar of the elitist's position. It also transcends the strict psychologistic delimitation of mental processes responsible for the aesthetic difficulty discussed in chapter 2. Inherent in that delimitation is the implication that social phenomena result from the collective interaction of physiologically predetermined consciousness which subsequently come to be socially mediated. It is in this way that the psychologistic delimitation of mental processes becomes essential to an elitist view of musical processes. The propensity to maintain an elitist view of music prevents Langer and Meyer from positing an exteriority or 'outerness' which consists of *intangible* and *directly imperceptible* social structures.

In this way, the centralized social structures of industrial societies prevent a transcendence of the categories of analysis which are its dialectical correlates. It might be thought that failure at such transcendence results *solely* from the effects of those centralized social structures.

However, it will be argued in the following section that, in a rather more advanced form, *and as it is applied to social-cultural analysis*, the inner-outer, mental-physical dichotomy itself actively militates against music being assigned a social significance in anything like a satisfactory fashion.

Music and the Industrial World Sense

If prevalent modes of thought and social organization in industrial societies are dialectical correlates, then the relationship of the psychologistic view of music to the dominant world sense of industrial societies should display two related features. The world sense should at least allow for the 'asocial' understanding of 'serious' music which is essential to the elitist's position. In addition, in order that the centralized structures of industrial societies should not come under scrutiny, they should *actively militate* against the formulation of any social theory for the significance of music. It is this latter feature which is explored in this section.

The elitist's position depends on a strict differentiation between cultural and social processes. This differentiation is predicated on the dichotomous epistemology set out previously. The elitist divides social process between those elements which are 'material' (the people and the environment on which they depend), and those which are 'mental' (the meanings conveyed through symbolic exchange). This distinction between the 'socio-economic' and 'cultural' aspects of social process depends on a multi-level interpretation of the dichotomous epistemology. Firstly, there is a tendency in industrial societies for the 'matter' (or content) of a message to be given a higher rational priority than the medium (or form) of its conveyance. But because the 'matter' of a message is divorced from the materiality of its 'inconsequential' conveyancing medium (all symbolic transfer involves some articulation of the material universe), it appears metaphysical in comparison with the materiality of people and the goods they manufacture. (Were the materiality of symbolic transfer not discounted in this fashion, such division of the social process would be impossible.)

Having made this division, the elitist is obliged to *restrict* the notion of the social process to the material half of their split, and the notion of cultural process to the mental. Were they to suggest that society and culture were somehow immanent 'in' each other (which for political reasons they are not disposed to do), they would be suggesting that both society and culture were explicable in terms of *both* halves of the dichotomous epistemology. This would be to transgress the fundamental condition of the dichotomy. In this fashion the metaphysics of high culture come to be inaccessible to the material-factual modes of thought which underlie 'mass' industrial society.

This division is difficult to establish categorically, since all culture presupposes some manipulation of the physical environment, and all actions are incipiently symbolic and therefore 'cultural'. However, *this* particular application of the dichotomous epistemology merely *facilitates* an 'asocial' view of culture (and therefore 'serious' music), and was, in all probability, not as instrumental in the *active* creation of that view as the emergence of a heavily centralized social structure. Further, because people in industrial societies live within these societies' dominant world sense, the categories of understanding specific to that sense are not as clearly or consistently interpreted as *post hoc* analysis might seem to require that they should be.

An illustration of this is to be found in the elitist's idea that 'non-serious' forms of music contain a social element. The elitist cannot consign these 'inferior forms of culture' to the material-factual world of mass society. If they did so, they would be admitting that they were generically different phenomena to their own forms of culture, and there would be no point in making any value judgements concerning them. However, the elitist cannot make a clear distinction between popular culture and its social 'content'. Apart from political considerations, such a distinction would contravene the fundamental conditions of the dichotomous epistemology. While the elitist's view of high culture must be based on this dichotomous epistemology, their view of popular culture cannot help but be predicated on the epiphenomenal. 'Non-serious' musics cannot be completely explained in terms of the material-factual modes of thought which are taken to underlie mass industrial society, yet they nevertheless remain secondary symptoms or manifestations of those same modes. This point is taken up again in the next section of the chapter.

Bryn Jones has observed that 'the field of cultural analysis is [currently] dominated by four major tendencies' (Jones, 1974, p. 25). Two of these, which Jones refers to as the 'conservative' and the 'liberal-humanist' correspond to the elitist position (Jones, 1974, pp. 25ff). The remaining, the 'technical-rationalist' and the 'vulgar-marxist', are predicated respectively on the universal and epiphenomenal epistemologies, and between them actively militate against the acceptance of a social theory for the significance of music.

The 'technical-rationalist' approach finds expression in

positivistic sociology and social psychology [and] introduces a supposedly scientific quality to its research. It has liberal aims, notably in the sphere of social policy, and employs scientific terms. Its classic study is the scientific analysis of the effects of mass media on the audience. The cultural object is reduced to its quantifiable elements by content analysis; the participants are reduced to their socio-economic categories or ranged along various axes of sociological variables by such techniques as audience research; and the activities are reduced to clinically isolated simple communication flow models such as those developed in psychology. It has an absent theoretical heart, its place taken by a set of routinised research practices. Its social engineering and reformist outlook imply an unquestioned adherence to consensual aims founded on myths of democratic decision making. (Jones, 1974, p. 26)

Whether other forms of culture and art are amenable to such analysis must remain an open question. Music, however, poses a problem. This is not because of the central aesthetic difficulty in attempting a 'content analysis' of music. Because their outlook is rooted in the universal epistemology, the 'technical-rationalist' is constrained to deny the existence of the emotional phenomena on which notions of musical significance usually rest, and so, *in the case of music* the relevance of the distinctions between symbol and meaning, the inner and the outer (these categories are permitted to the 'technical-rationalist' so long as all phenomena subsumed under them are susceptible to material-factual modes of analysis). The 'technical-rationalist' may take refuge in the fact that music's 'quantifiable elements' are taken to be elucidated through the traditional analyses of music theorists. The findings of such analyses are taken to be *identical* with the unidirectional information flow involving society, people and symbols. This line of thought parallels that used by Meyer to overcome the absolutist's position, with the exception that any *mental* qualities symptomatic of 'psychological constants' are replaced with physico-chemical 'psychological' characteristics determined by the rational social process. Since this *particular* line of thought negates all epistemological dichotomies, it is impossible to bring the same charges of inconsistent interpretation that were earlier laid against the theories of Langer and Meyer. The central problem with this line of thought is that technical-rational analysis of music can never elucidate that music's significance (this because music does *not* possess rational and internally sufficient laws grounded in physical reality). This lack of success is admitted by Meyer in his discussion of ethetic relationships. However, Zuckerkandl brings to bear an argument which puts the matter beyond reasonable doubt.

Zuckerkandl argues that there exists a difference between a series of tones which are musical nonsense and a series of tones which make up a melody. In the latter case the series of tones convey a 'meaning' which is lacking in the former. The melody 'has something' that the random series of notes does not. Zuckerkandl then argues that what the tones of a melody 'possess' is a dynamic quality. They create a feeling over and above their simple existence which reveals a great deal about their relationship to other tones in the melody. It is this dynamic quality which cannot be described or quantified in physical terms. A physical description of a tone is the same whether the tone is isolated from other tones, part of a random series, or part of a meaningful melody. Because of this, the musical quality of a tone is beyond the realms of explanation in physical reductionist terms.

> Among the qualities that belong to the tone as an acoustical phenomenon there is none that is not determined by a particular element of the physical process and only changes, and always changes, if something changes in the physical process. Nothing in the physical event corresponds to the tone as a musical event. (Zuckerkandl, 1956, p. 22)

'When we hear a melody', therefore, 'we hear things that have no counterpart in the physical nature' (Zuckerkandl, 1956, p. 23). Although the physical properties of a tone may be made explicit in a visual fashion, music presents us with 'something' not easily accessible to material-factual modes of thought.

This is the difficulty encountered by Silbermann in his book, *The Sociology of Music*. With its emphasis on a scientific method, and its concern with the social determinants of music, the structure, function and behaviour of socio-musical groups, and the need for socio-musical planning, the book conforms to Jones's description of the 'technical-rationalist' approach. It is the 'scientific' method which concerns us here. For Silbermann, society and its study (and this includes music) can only exist insomuch as they are explicitly rooted in the material-factual world.

> Sociology is the study of social life as much, of its forms and origins, its processes and aims; and it studies the social wherever it may directly be perceived and grasped. Thus, for instance, everything contained in the concept of 'society' is perceptible and tangible. Under this heading comes every type and degree of human relationship, whether organized or unorganized, conscious or unconscious, direct or indirect. Culture – for our purposes music –

with all its modes of effectiveness, may also be grasped directly, and the study of culture is thus the study of a social force. (Silbermann, 1963, p. 37)

Human affairs should be investigated in a scientific and objective fashion, and speculation about the nature and origin of social 'facts' should be avoided.

Since ours will be an approach in which disputes over methodology will be left aside and practical and applicable sociology will be pursued, we shall be less concerned to define the sociology of music in itself than to describe its tasks through penetration into the matter itself. We shall therefore employ concrete results of research without yielding to the temptation to indulge in philosophical speculation about them; although this might well give an impression of subtlety, it would also stand in direct contradiction to that principle of sociology which enjoins us to study human affairs dispassionately and objectively. The sociologist of music must ever be ready to take up a scientifically objective attitude to socio-musical facts, to observe them independently of his own desires and interests, and to steer clear of any kind of religious, racial, national or class prejudice. (Silbermann, 1963, p. 46)

Silbermann thinks of musical experience as a 'social phenomenon'. In so doing, he runs into the problem just outlined. Although sound – and, therefore, in one sense, music – is directly perceptible and, within the broader sense of the word, 'tangible', it is doubtful whether musical experience can be so described (this because of the intangible and directly imperceptible social structures immanent 'in' all musical communication). Yet because Silbermann thinks of musical experience as a 'social phenomenon' he cannot relegate it, as Langer and Meyer do, exclusively to the realm of inner psychology. At the very least, musical experience of the inner world must have correlates in the external world.

Silbermann gets round this difficulty through the epistemological vacillation described in chapter 3. He invokes the dichotomous epistemology in asserting the validity of emotion in music: 'The countless possibilities of emotional experience have in many cases been wilfully suppressed, and it is with such negative attitudes as these that we must take issue in the strongest possible manner' (Silbermann, 1963, p. 63). Yet he maintains the universal by implying that emotional experience is dependent on the perceptible and tangible phenomena which 'exclusively' constitute 'social' life. Although he does not say that 'the arts are merely "the designs embossed upon the texture of social life"', and although he admits of 'a reciprocal action between the musical experience and the groups which consume it', the emphasis placed by Silbermann on the 'social determinants' of musical experience leads one to think that the reciprocal action is only possible because of the initial dependency just mentioned.

'In what way is the musical experience socially determined?' and 'In what way does the musical experience socially determine other elements?'; to the treatment of these fundamental questions, the words of Romain Rolland are very relevant: 'Art is not influenced by art alone, nor by thought alone, but by everything which surrounds us – people, things gestures, movements, lines and light'. In fact, the musical experience is dependent upon so many factors that the attempt to grasp and describe them sometimes leads to despair. (Silbermann, 1963, p. 83)

The validity of imputing this epiphenomenal line of thought to Silbermann is underlined when he claims that 'sociological analysis of music as such [is] extremely difficult, if not impossible.'

Hence then the failure of those pseudo-sociologists who, in spite of frequent warnings, persist in undertaking the impossible: in trying to analyse music as such sociologically. Music, as the inner concern of the composer, the musician or even of the whistling amateur, *has not the slightest value as reality*. Only when this inner concern becomes objectified, when it takes on concrete expression, has it value as a social reality, only then does it express the 'something' (I use the word deliberately) which must be understood or which will call forth a social effect. (Silbermann, 1963, p. 68)

The notion that 'music ... has not the slightest value as reality' seems at odds with the earlier statement that 'culture – for our purposes music – with *all* its modes of effectiveness, may be grasped directly ...' (italics mine). This disparity points to the difficulty of attempting to analyse musical experience according to the canons of a positivistic sociology. The only means by which positivistic sociology can accommodate musical experience is by momentarily adopting the infrastructure-superstructure model associated with traditional forms of Marxism. That is, because music is viewed as a secondary symptom or manifestation of rational social process, there is no need for musical experience to be analysable in terms of material-factual modes of thought. It is this infrastructure-superstructure model which constitutes Jones's final tendency in cultural analysis.

> The conventional wisdom of orthodox Marxism has consistently devalued the significance of culture, seeing it, in the main, as simply the reflection of the base, the economic infrastructure of society. So culture is produced by the economic relations in a fairly direct way, and is thus mere illusion or delusion, bourgeois ideology or false consciousness. The economist version of Marxism has its roots in some of the more positivistic assertions by Marx about the place of ideology. What is left out, however, is any sense of the relative autonomy of the superstructure, of the reciprocal determination of the base by the superstructure which precludes any such undialectical analysis as that conducted by *vulgar* Marxism. (Jones, 1974, pp. 26–7)

This tendency in cultural analysis is predicated on the epiphenomenal epistemology. By asserting that culture is a secondary symptom or manifestation of the material processes of society, and by acknowledging that the bourgeois elitist invokes a strict society-culture dichotomy in order to pass moral judgements on society as a whole, the Marxist is able to claim that the bourgeois concept of art is an illusion and therefore one aspect of its ideology. However, *some* Marxists seem unable to accept that symbols act back on society in any other sense than that they reflect and reinforce a pre-existing social structure.

Yet the infrastructure-superstructure model need not be restricted to Marxism. It is (and this is the main point towards which this section has been moving), the only remaining mode of thought founded on the industrial world sense by which music may be assigned any sort of social significance. If the *traditional* aesthetician or music theorist seriously considers the notion that the significance of music is social, then this is the mode of thought that comes into play. However, to the traditional aesthetician or music theorist, this mode of thought in turn guarantees the 'asocial' nature of music. For it is nothing if not synonymous with the view that a symbol has meaning because it refers to something outside itself, in this instance some process in the infrastructure. The music theorist or historian who acknowledges a social influence on musical style is thus placed in a dilemma. They may be all too aware that fundamental stylistic changes frequently correspond to fundamental social changes. However, they are prevented from situating the significance of music in its full social context because such a situation invokes the notion of extra-musical concepts. This dilemma is reflected in Meyer's attitude towards the subject:

Yet the explanations furnished by reference to political, social and cultural history tell only part of the story. For stylistic changes and developments are continually taking place which appear to be largely independent of such extramusical events. Although an important interaction takes place between the political, social and intellectual forces at work in a given epoch, on the one hand, and stylistic developments on the other, there is also a strong tendency for a style to develop in its own way. If this is the case, then the causes of these changes must be looked for in the nature of aesthetic experience, since for composer and listener style is simply the vehicle for such an experience. (Meyer, 1956, p. 65)

Meyer seems to be saying that, although the aesthetic experience must remain independent of social forces, it is impossible for the composer, as a member of society, to remain uninfluenced by such forces. Meyer therefore allows for a reverse information flow by which society informs the composer, but this reverse flow is only seen as affecting the particular manner in which musical values (the unsullied aesthetic experience as it appeals to innate psychological constants) are communicated. This view of the relationship between aesthetic experience and social forces is made explicit in another context.

One must therefore distinguish between moral values and individual values. Moral values deal with what will probably be good or bad for men taken as a group. Individual values are concerned with experience as it relates to particular men and women. The two should not be confused. For a concern with moral values such as the social sciences exhibit (and their inductive-statistical method makes this all but inevitable) leads to a normative, relativistic view in which values change from culture to culture and from group to group within the culture. A concern with individual values such as one finds in the humanities leads, on the other hand, to a universal view of value, though recognising that ultimate value goals may be reached by somewhat different means in different cultures. Indeed it is because the individual dimension of values is universal that, where translation is possible (as it is not in music), one is able to enjoy and value art works of another culture. Lastly, in contending that the ultimate value of art lies in its ability to individualise the self, I am conscious of my opposition to those who, like Plato, Tolstoy and the Marxists, would make aesthetic value a part of moral value. (Meyer, 1959, pp. 499–500)

Meyer's position illustrates the fashion in which the centralized structures of industrial societies and their dominant world sense 'coalesce' to prevent a social significance being assigned to music. Not only is a belief in objective musical values a necessary adjunct of centralized social structures. The exclusive 'interiority' associated with such values is essential if music, *in terms of the dominant industrial world sense*, is not to be assigned extra-musical significance.

The influence brought to bear by the industrial world sense filters through in the analysis of *both* the musical *and* social spheres. It precludes the possibility that the significance of music should, in any *complete* sense (whether 'referential' or social), be extra-musical or extra-symbolic (since the extra-musical is taken to be exclusively constituted through objects, events and concrete concepts). Yet, taking this difficulty into account, and acknowledging the unsatisfactory nature both of 'asocial' and positivistic sociological theories for the significance of music, it *ultimately* prevents an analysis of the social-cultural process where the significance of symbols can be anything *but* extra-symbolic (that is, lodged ultimately beyond a symbol's materiality).

The inadequacy of traditional referentialism as a basis for musical analysis reinforces the intuition against which the critique in this part of the book has been set out: that, because of its inherently 'non-referential', fluid and dynamic nature, music is well suited to convey the intangible, directly imperceptible, highly fluid and dynamic nature of social structures as these structures are mediated and given life in both the external and internal worlds. Indeed, it is questionable whether a distinction should be drawn between 'music' and 'society'. It is obvious that in one sense or another music is in society. It is also the case that society is 'in' music, a point that will be explored further in chapters 5 and 11.

Music and Social Organization

So far this chapter has shown how the predominant world sense and centralized structures of industrial societies have prevented the adoption of an adequate social theory for the significance of music. But while the world sense and its concomitant social structures constitute necessary conditions for the maintenance of implicitly 'asocial' views, they are not sufficient. If the proposition that the significance of music is social is correct, then there must be some feature of the relationship between 'serious' music and other activities in industrial societies which prevents that sociality from being self-evident. This feature may be highlighted by considering the different situations of music in pre-literate and industrial societies.

The potential for the development of role-specific knowledge in industrial societies is higher than in pre-literate societies. One reason for this difference lies in the varying abilities that pre-literate and industrial people have to recede from the imposing massivity of everyday reality, and to develop a high division of labour. In pre-literate societies the division of labour upon which role-specific knowledge is predicated (see Berger and Luckmann, 1967, p. 158) occurs largely along lines of age and gender and may be said to be relatively undeveloped. It is a social rather than manufacturing division of labour. Consequently, the distancing and separation that occur in pre-literate societies between different bodies of role-specific knowledge and the universally shared knowledge appropriate to everyday reality seem to be less than in industrial societies. This reduced distancing is consistent with, and a dialectical correlate of, pre-literate people's less developed potential for receding from everyday reality. Industrial societies, on the other hand, are characterized by a highly developed division of labour. Although there exists a sizeable body of knowledge which is common to everyday reality, role-specific bodies of knowledge in industrial societies tend to be hermetically conceived and articulated, and to have a minimal of relationship with each other and the central core of everyday knowledge. This distancing and separation are a dialectical correlate of the potential in phonetic literacy for people to recede to a substantial extent from everyday reality.

This distinction may be highlighted through Berger and Luckmann's discussion of ideal-typical extremes regarding the scope and modes of institutionalization in different societies. On the one hand:

> It is possible to conceive of a society in which institutionalization is total. In such a society, all problems are common, all solutions to these problems are socially objectivated and all social actions are institutionalized. The institutional order embraces the totality of social life, which embraces the continuous performance of a complex, highly stylised liturgy. There is no role-specific knowledge, or nearly none, since all modes are performed with situations of equal relevance to all actors. (Berger and Luckmann, 1967, p. 97)

On the other hand:

> The opposite extreme would be a society in which there is only one common problem, and the institutionalization occurs only with respect to actions concerned with this problem. In such a society there would be almost no common stock of knowledge. Almost all knowledge would be role-specific. (Berger and Luckmann, 1967, p. 98)

Such societies do not exist. However, Berger and Luckmann conclude that 'primitive societies approximate the [first] type to a much higher degree than civilized ones.' Further, 'in the development of archaic civilizations there is a progressive movement away from this type' (Berger and Luckmann, p. 98).

Secondly, there are probably different attitudes towards creativity in pre-literate and industrial societies. In chapter 2 it was argued that because pre-literate people's knowledge is mediated in an oral-aural fashion, their relationship to their knowledge and their environment is characteristically slippery and elusive. Although pre-literate people may dislike the non-traditional, they must also be ready to react to a world which is dynamic and unpredictable. To this extent they may *intuitively* accept as necessary and even faintly desirable activities which we label as 'creative' or 'deviant'.

The situation in industrial societies is different. Creativity, which involves the spontaneous coming into being of something that was unpremeditated and unpredictable, is incompatible with the supremacy of an epistemology that tends to be scientistic, reductionist and deterministic. A unified field of 'cause and effect' cannot easily tolerate the capriciousness of creative events. Further, because industrial societies can 'control' the events of their world, they have found genuine creativity not only 'unnecessary', but a threat to the rational *status quo*. The unity and conformity essential to centralized social structures does not easily tolerate radical acts for their own inherent value.

Because of the 'lack of development' of a manufacturing division of labour and, consequently, of role-specific knowledge in pre-literate societies, the degree to which *any* activity can be distanced from the central core of everyday reality is significantly circumscribed. Moreover, because creativity has a marked degree of intuitive acceptance, there seems little desire to remove activities which *we* might label as creative from the central concerns of society. Pre-literate people therefore relate to music in its full social context. In literate civilizations with a highly developed manufacturing division of labour, and especially in industrial societies, the high development of role-specific knowledge allows different activities to be removed to a considerable distance from the central core of everyday reality. Further, because creativity is so incompatible with the deterministic rationality which constitutes the overriding mythology of industrial societies, the temptation has been to institutionalize the creative elements of the social process on the periphery of predominant social concerns in cultural and, to a lesser extent, academic activities. As a form of culture, music *in general* has tended to suffer this fate. This assignation of a socially peripheral role to music is consistent with the traditional assignation of a higher rational priority to the material-factual side of the dichotomous epistemology.

Although few people would say that any type of music in industrial societies is of *fundamental* social significance, there is a tendency to think that 'popular' forms of music are of more social 'relevance' than 'serious' forms. Reasons for this attitude have already been discussed. In order to understand how the organization of industrial societies further permits this attitude, it is necessary to refer to the phenomenon of cultural lag. This phenomenon results from the ability of literate people to commit new ideas to paper at various times in history. (In pre-literate societies, on the other hand, where all knowledge is mediated in the continuing present of face-to-face situations, the possibilities for cultural lag are minimal.) Coupled with highly developed role-specific knowledge, the consequence of this phenomenon in industrial societies is that a new piece of role-specific knowledge may take a long time to filter through to the core of everyday reality if, indeed, it filters through at all.

But the 'historical time' to which such knowledge belongs need not, from the point of view of the common stock of knowledge, be in the past. The more 'advanced' or 'consciously creative' a piece of knowledge is with regard to that common stock, the more it will 'belong to the future' and be irrelevant where the majority of people are concerned. This kind of relationship seems to exist between contemporary high culture and the population in general, as Marshall McLuhan indicates:

> The percussed victims of the new technology have invariably muttered cliches about the impracticality of artists and their fanciful preferences. But in the past century it has come to be generally acknowledged that, in the words of Wyndham Lewis, 'The artist is always engaged in writing a detailed history of the future because he is the only person aware of the present. . . .' The ability of the artist to sidestep the bully blow of new technology in any age, and to parry such violence with full awareness, is age-old. Equally age-old is the inability of the percussed victims, who cannot sidestep the new violence, to recognise their need of the artist. . . . The artist is the man in any field, scientific or humanistic, who grasps the implications of his actions and of new knowledge in his own time. He is the man of integral awareness. (McLuhan, 1964, p. 70–1)

This trend has been apparent in 'serious' music since the beginning of the nineteenth century, and is in evidence today. The latest techniques in high-culture computer music, for example, are less likely to impinge on collective awareness than, say, the kinds of music played on AM Radio.

To make this kind of distinction between 'serious' and 'popular' music is not to admit absolute and 'arbitrary' cultural values by the back door. The distancing or lack of distancing being described is associated with the existence of *differing* cultural realities which cannot admit of one, universal set of cultural criteria. It is the *traditional* elitist view which utilizes this difference in degree of distancing to maintain and reinforce its own position. Further, the difference in distancing does not coincide in all instances with traditional categories of 'popular' and 'serious' music. Some 'popular' artists distance themselves from the central core of everyday reality more than some 'popular' classical composers, and are just as much 'people of integral awareness' as many, more 'serious' classical composers. It is the *general* coincidence of degrees of distancing with traditional categories of 'serious' and 'popular' music which allows the elitists to hold their position.

The placing of 'serious' music on the periphery of social concerns does not mean that its lines of communication with the remainder of society are cut. Neither does it mean that its significance is inherently 'asocial'. It is precisely because 'serious' music has this peripheral status that aestheticians and music theorists have been able to slide surreptitiously into the position of thinking it 'asocial', and so of maintaining successfully that its significance is ultimately located in an essential and mystical reality. Equally, 'popular' forms of music are seen as retaining a social significance, not only because their positions vis-à-vis core reality are less peripheral, but also because their 'inferior value as music' precludes them from revealing 'inner truths'. These correlations are nicely indicated by Francis Routh:

> The term music is taken to include as many aspects of the composer's work as fall under the heading art-work. An art-work is one which makes some claim on our serious attention. This implies a creative, unique purpose on the part of the composer, and an active response on the part of the listener; it implies that the composer possesses and uses both vision and technique, and that the listener in return is expected to bring to bear his full intelligence. This excludes non-art music, such as pop music, whose purpose is chiefly, if not entirely commercial. Pop groups are big business; they are socially significant; there is no question that they form a remarkable contemporary phenomenon − but this does not make the result into an art-work, and to consider it as if it were is an illogical affectation. (Routh, 1972, pp. x–xi)

Conclusion

It is now clear why music theorists and aestheticians tend not to locate musical significance as an integral aspect of socially constructed reality. Not only does such location go against any possible interpretation of the industrial world sense, it also brings under scrutiny the centralized structures of industrial societies. If a musicologist or aesthetician questions not only what they say about music, but in so doing questions also their right to speak exclusively to and on behalf of other people, they put themselves in the unenviable position of questioning the legitimacy of their own socially designated role. Musical processes tend to be conceived as absolute, permanent, and discoverable beyond the vagaries of human thought and perception because such an approach aids mystification and so role security. To ignore the social nature of music is to articulate the predominant modes of thought and social organization of industrial societies.

These tendencies result from the inability of most musicologists, music theorists and aestheticians to follow through on the implications arising from the related aesthetic and political problems surrounding the 'meaning' of music. Given the characteristics of the dominant world sense of industrial societies and their associated social structures, there can be little doubt that these problems have been intransigent. Because of its characteristics as a social medium *in sound*, music, more than most other phenomena, has highlighted the assumptions and deficiencies of our social organization and our traditional outlook on the world.

Although it seems a far from complete or satisfactory approach, the question of meaning in the literate and plastic arts *can* be dealt with on a purely 'representational' basis. 'Meaning', in other words, can be 'adequately' located in 'content'. As a consequence, 'social' analysis of these art forms becomes easier and, moreover, of little danger to traditional social structures, because it is carried out in terms of the categories interdependent with those structures (that is, the categories of 'form' and 'content'). What is said within a structure is of little consequence to the structure unless it actively questions the assumptions upon which the structure is grounded. *It is precisely the very great difficulty of coming to grips with the 'meaning' of music in terms of 'form' and 'content' that has paradoxically made arbitrary and central definition with regard to music so very easy and, in some cases, so very extreme.*

To put it another way, there can be two responses to the difficulty of the 'meaning' of music. One is to avoid the difficulty. In this case, because traditional ways of understanding the world are unsuited for an adequate understanding of music, it becomes difficult to use the categories of that world sense to question elitist and idealist theories. The other response is to confront the difficulty, and construct a sense of the world which allows for an adequate understanding of the musical process.

Part II

Music as Social Text

5 Meaning in Music

Introduction

Part I undertook an analysis of the forces which militate against an acceptance for the proposition that the meaning of music is social. This proposition requires an approach to understanding the sociality of music which is not grounded in the categories of analysis fundamental to the dominant world sense of industrial societies.

If it is to be accepted that music is inherently social, there arises a need to conceptualize *cultural* processes in such a way as to make possible an understanding of 'how the social gets into music'. Such a conceptualization cannot rest on notions of the epiphenomenal. Although an epiphenomenal conceptualization of cultural processes seemed the most promising in terms of understanding the social character of music, it was flawed in locating the meaning of music outside music in social processes themselves conceived as essentially non-musical. Musical meaning, in other words, was taken to be located in extra-musical processes. However, an epiphenomenal conceptualization did retain the advantage of offering up the *possibility* of a social theory for music, while at the same time guaranteeing conceptual space for an appreciation of the specific qualities of music as a form of human communication. There was conceptual space sufficient to accommodate Zuckerkandl's 'dynamic qualities'. A starting point for developing alternative theories for the sociality of music might be to retain the advantage of an epiphenomenal conceptualization while problematizing its categorical basis.

It is difficult to discuss the relationships between society and culture without invoking the broad tradition of Marxist and Marxist-informed scholarship. The notion of culture as 'epiphenomenal' suggests immediately the categories of infrastructure and superstructure. However, much water has flowed under the bridge since Jones's article of 1974. Marxist discussions of culture have become markedly more sophisticated than it was possible for him to indicate. Symptomatically, Jones's article appeared in volume 6 of the *Working Papers on Cultural Studies* published from the Centre for Contemporary Cultural Studies at the University of Birmingham. It is through the work carried on in and around this Centre that Marxism as a scholarly tradition has faced squarely and comprehensively the question of the role played by culture in processes of social reproduction. It is as a result of the work of the 'Birmingham school' (a school whose ramifications have always stretched considerably beyond the 'time' and 'place' of Birmingham) that the question of the relationship between society and culture, between 'infrastructure' and 'superstructure', has been problematized and conceptualized in increasingly subtle and complex ways.

It is not unnatural to look to this tradition in confronting the central difficulty of traditional music aesthetics. This is what this chapter undertakes. The first two sections elaborate a theory for significance in music in a way which avoids the problems outlined in part I, but which also postpones any explicit reference to Marxism as an intellectual tradition. The following section argues that this theory is entirely consistent with the broad tenets of cultural studies as that discipline developed from the early work of Raymond Williams. It points to the manner in which the following four chapters owe much to the work of the 'Birmingham school' as it developed through the 1970s and early 1980s. This influence includes that of the feminist scholarship to originate from Birmingham.

The final section moves away from questions of theory to consider briefly a methodological issue fundamental to any academic analysis of music, and one which has been rendered especially relevant to this book as a consequence of the discussions in part I concerning the consequences of literacy. This issue has to do with the legitimacy and appropriateness of writing about music.

It is in these ways that the chapter serves as an introduction to part II, concerned as it is with the analysis of music as social text, and the presentation of those analyses through the medium of print.

Symbologies

The positive feedback operating in post-Renaissance societies between visual stress and written language has been responsible for repressing important facets of life and experience to a 'collective unconscious'. As a consequence of this process, 'educated' people in industrial societies (overwhelmingly men) have tended to relate to the world in material and reified terms – terms which they have not unnaturally equated with the rational objectivity of typography. This outlook has acted back on language so that in all its forms – even the spoken form responsible for the vastly different world sense of pre-literate people – it is ultimately conceived in terms of, and measured against the norm of rational objectivity. The 'oral' and 'emotional' in life and language has at best been relegated to a position of secondary importance.

The emphasis placed by industrial societies on rational, verbal objectivity has led these societies to relegate in significance the realizations of any symbolic mode which implicitly challenge their dominant world sense. The unspoken – or more appositely, unwritten – assumption is that everything that is real can be expressed in objective, rational language and its extensions, and that reality as embodied in the rational word is somehow higher than, or ontologically prior to, any other evidence of reality accruing from other sources. But although language constitutes a most important symbolic mode for maintaining the technologically developed civilizations of industrial societies, it does not follow that reality as comprehended through language is more real than that articulated through other modes of communication, nor, concomitantly, does it follow that language is potentially an exclusive mode in the sense of all other non-verbally coded experience being reducible to verbal terms.

Different symbolic modes *emphasize* different aspects of reality by reason of their different media. However, language and other symbolic modes do not contribute their different realities to the total field of meaning in a society additively. Meanings in society display two aspects: *relata* and *relationships*. These terms are explained by Duncan:

> It has long been realised that any mode of social analysis will produce at least two types of entity: first, analytical elements called 'social facts' which can be observed easily enough, and second, the entities (not so easily observed) that arise in a system because analysis was made in the particular way in which it was made. In more specific terminology the easily observed elements are called relata, while the elements 'underlying' the system are called relationships of those relata. (Duncan, 1968, p. 46)

Structures in society are revealed to people through the relata (other people and symbols) that they perceive, but the structures would not exist unless the relata were maintained in certain relationships that people cannot *directly* perceive but can sense in consciousness through the individual constructions made possible by the presence of symbols. Language as conceived by 'educated' men in industrial societies has emphasized relata at the expense of relationships because relata display a materiality consanguineous with the objects of the material universe – objects, however, which are not *necessarily* maintained in structural relationships. This emphasis induced those people to apply a materialist and reductionist philosophy to human existence, an application which still finds expression in positivistic social science. Yet language does not simply signify objects and reified concepts, as its rational written form might imply. Objects and reified concepts are the word-embodied materials or relata in and through which cultural constructs are articulated. Music tends to emphasize relationships at the expense of relata, because its own relata are 'abstract' or non-referential. Different symbolic modes, therefore, are capable of encoding similar structures but may, because of their method of encoding, stress different aspects of these structures.

In *Symbols in Society*, Duncan makes the following observation:

> All we know about the meaning of what happened, or is happening, in a social relationship is what someone says about its meaning. 'Saying' involves many kinds of expression. A diplomat *participates* in foreign negotiations. Historians *describe* a battle. An Australian savage *dances* the history of his tribe. The Indian *paints* his myths of tribal origin in sand. Witnesses verify what 'really happened' through creating expressive forms in which they depict the event. Ascriptions of meaning to forces, processes, energy, or cathexis are based on analogies, not on direct observation of concrete human acts. Like all analogies, such ascriptions are interpretations, not observations. If we follow the canon of parsimony in science, we must, in our study of society, turn to the most directly observable of all social data, namely, the symbols we use in social relationships. (Duncan, 1968, p. 50)

Consequently, not only must 'interpretations of forces "beyond" symbols ... still be interpretations of symbols' (Duncan, 1968, p. 50), but 'when we say that there is some reality in human relationships which lies "beyond" symbols, we are still bound by symbols in our "report" of the operations of the "extrasymbolic" phenomena we have observed' (Duncan, 1968, p. 51). Symbols display a logical status qualitatively different from that of the social relationships they signify. When we realize that 'concrete human acts' are themselves a means of 'saying' something about the social context of their articulation, that difference becomes clear. Whereas symbols can be seen, touched or heard, social relationships, Duncan's '"extrasymbolic" phenomena', cannot be directly perceived, although they are immanent 'in' directly perceptible symbols. One cannot see social relationships (within the literal meaning of that word), nor, for that matter, can one touch them or hear them. Structures in society are only *revealed* to people *through* the symbols they perceive, and, as such, society is quintessentially symbolic.

The role of symbols in society is to 're-present' the intangible, fluid and dynamic set of social relationships within which we live. But because the utterance (or 'outerance') of a symbol involves articulation of the material universe (if it did not, the symbol would be imperceptible), any form of communication freezes and so dilutes the fluid complexity of social relationships. All symbolic exchange involves a degree of objectivation.

Whereas sight, the medium of literate and plastic cultural forms, emphasizes the distancing and separation of (frequently static) objects in space, sound, the medium of music, emphasizes the immediate and dynamic flow of undifferentiated temporality. While predominantly literate modes of thought and social organization might be unsuited to an understanding of the musical process, it conversely seems that, because of its inherently fluid and dynamic nature, music is well suited to convey the dynamic power of social relationships as experienced in real time. It may be asserted that music objectifies social processes less than most other symbolic modes.

Music seems most faithfully to reflect the intangible, fluid and dynamic characteristics of social relationships. However, these relationships could not exist without the people, symbols and goods that have a separate and distinct material embodiment in visual space. The fact that literate and plastic cultural forms in general make an initial reference to people and their symbolic utterances should not obscure the reference that is thereby made to the relationships articulated through those people and their mutual externalizations. It may well be that all art 'approaches to the condition of music', but this tendency is not sufficient reason to assign music, in Schopenhauer-like fashion, a privileged place among cultural forms. While music may most closely approach the fluidity and dynamism of social relationships, it is incapable of referring directly to the people, symbols and goods which are co-extensive with those relationships. All that may be concluded, therefore, is that because of their different media different cultural forms emphasize different aspects of the social process.

The relationship of music to underlying categories of analysis in industrial societies is in no way unique or singular. If 'literate' modes of thought and social organization preclude an 'adequate' understanding of musical process, then it should follow that they preclude an 'adequate' understanding not only of the *full* significance of other cultural forms, but also of the *full* significance of other, everyday forms of communication. In this respect Jarocinski's observation that a symbol 'conveys an imprecise meaning which can be interpreted in various ways', and that 'the transportation of its meaning has a dynamic character' (Jarocinski, 1976, pp. 23–4), is particularly pertinent. 'Literate' categories of analysis, in favouring precisely locatable objects and precisely definable ideas, cannot tolerate the 'imprecise' and truly dynamic. That predominant modes of thought and social organization in industrial societies tend to preclude a full understanding of the essentially symbolic processes of society is hinted at by Duncan when he ironically says that 'communication . . . must be explained by everything but communication . . . it must have, as we read so often, a "referent" . . .' (Duncan, 1968, p. 31).

As it affects individual consciousness the presence of symbols in society presents two aspects. Firstly, there are the constructions instigated by the reception of socially efficacious symbols. Secondly, there are those constructions which result in socially efficacious utterances and externalizations. It is essential to emphasize that the dialectic process of consciousness indicated here cannot function without an element of creativity. By creativity is meant the formulation of a structure in consciousness which is facilitated and preconditioned by the structures of previous symbolic mediations, but whose *precise* configuration could not have been predicted at the deterministic level of materiality appropriate to symbols themselves. Without this inalienable element of creativity the meaning of symbols would remain non-negotiable, and processes of signification would lose the imprecision or dynamism referred to by Jarocinski. Creativity may be efficacious at any level of generality, whether that of a comparatively inconsequential situation in everyday life, or that of the largely unconscious articulation of a group or society's assumptive framework. This possibility for creativity is indicated by the claim of Lévi-Strauss (1968, p. 79), that 'between culture and language there cannot be *no* relations at all, and there cannot be 100 per cent correlation either.' Lévi-Strauss's argument may be extended. If the correlation between culture and symbol were 100 per cent, societies would be reduced to the determinism and predictability inferred through the dominant world sense of industrial societies. The rigidity of societies would make dialecticism an impossibility, and it is difficult to see how societies could come into existence or survive under such circumstances. The creative element of individual minds is thus a necessary precondition for structural changes in society.

The 'Meaning' of Music

Insomuch as evidence of the existence of society or culture is revealed to us only through the symbols we perceive, culture and society can only be regarded as being immanent 'in' the potentially creative articulations of specific symbols, no matter to which realm of social activity they pertain. Since these articulations originate from and are only efficacious 'within' individual minds, society must also be regarded as being immanent 'in' individual consciousness. Society as a process of order-in-change is immanent 'in' and 'through' the dialectic interaction of people and symbols.

The meanings of society are encoded and creatively articulated by music to an extent that denies the assumptive assignation of a higher rational priority to verbally encoded meanings. Music has meaning only insomuch as the inner-outer, mental-physical dichotomy of verbally referential meaning is transcended by the immanence 'in' music of *abstracted* social structures, and by the articulation of social meanings in individual musical events. Music stands in the same relationship to society as consciousness: society is creatively 'in' each musical event and articulated by it.

Any meaning assigned to music does not and cannot result or depend on the existence of physically external referents. In this sense music is its own meaning. But this does not imply, as Langer would have it, that music is an 'unconsummated symbol', for the presence of permanent contents that Langer requires for the fulfilment of the function of meaning in a symbol must surely be rooted in the inner-outer, form and content dichotomy of the verbal-physical world. Restricting musical meaning to the 'inner life' as Langer does, and denying an 'outer', transcendent or social meaning is surely a product of the dominant epistemology of industrial civilizations. Music is not an informationally closed mode of symbolism relevant only to 'emotive, vital, sentient experiences', or 'inherent psychological laws of "rightness"', but an open mode that, through its 'abstract' nature, is singularly suited to reveal the dynamic structuring of social life, a structuring of which the 'material' forms only one aspect. Music is consummatory because of the social meaning immanent in the individual consciousnesses and musical events of a society and, conversely, because social meaning can only arise and continue to exist through symbolic mediations in consciousness – mediations of which music forms a part.

It would be wrong to imply that Langer's and Meyer's psychologistic views of music go *absolutely* no way towards transcending the form and content dichotomy. In maintaining that there is a structural conformity between music and minds their position is not totally dissimilar to the one advanced here. The crucial difference is that they have implicitly assumed mind to be a delimited entity. But as the following statement by Gregory Bateson indicates, it is possible to arrive at a concept of mind consistent with the views expressed in this chapter:

> The individual mind is immanent but not only in the body. It is immanent also in pathways and messages outside the body; and there is a larger Mind of which the individual mind is only a sub-system. The larger Mind is . . . immanent in the total interconnected social system. (Bateson, 1973, p. 436)

The superimposition of the structures articulated by a particular musical event onto a suitably predisposed mind is an important aspect of most musical communication. But equally important is the social interaction responsible for the particular structural disposition of that mind.

It would be unfair to Langer to imply that her notion of music as an 'unconsummated symbol' is without insight. Langer, following Wagner, tends to categorize experiences-in-consciousness into the 'unspeakable' and the 'speakable'. The former, *implicit*, category consists of those experiences which can only be sensed in consciousness and not specifically referred to; the latter, *explicit*, category of those objects and concepts which may be definitively indicated. Music is equated with the implicit category, writing with the explicit. To this extent, Langer's thinking on music and writing conforms to the dichotomous epistemology. Now while it remains true that music may emphasize the implicit and writing the explicit, it does not follow that music cannot encode the explicit, nor that writing cannot encode the implicit. Different symbolic modes are capable of encoding similar structures, but may, because of their method of encoding, stress different aspects of these structures (for the purposes of illustration, the explicit may here be equated with relata, and the implicit with the relationships 'underlying' those relata).

A brief discussion of 'explicitness' and 'implicitness' as possible paradigms for social and musical analysis is undertaken in the concluding section of this chapter. However, the following further relationship between media and world senses may be indicated in order to properly situate Langer's notions of the explicit and implicit. There are those media which communicate implicitly and those which communicate explicitly. There are those world senses (such as the 'pre-literate') which tend towards the implicit and those (such as that of industrial societies) which tend towards the explicit. Music is capable of implicitly coding an explicit world sense, a process evidenced throughout the entire tradition of functional tonality. Langer's concept of the implicit and the explicit thus has substance. But her tendency *rigidly* to equate music with implicitness, and writing with explicitness, her consequent implied denial of the social processes immanent 'in' music, and her subsequent failure to assign any *real* significance to music, once again points to the inadequacy of the view that music is an 'unconsummated symbol'.

The Deconstruction of Music as Social Text

There are two possible ways of interpreting significance in music in terms of a traditional Marxist perspective. Either, following Cohen (1978, pp. 216–17), one may argue that the superstructure is comprised of those non-economic institutions whose character is explained by the nature of the economic structure. Given the difficulties of interpreting all ideational, cultural and artistic processes in terms of overdetermination by the economic structure, one may then argue that certain ideational, cultural and artistic processes are *not* subsumed in the class of those non-economic institutions whose character is explained by the nature of the economic structure. As Cohen observes, there are times when Marx seems to move in this direction in his understanding of art and culture:

> ... the cultural production of class society, though restricted by its class affiliations, remains an expression of the highest human faculties. Historical works of art and thought are not a set of ideological instruments whose value is that they help to sustain class hegemony, and the proletariat does not banish traditional culture. It appropriates and extends it in [the] future. (Cohen, 1978, p. 205)

Or, again following Cohen, one may argue that the superstructure is comprised of all non-economic institutions, in which case the question will arise as to the extent to which the superstructure, including, presumably, culture, art and music, is overdetermined by the economic structure.

On this latter reasoning, the central aesthetic difficulty of understanding significance in music arises once more. The position argued here averts the difficulty by 'collapsing' infrastructure and superstructure into one another while at the same time avoiding the idealist overtones of assuming artistic and cultural processes to lie essentially outside the influence of social relations of production, patiently awaiting, as an 'expression of the highest human faculties', a social form within which they will be available, relevant and comprehensible to all. This position refuses to make the kind of unqualified distinction between musical and social processes that is implied through our separate linguistic and epistemological categories of 'music' and 'society'.

The position adopted here resembles that developed by Raymond Williams. Williams begins by noting the tension inherent in British Marxist literary criticism of the 1930s between idealism and materialism. Idealist overtones are maintained by assigning culture and art an autonomy which allows them, despite ultimate dependence upon material conditions, to embody the future as against the regressive restrictions of the infrastructure. The millenarianism of this version of Marxist literary criticism has much in common with the millenarianism of Romanticism. As Williams observes, it 'seems relevant to ask English Marxists who have interested themselves in the arts whether this is not Romanticism absorbing Marx, rather than Marx transforming Romanticism' (Williams, 1961, p. 265). Williams removes this tension by, essentially, conflating an 'ideal' notion of culture 'in which culture is a state or process of human perfection, in terms of certain absolute or universal human values' (Williams, 1965, p. 57) with a 'social' notion of culture 'in which culture is a description of a particular way of life which expresses certain meanings and values not only in art and learning but also in institutions and ordinary behaviour' (Williams, 1965, p. 57). As Williams concludes, 'any particular definition ... which would exclude reference to the [other], is inadequate' (Williams, 1965, p. 59). Thus:

> ... an ideal definition which attempts to abstract the process it describes from its detailed embodiment and shaping by particular societies ... seems to me unacceptable. ... Again, a 'social' definition, which treats either the general process or the body of art and learning as a mere by-product, a passive reflection of the real interests of society, seems to me equally wrong. (Williams, 1965, pp. 59–60)

A problem in resolving these competing and incompatible definitions is that the creativity and individuality which many would argue to be inalienable characteristics of cultural processes are assumed by those critical of the traditional 'high' culture position to be necessarily symptomatic of an idealist approach. Equally, those critical of Marxist perspectives on art and culture argue that any attempt to analyse cultural processes as being social in their significance results in the creative and the individual – those characteristics taken to form the central aesthetic core of art and culture – being filtered out of existence. Art and culture are thus conceptually destroyed. The opposed problems of autonomy and determination can only be solved by refusing to make a qualitative distinction between different areas of social process, with one area retaining prime causation over others. All areas are qualitatively similar and all areas are *relatively* autonomous. Williams demystifies the social and cultural processes which constitute rather than simply inform art, and defetishizes art as an autonomous power, unresponsive to the social and cultural processes which both inform *and* constitute it. The question is not how art and society relate. This question cannot help but be grounded on more subtle forms of mystification and fetishization. The essential realization is that, along with many other processes, art *is* society.

> It was certainly an error to suppose that values or art-works could be adequately studied without reference to the particular society within which they were expressed, but it is equally an error to suppose that the social explanation is determining, or that the values and works are mere by-products. We have got into the habit, since we realized how deeply works or values could be determined by the whole situation in which they are expressed, of asking about these relationships in a standard form: 'what is the relation of this art to this society?' But 'society', in this question, is a specious whole. *If the art is part of the society, there is no solid whole, outside it, to which, by the form of our question, we concede priority.* (Williams, 1965, p. 61, my italics)

Williams's position is compatible with that developed earlier in relation to music. There is no such 'thing' as society. The only 'things' we can directly perceive are the material articulations of symbolic discourses through which the multidimensional logics of immaterial, fluid and dynamic social interactions are revealed and presented to us. Equally, Williams sees human creativity as an essential part of social process (Williams, 1965, pp. 88ff). Creativity and sociality are not antithetical, but mutually necessary, a position which has also been argued specifically in relation to music (Vulliamy and Shepherd, 1984a and 1985). Finally, the idea that all human activity is quintessentially social leads to the realization that there is an order, a logic which underpins the activities of a society, and which can be teased out by analysis of different social institutions whose relationship, on the surface, may seem tenuous.

I would then define the theory of culture as the study of relationships between elements in a whole way of life. The analysis of culture is the attempt to discover the nature of the organization which is the complex of these relationships. Analysis of particular works or institutions is, in this context, analysis of their essential kind of organization, the relationships which works or institutions embody as parts of the organization as a whole. A key-word, in such analysis, is pattern: it is with the discovery of patterns of a characteristic kind that any useful cultural analysis begins, and it is with the relationships between these patterns, which sometimes reveal unexpected identities and correspondences in hitherto separately considered activities, sometimes again reveal discontinuities of an unexpected kind, that general cultural analysis is concerned. (Williams, 1965, p. 63)

This concept of pattern is suggestive for an analysis of music, because it dispenses with the troublesome notion of the 'referent' *at the same time* as transcending the 'inner-outer' dichotomy (on which the notion of the 'referent' is ultimately grounded) by understanding that the location of significance in any symbolic discourse is simultaneously 'inside' and 'outside' it. The concept transcends the limitations of 'patterning' or 'structure' as in the work of Langer and Meyer. Within the tradition of British culturalism, Williams's insistence on 'identities and correspondences in hitherto separately considered activities', on a congruence between different patterns as materially articulated, lays the foundation for the concept of the structural homology later developed by Willis (1975 and 1978). Willis's application of this concept to the analysis of certain forms of rock music is not without its problems (see chapter 7), but the fundamental insight remains crucial in opening the way for the understanding of many genres of music as socially constituted.

There is a problem with the model of cultural analysis developed by Williams. By 'collapsing' infrastructure and superstructure, Williams filters out the possibility for conflict and the exercise of political power between different areas of social activity. The model of cultural analysis to emerge from Williams's earlier work thus tended to be consensualist and conservative on the one hand, and one-dimensional on the other. There was little 'depth' or 'thickness' to the understanding of symbolic articulation.

This tendency towards consensualism was significantly weakened in a later essay by Williams (1973). In this essay, Williams recontextualized his emphasis on a 'whole way of life' within Gramsci's concept of 'hegemony' (Gramsci, 1971), thus creating space for dimensions of struggle and confrontation to emerge in a more unfettered fashion. The acknowledgement of imbalances in political power at various historical moments thus reveals a concern for the specificity of concrete cultural processes evident previously in the work of Gramsci. However, although this re-situation of a concept fundamental to Williams's theory of culture guarantees a certain 'thickness' where an understanding of social and cultural contexts is concerned, it does leave a lingering sense of one-dimensionality in the understanding of symbolic articulation. There is evident within the tradition of British culturalism in general a tendency not to get beneath the surface of symbolic articulation, not to develop a sense of 'thickness' or 'depth' where internal processes of signification are concerned. There are few developed protocols within this tradition through which internal processes of signification can be approached as themselves sites for struggle and confrontation. This sense of 'depth' or 'thickness', of the articulation of signification from within the internal processes of symbols is supplied by semiological analyses of cultural artifacts. Since semiology represents, at base, a set of tools rather than a school of cultural theory, it is nonetheless possible, as Hebdige (1979) and Brake (1980) have demonstrated, to situate semiological approaches within a culturalist perspective. A sense of conflict and political power can thus be reinserted into a culturalist perspective not only by seeing conflict and power incorporated within processes of signification (Hebdige, 1979; Brake, 1980), but also, in drawing on Gramsci, by viewing the social and cultural processes which contextualize and inform processes of signification as themselves sites of confrontation and struggle.

Although the analyses presented in chapters 6 and 7 rest to a large extent on the notion of the structural homology, transcending, as it does, the limitations of more traditional approaches towards understanding signification in music, they attempt to avoid the sense of consensualism and one-dimensionality implicit in Williams's earlier work by invoking concepts of ideology, hegemony and resistance. However, the discussions presented in chapters 6 and 7 do not invoke *at the level of 'language'* many of the technical semiological and structuralist categories which have done so much to provide a sense of 'depth' and 'thickness' in the analysis of signification in other cultural and artistic media. Structuralist and semiological accounts of signification inevitably involve 'denotative' and 'referential' starting points without which more subtle and sophisticated levels of analysis having to do with the dynamic and creative reinscriptions of purely abstract structures would not be possible. While some musics of the world, for example, that of the Kaluli of New Guinea (Feld, 1982), display aspects of signification that may be approached using established modes of structuralist and semiological analysis, many other musics of the world including that of the functional tonal tradition, display a central core of signification that does not admit of such analysis. Many semiological and structuralist categories of analysis thus give rise, in an admittedly more subtle form, to the central difficulty in the aesthetics of music discussed earlier. For musics displaying this core of non-denotative and non-referential signification (and it is arguable that most do), it is necessary to evolve modes of analysis which take as their starting point purely abstract and 'structural' notions of signification.

One final problem emerges from assessing the applicability of cultural theory to the analysis of signification in music. The majority of cultural theory has developed from and been applied to the analysis of modes of communication that are *visual*. Although music, by definition, is encoded in patterns and textures of sound, some musical parameters, as Wishart (1977a) has argued, are more susceptible to fully analytic, *visual*, notation than others. The parameters of frequency and duration, that which Meyer (1959) refers to as the 'syntactical' as opposed to the 'sensuous' in music, can be pinned down on the page in a way in which amplitude and timbre cannot. The insusceptibility of timbre to analytic notation is particularly symptomatic. For timbre, more than any other musical parameter, appears to be the nature of sound itself. While it is possible to conceive of sound with infinite and thus, in a sense, 'no' duration at all, sound without fixed pitch and sound without gradations of amplitude, it is not possible to conceive of sound without timbre. It is the texture or grain without which sound cannot reach us, touch us or move us. It is the vibratory essence that puts the world of sound in motion and reminds us, as individuals, that we are alive, sentient and experiencing. If rhythm and pitch can be regarded as durations and extensions of timbre, then rhythm and pitch as musical parameters are distanced from the core of musical articulation and come to contain and contextualize it in one way rather than any other.

The concept of the structural homology is a concept that constitutes a visual analogy for a set of processes, social, cultural and musical, of which the visual forms only one aspect. The notion of 'pattern' or 'structure' can, and often does, imply a silence, a vacuum, between the delineations of the particular pattern or structure in question. However, social, cultural and musical realities are continuous, substantial in that they do not of necessity display gaps and silences. The articulation of social and cultural realities involves *all* the senses, and we are continually reminded, in our quintessentially symbolic existence, of the way in which the world rubs up against us and continually stimulates us to active participation.

It is the tactile core of sound, timbre, that reminds us that the gaps and silences between the delineations of structures, whether social, cultural or musical, are not gaps or silences, but directionally charged fields of meaning and experience that speak to our sense of identity and existence. If it is the syntax of music, the relationship of individual sonic events as deployed in time and space, that speaks to the socially structured context of existence, then it is timbre, the essence of individual sonic events, that speaks to the core of existence. In basing its analyses on the visual analogy of the structural homology, the work presented in chapters 6 and 7 concentrates more on the way that social contexts are encoded and articulated through the 'visual' parameters of music, rhythm and pitch, than they do on the way that timbre, the tactile core of sound, encodes and articulates the logics through which individuals creatively embrace the social world and construct a unified and manageable experiential core of personality and reality. Although the work presented in chapter 7 refers to the way in which a sense of individuality-in-community is articulated within many genres of popular music through individuated timbre characteristics, the way in which timbre in itself articulates social and cultural messages is not fully examined. To the idea that analyses of signification in music need to take as their starting point concepts which are purely abstract and 'structural' needs to be added the idea that they also take as their starting point concepts which allow for the articulation of signification through purely abstract and fluid tactile dimensions. This idea provides the basis for the analyses presented in chapter 8.

If the concept of the structural homology is capable of transcending the traditional, central problem of music aesthetics, and of providing a conceptual tool in terms of which to understand the way in which the 'structural', syntactical dimensions of music speak to the structural contexts of individual existence, then it clearly has limitations in teasing out the timbrel articulations of individual personalities and realities as socially constituted. In analysing music as but one site for the playing out of ideological struggles, it becomes necessary to invoke not only the notion of the structural homology but, at the level of *myth and myth alone*, notions of explicitness and implicitness as filtered through Barthes's concepts of 'readerly' and 'writerly' texts. Such concepts, by highlighting the degree to which the consumer is encouraged to enter into processes of meaning construction, allow for the development of a typology of timbres in terms of degrees of 'openness' and 'closedness' which in turn facilitates an initial understanding of *gender types* as negotiated through music. The assumption is that it is not possible to gain an idea of the musical constitution of the self without an understanding of the musical articulation of gender. As empirical evidence suggests (Shepherd, 1986), gender may well be a more important and clear-cut variable in terms of which to grasp the musical articulation of social and cultural realities as individually negotiated and constituted than class, which speaks primarily to the structural location of such negotiations. This point is taken up again in chapters 8 and 9.

The analyses presented in the following four chapters therefore move from the general to the particular, from the musical articulation of the broadest of social contexts to that of specific and individual personalities and realities. Chapter 9 in particular addresses this latter question of the musical articulation of individual subjectivities as socially mediated, and so explores an important dimension of the position set out in this chapter, namely, that musical sociality is manifest not only in the external social world, but in the internal social world as well. Ultimately it is individuals, albeit under massive social and cultural pressure, who put the world of musical sociality (both external and internal) into motion.

In developing a theoretical perspective for the deconstruction of music as text it will be necessary to have recourse to concepts developed within the traditions of both culturalism and structuralism. It will be important also to ensure that such concepts are firmly grounded in the concrete actualities of struggle, conflict and resistance that constitute much of the fabric of social relations. In assessing the balance between (*inter alia*) class and gender or homology and texture in the musical articulation of social and cultural realities, it will be necessary to locate the theoretical discussions in actual musical events as situated in concrete social and historical moments. It seems unlikely that instances of ideological struggle repeat themselves. As a consequence, theoretical considerations need to be tailored in their details to each instance of the textual mediation of power. This point is exemplified through the analysis presented in chapter 9.

Writing about Music: The Implicit-Explicit Paradigm

In her book, *Purity and Danger*, Mary Douglas warns against analysing pre-literate cosmologies as if they were systematic philosophies, subscribed to consciously by people.

> The anthropologist who draws out the whole scheme of the cosmos
> ... does the primitive culture great violence if he seeks to present
> the cosmology as a systematic philosophy subscribed to consciously
> by individuals. We can study our cosmology – in a specialised
> department of astronomy. But primitive cosmologies cannot be

rightly pinned out for display like exotic lepidoptera, without distortion to the nature of a primitive culture. (Douglas, 1970, pp. 110–11)

In terms of the way that Langer conceptualizes the 'implicit' and the 'explicit', and in terms of previous observations concerning sound, pre-literate worlds, literacy, visuality, the dominant world sense of industrial societies and music, a similar warning could be uttered in respect of writing about music. The fluidity, dynamism and 'abstract' qualities of music could become prisoner to the reified and denotative concepts that lie at the basis of language. However, the relationship between world senses, media, and modes of analysis is more complex than that suggested by Langer's notions of the 'implicit' and 'explicit'.

The criticism levelled against these categories as developed by Langer is that they saw the 'speakable' and 'explicit' on the one hand, and the 'unspeakable' and 'implicit' on the other, as distinct experiential worlds having little connection with, or influence on, one another. The position developed earlier sought to transcend this categorical splitting by establishing that specific world senses could tend either towards the explicit or the implicit, that various media, in terms of their inherent technical characteristics, could tend either towards the explicit or the implicit, but that, notwithstanding these tendencies, it was possible for an 'implicit' medium to articulate an 'explicit' world sense and for an 'explicit' medium to articulate an 'implicit' world sense. Since the analyses of the following three chapters are grounded in notions of implicitness and explicitness, it becomes necessary to consider these notions further.

Notions of implicitness and explicitness can be applied to at least four levels in human realities and their associated discourses. Firstly, they can be applied at the level of world senses themselves, those complex totalities which maintain, reproduce and articulate themselves in terms of some deep-seated set of logics. Whereas pre-literate worlds – lived within, powerfully tied to the individuals who occupy them – tend to display senses that are implicit, industrial worlds, with their desire to distance and control unilaterally environments and the individuals who occupy them, tend to display senses that are explicit. These tendencies were more thoroughly discussed in chapters 2 and 3. Secondly, notions of implicitness and explicitness can be applied to the inherent technical characteristics of media themselves, to the extent to which such characteristics can or cannot lead, on the one hand, to a dynamic articulation of that which is fluid and abstract and, on the other, to a denotative labelling and precise fixing of discrete elements of the world and the relationships that obtain between them. This difference relates also to the extent to which they can or cannot reproduce the tactile qualities of textures and the silent inscrutability of 'structures'. Sounds admissible to functional tonal music are severely constrained so that they may more clearly evoke the syntactical (Wishart, 1977a), for example, while language as used by French Symbolist poets reaches considerably beyond its denotative base in order to evoke the textural. Thirdly, notions of implicitness and explicitness can be applied to the manner in which different media articulate different world senses. *Despite their inherent tendencies towards implicitness and explicitness*, different media could articulate radically different world senses. This articulation is achieved not only in terms of the ways in which different media, implicitly *or* explicitly, evoke structures *or* textures. It is achieved also in terms of the balance between textural and structural elements in symbolic expression, and the order of relationships obtaining between them. Thus language, in its literary mode, may evoke structures that are implicit in the sense of articulating relationships between discrete semantic elements that are thoroughly ambiguous. To invoke the language of semiotics, the signified is questioned or repressed. It may also, through formal literary devices such as alliteration and onomatopoeia, evoke textures by concentrating the mind on its qualities as sound. Additionally, it may stress its textural qualities through an obfuscation and therefore backgrounding of its discrete semantic elements. Lack of 'commonsense' meaning directs the mind elsewhere. Finally, notions of implicitness and explicitness can be applied at the level of analysis itself. Analysis in the world of post-Renaissance, industrial intellection tends to be an overwhelmingly explicit procedure.

What remains to be undertaken is an exploration of the way in which notions of implicitness and explicitness can be applied to concepts of structure and texture at the level both of different world senses and of the musical articulation of those senses. A sense of what is meant by 'implicit' and 'explicit' can be gained through a comparison of 'pre-literate' and 'industrial' world senses as elaborated in chapters 2 and 3. However, it is important to realize that the 'characteristics' of this implicit-explicit opposition or paradigm cannot be explicitly or directly stated without reifying it and therefore compromising its explanatory power. An important aspect of the position developed earlier in this chapter was that the totally intangible, fluid, abstract and dynamic set of social relationships within which we live can only be revealed to us through the objectifications and reifications of concrete symbols. To attempt to state the 'characteristics' of the implicit-explicit paradigm would serve only to entrench this objectification and reification by freezing such 'characteristics' in a symbolic mode – print – which has limited tolerance for that which is fluid and dynamic. As the different aspects of a specific world sense are all dialectically related, so the complex totality of the non-objectified social structurings of which they are evidence may only be sensed through them 'in' those processes of consciousness which are *not* symbolically imminent. It is these non-objectified processes of consciousness which approach most closely the non-objectified nature of social process, and which are therefore most appropriate for sensing such culture-specific processes in a 'seamless' and inseparable fashion. This level of abstraction is not easy to approach because it cannot be *directly* conveyed in terms of actual symbols, let alone in the highly reified and phonetically literate world sense of industrial societies. 'Rationally', social structuring can only be *approached* through the objectification of symbols. 'Irrationally' and ultimately, realization depends upon the *creation* of constructs 'in' *individual* consciousness, or, as some people might prefer it, upon intuition.

As developments in structuralism as an intellectual movement have demonstrated, analyses of literature, art and culture can be couched in terms which themselves approach the qualities of 'literariness' or 'artistry' being elucidated. As Feld's work (1982) illustrates, it is possible to discuss pre-literate worlds and their musics in such a way as to render them explicitly understandable to the Western academic mind, while retaining a strong sense of their organic and 'lived-within' nature. To this extent such analyses become implicit in their expressive powers. No such attempt has been made in the writing of this book. Firstly, its subject matter lies only partially within the realm of the implicit. Secondly, the dominant epistemological and musicological positions which form its backdrop themselves tend heavily towards the explicit. While the modern (or even postmodern) Western mind is capable of restructuring the implicit from an analysis couched explicitly, it is more difficult to see how such a mind could benefit from descriptions and criticisms of the explicit couched implicitly. In particular, criticism of positions grounded and expressed explicitly can only be criticized with effect in terms of arguments likewise grounded and expressed. Having said that, however, it should be remembered that the reality of an analysis lies not in the text through which it is embodied, but in the meanings and realizations that a reader is able to construct for themselves in and through the text in ways which may not be symbolically imminent.

6 Functional Tonality: A Basis for Musical Hegemony

Introduction

The aim of this chapter is to elucidate the social and cultural significance of functional tonality as a musical system during the historical moments of its emergence. Only through engaging in this analysis is it possible to gain a sense of the potential in the system for the cultural and musical hegemony that is exercised in contemporary industrial societies and, as a consequence, throughout the world. There is hardly an instance of *transnational* popular music whose technical characteristics are not at least compatible with the characteristics of the harmonic-rhythmic framework that has been imposed by or received from music composed in the functional tonal tradition. In order to understand functional tonality as an emergent cultural and musical system, it is necessary to engage in a cultural analysis of the hegemonic musical system which preceded it, that of medieval sacred plainchant. The chapter then proceeds to construct a theoretical model for the evolution of functional tonality from its *political* predecessor.

The Case for the Underlying Pentatonic Structure of Plainchant

This chapter argues that the largely implicit world sense of early medieval society was articulated musically through structurally implicit monody; that, as classic feudalism gradually broke down and began to give way to increasing urbanization, mercantilism and incipient forms of capitalism, so, too, the implicit monody of plainchant began to disintegrate and state, harmonically and explicitly, the internal conditions of its structure; and that, as the intellectual preconditions necessary for the development of industrial capitalism became fully established during and after the Renaissance, the emerging explicitness of late medieval and early Renaissance polyphony gradually syncretized into the homogeneous and explicit structure of functional tonality.

There is a temptation to understand the implicit nature of medieval plainchant and the explicit nature of functional tonality as being tied in some fixed way to conditions of monody and harmony. Although there was, in the case of this particular social-musical transition, an 'alliance' between implicitness and melody on the one hand, and harmony and explicitness on the other, no such alliance is given or inevitable. If it is a condition of the concepts of 'implicitness' and 'explicitness' that they cannot be definitively stated through symbols without injury to their inherently fluid, dynamic and abstract nature, it follows that there can be no easy one-to-one relationship between implicitness and explicitness on the one hand and, on the other, the technical characteristics of any symbolic medium, including that of music, through which conditions of implicitness and explicitness receive material articulation. The very terms in which Williams laid down the groundwork for the concept of the structural homology demonstrates that the meaning or significance of any symbolic utterance can never be totally intrinsic or immanent to that utterance. No symbolic system maps in a fixed and frozen fashion the world sense or social reality to which it gives expression and life. There are, as a consequence, varying degrees of plasticity in the range of significations that can be 'pushed' through any material utterance or signifier, and concrete musical utterances can never contain completely within themselves the conditions of implicitness or explicitness they 'express'. Meanings are always, to one degree or another, negotiable. While this chapter pushes 'purely' technical explanations for various musical developments as far as is possible, the ultimate impossibility of explaining changes in musical 'languages' and styles through 'purely' technical analyses points to the necessity of remaining sensitive to the way in which such 'languages' and styles constitute sites for the *active negotiation* of cultural and social meanings. While the 'easy' equation of melody and implicitness on the one hand, and harmony and explicitness on the other may provide the reader with an easy way into understanding the musical articulations of these social and cultural 'conditions', the equation should not be taken as representative of a fixed mode of social-musical articulation. This point will be taken up again later in the chapter.

Although the advent of literacy substantially altered people's orientation towards themselves and the world, a strong residue of orality prevented any development of a 'consciously' or 'rationally' organized harmony or metre until the late Middle Ages. The phonetic literacy of ancient Greece, for example, provided the conceptual framework within which Pythagoras could evolve the mathematical basis of Western melody and harmony, and within which it was possible to step outside the all-encompassing confines of the melodic line (or, in some cases, of implicit harmony). Yet the orality which underlay the society would not allow further musical exploitation of the discoveries made by Pythagoras. As Mellers has observed, the 'passionate religious mystical matriarchy ... remained at war with, and was too powerful to be absorbed by its new, empirical, rationalistic patriarchy' (Mellers, 1968, p. 8). This dualism was reflected in the music, as Peter Crossley-Holland points out: 'practising Greek musicians, although by no means unaware of the role of the mind in defining their materials, naturally placed more emphasis on the evidence of their ears than on the mathematics of the specialist theorists' (1960, p. 100).

Again, in early medieval society, although a degree of 'objectivity' and 'reason' were used to maintain a theocratic world, the orality which was still strong and at the basis of the theocracy prevented any development of 'consciously organized' harmony. People thought of themselves as being at the centre of the universe, and even the learned stock of knowledge was still reinforced orally. A student in a university 'proved his ability in logic, physics or natural philosophy, ethics, metaphysics, law or medicine, as well as in theology, by disputation and possibly a final oral examination in a disputation-like form. There were no written papers, written exercises or written examinations at all. Writing was used a great deal, but in connection with oral expression' (Ong, 1967, p. 59).

It would be impossible to begin a discussion of any Western musical language without mentioning at least the bare essentials of the Pythagorean discoveries, since it is the *social organization* of the natural phenomena brought to people's notice through these discoveries that results in those languages. The discoveries are as follows: when a note is sounded, harmonics are given off above the fundamental, in vibration ratios of 2 to 1, 3 to 2, 4 to 3, 5 to 4 and so on. These ratios constitute the octave, and then *approximately* (as a consequence of social organization)

Example 1   The Harmonic Series

(N.B. The notated pitches are only approximate.)

the fifth, the fourth and the major third of the functional tonal system. These ratios are the beginning of a series of gradually diminishing intervals that constitute the harmonic series (see example 1).

As social constructions utilizing this series, the underlying structures of most Western musics possess the common element of being variously grounded upon the intervals of the octave, the fifth and the fourth (with these latter intervals undergoing minor adjustments to fit particular systems and situations). The keynote in functional tonality is dependent on the primacy of the octave, and is harmonically defined by its relationship to the dominant (at the fifth) and subdominant (at the fourth). The fundamental interval of ancient Greek music – at least in its theoretical aspect – was the fourth of the tetrachord, two of these tetrachords being put together – 'either disjunctly with a note to join them, or conjunctly with a tone to complete their downward series' (Crossley-Holland, 1960, p. 102) – to form the octave scale or *harmonia*. But there also exists another structure, that of pentatonicism, which is based on the intervals of the fifth and the fourth, and which, it is argued, provides the structure underlying a great deal of medieval music.

The first step in this argument is to put forward the case for the underlying pentatonic structure of plainchant. Before doing this however, the indigenous nature of the octave, fifth and fourth, to the music of the Western world in general, and to medieval music in particular, may be illustrated by reference to early organum (that is, parallel singing at the interval of a fifth or the interval of a fourth), and to the reasons that can be put forward for its development. Starting with a monodic line, and assuming that the properties of the harmonic series influenced the manner in which people of different voice ranges sang with each other, it is not difficult to speculate on how parallel singing at the octave, fifth and fourth originated. Not only are the octave, the fifth and the fourth the intervals (audible as harmonics) which occur first in the harmonic series, but the fifth and the fourth provide convenient 'half-way' points between the two notes of the octave (which is the most 'natural' interval for parallel singing) for those whose voice range does not easily fall within either of the two lines of the octave. Reese substantiates this analysis:

> Another explanation [for the 'origins' of parallel organum] is offered by the natural ranges of the four main classes of human voices, which, roughly speaking, lie at pitch levels a fifth away from one another, in consecutive order from bass to soprano. The congregations that sang responses at services did not consist of trained singers, but sang with the ranges they found comfortable. Machabey, on the basis of this, writes: 'The division of men's voices

into two parallel lines, and of the high-pitched (women's and boys') voices into two other lines paralleling the first, must have followed as a matter of course, without the executants noticing it'. In 1908 in France, he heard an untrained congregation singing in organum without, apparently, intending to. The men and women each broke into two groups singing a fourth or a fifth from one another according to the texture of the melody. (Reese, 1940, p. 250)

The interval which is midway between the two notes of the octave (that is, the interval comprised by the defining note of this octave and the sixth note of the semitone scale) is the augmented fourth of the tempered scale. This is the only interval that is not even approximated between two adjacent notes of the harmonic series. Moreover, if it is conceived in terms of two non-adjacent notes, the vibration ratio is never the same (5:7, 7:10, 12:17 etc.). In comparison to the fifth and the fourth, which can be conceived as maintaining exactly the same ratios throughout the harmonic series, the unstable augmented fourth seems less of a natural choice as an interval for parallel singing.

The interval of the fourth is one removed from that of the fifth in the harmonic series. It could be argued, in the case of parallel organum, that the fourth arises as the inversion of the fifth. Hughes gives this impression in discussing the organum of the *Musica Enchiriadis* (see example 2):

From the *Musica Enchiriadis* we learn about four types of organum: (1) in parallel fifths, with the plainchant melody on the top line; (2) in the same, with the higher voice, or *vox principalis* doubled at the octave below and the lower voice, or *vox organalis* doubled at the octave above, thus resulting in a four part effect . . .; (3) taking either the higher or the lower pair of these four voices and running on in parallel fourths . . .; (4) a variant of this last method. (Hughes, 1955, p. 278)

Example 2 A Section of the *Musica Enchiriadis*

By inversion, the occurrence of the perfect fifth underlines the existence of the perfect fourth, even if the fourth cannot be said to arise by reason of its position in the harmonic series. Even then, it does not seem legitimate to conceive of a perfect fourth on the fundamental, since no such fourth occurs either in the harmonic series or by inversion of the fifth. However, it could be argued that, once the fourth was established as an equal partner of the fifth, it would not be a great development for the fourth to become established in its own right as an interval directly relating to the fundamental. Notwithstanding this theoretical 'difficulty', there still remains much evidence that the fourth, for whatever reason, was as much a natural modification of the original melodic line as the fifth.

Given the indigenous nature of the fifth and fourth to Western music, it is possible to see how the pentatonic scale could have come into existence. If one takes the fifth and fourth on the original fundamental, and treats them in turn as fundamentals with their own fifths and fourths, then one arrives at a structure of five notes (see figure 1). It might seem that this is a somewhat cursory explanation for the origins of the pentatonic structure in early medieval society. Surely there are more detailed causes and influences. There are two related answers to this criticism. Firstly, there can be no ultimate and complete explanation for the occurrence of any social symbol. All that can be said is that *this* pentatonic structure, as specifically articulated in the plainchant repertory, was *creatively* evolved in early medieval southern Europe as part of the continuing construction of social reality. Given this construction of

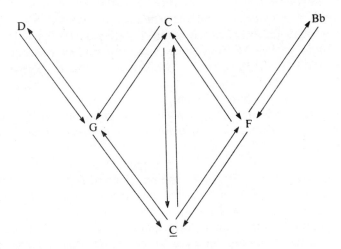

Figure 1

reality, *other* structures with similar features and articulating similar meanings might have come into being. Secondly, even if it were possible to adduce detailed causes for the creation of this structure, such causes would never furnish a complete explanation, and would only be dialectical *symptoms* of continuing structural change, rather than causes in the *strict* meaning of that word.

One of two further questions might also arise regarding the structure in figure 1. Having accepted the indigenous nature of the octave, fifth and fourth to Western music, why is it that the progression of fifths and fourths shown in figure 1 stops at the second level? The second question is this: once having generated a fifth and a fourth from the original fundamental (the underlined 'C' of figure 1), why is it that another fourth and fifth are generated above the G and F rather than other subsequent intervals of the harmonic series? This alternative suggestion does not negate the primacy of the fifth and the fourth, and would permit the introduction of other intervals (audible as harmonics) into the underlying structure. There are no intra-musical answers to these questions, for the organization of musical structures is ultimately a dialectic correlate of the social reality that is symbolically mediated by and through the music of a particular society. *The answers will only emerge as an attempt is made to demonstrate the way in which pentatonicism and functional tonality have respectively mediated medieval and industrial world senses.*

There are three pieces of evidence which support the hypothesis that Gregorian chant in particular, and medieval music in general, have an underlying pentatonic structure. Firstly, many chants are purely pentatonic: 'Whether or not virtually the entire ancient repertoire was based on a pentatonic groundwork ... the fact remains that a considerable number of Gregorian melodies are clearly pentatonic' (Reese, 1940, pp. 159–60). Furthermore, medieval German songs also display a pentatonic character (Reese, 1940, p. 233), a feature which, according to Westrup, has 'obvious associations with Gregorian chant' (1955, p. 259). But even where a Gregorian chant does not display pure pentatonic formulae throughout, there is often convincing evidence from opening phrases and subsequent motives that the pentatonic structure plays a generative role in that chant.

Furthermore, many Gregorian compositions betray their pentatonic origin through characteristic opening phrases of a purely pentatonic nature (usually sung by the cantor alone). These produce an impression of being 'principal themes' and are sometimes subsequently developed on a six or seven-tone basis. One finds a still greater abundance of the so-called 'trichordal' motives – the nuclei of pentatonic formations. These are composed of three notes within the interval of a perfect fourth and contain no semitones. Thus C–D–F, D–F–G, G–A–C, A–C–D, as well as their various permutations and transpositions, used either consecutively or intermittently are trichordal motives. (Yasser, 1937, p. 181)

An objection which can be raised against the hypothesis of pentatonically structured medieval music is that frequently more than the five notes of the pentatonic scale are in evidence. It seems likely, however, that the remaining two notes of the natural gamut which may appear in a chant do so in the role of passing notes.

Still another important piece of evidence should be taken into account in determining the true scalar basis of medieval music. We refer to the *quilisma*, the symbol for which is today generally believed to have indicated the sounding, within a minor third, of a very light and transient ornamental note. (Yasser, 1937, p. 182)

As Yasser indicates (1937, pp. 182–3), a precedent for this procedure is to be found in the Chinese *pien*-tone. There is statistical evidence in support of the theory.

Out of nearly 1600 Gregorian items which at present constitute the principal musical material of the Catholic liturgy, only a little more than 700 contain no quilismas at all. The number of those which do contain quilismas, impressive as it is (amounting to almost 900), must have been greater at the time when, as is supposed, the use of the quilisma was universal for all melodies that employed more than five notes within an octave. The total number of quilismas found in the 900 compositions referred to is 3100, of which 81.5 *per cent* are placed within minor thirds, 17 *per cent* within major thirds, and 1.5 *per cent* within perfect fourths. (Yasser, 1937, p. 344)

The passing note theory does much to explain B flat as the sole example of notated 'chromaticism' in early medieval music. It can be heard as one of the two possible passing notes between A and C: 'The *pien*-tone theory ... shows that B flat is not merely a faintly undesirable substitute for B natural ... but its peer; and the melodies themselves, with their frequent use of B flat, bear this out' (Reese, 1940, pp. 160–1). Finally, if the original objection is maintained by asserting that passing notes destroy any feeling for pentatonicism, and create an incipient feeling for functional tonality, it may be pointed out that the existence of chromatic passing notes in functional tonal music does not immediately imply the destruction of tonality and the creation of atonality. It is not necessary, in order to demonstrate the existence of a musical structure, that only the notes of that structure be present in the music itself. What is necessary is to indicate that the structure, as articulated by and through the music, determines both the relative importance and function of the notes, as well as the more general characteristics of the archetypal melodic (and harmonic) formulae.

This line of argument has been substantiated by Chailley. Chailley's position is that the traditional eight modes of plainchant are extensions of pentatonicism:

> What is a Gregorian mode? In the light of the following article we are able to reply with the utmost conciseness: it is a formulary pattern originating from the ornamentation of a melodic shape which links a tonic note with a recitation note or tenor (latterly called the dominant) in a fixed pentatonic scale. This pentatonic scale is freely completed with weak notes which are more or less mobile. (Chailley, 1970, p. 85)

These modes cannot be regarded as tonal formations in quite the same way as functional tonality can. Whereas functional tonality is a musical language universally evident in European art music between approximately 1600 and 1880, many individual chants are either modally ambiguous, or do not convincingly fit into any mode at all. Moreover, without denying that much plainchant does fit into modal analysis, and may therefore be said to articulate different concepts of time-space within that more generally articulated by the generative pentatonic structure, it seems likely that the theoretical concept of the eight modes had as much to do with theological numeric symbolism as with rationalizing strictly musical evidence (Werner, 1948, pp. 211–55). The theory of functional tonality, on the other hand, was completely derived from the music of the functional tonal period and is consequently universally applicable to that music.

Chailley takes as his point of departure two 'facts' which, in his opinion, have been largely ignored by traditional theory: the pentatonic nature of very old melody, and the historical importance of chanting the psalms, and so of the reciting note or tenor used in that chanting. The importance of the tenor lay in the tendency of most chants to move around it before descending to the final. These legacies, argues Chailley, were influential in the development of both the Gregorian chant and the eight modes, these latter evolving from the interaction of four factors.

1   The range defined by the tenor and the final (the final gradually replaced the tenor in importance and traditionally became the somewhat unsatisfactory method of assigning a mode to a chant). This range could be a minor or major third, a perfect fourth, a perfect fifth (these perfect consonances being the most 'fertile' generators of modes) and, exceptionally, a minor sixth.

2   The shape of the melodic kernel whose range has been fixed by the tenor and final. If one takes a strict pentatonic scale (and Chailley is very precise in his definition: 'the basic scale being that of a pentatonic scale without any semitones in which the unfilled minor thirds are optionally divided by weak and often movable *piens* whose exact placement within the minor third would seem to be fixed by attraction [to more important notes]'), then, by starting in turn on each of the five notes it is possible to arrive at different internal shapes for the intervals of the fourth and fifth (this explains their 'fertility'). In the following scheme 'T' indicates a whole tone and '3' a minor third.

Perfect fourth

C D F G A C   =   T 3 T T 3   ⎫
G A C D F G   =   T 3 T 3 T   ⎬   Shape 'I'

D F G A C D   =   3 T T 3 T   ⎫
A C D F G A   =   3 T 3 T T   ⎬   Shape 'II'

    The remaining 'scale' does not give an initial interval of a fourth.

Perfect fifth

F G A C D F   =   T T 3 T 3   Shape 'I'

C D F G A C   =   T 3 T T 3   ⎫
G A C D F G   =   T 3 T 3 T   ⎬   Shape 'II'

D F G A C D   =   3 T T 3 T   Shape 'III'

The remaining 'scale' does not give an initial interval of a fifth.

3   The fixing by attraction of the weak notes to be found in the two intervals of a minor third created by a pentatonic scale.

4   The manner in which the range of the melodic kernel was extended to give the *ambitus* (range) of a chant. This determined whether a mode was authentic or plagal.

There is insufficient space to reproduce all of Chailley's arguments. Nevertheless, Chailley's analysis has the advantage over the traditional classification of accounting for modally ambiguous chants and chants which do not fit properly into the modal scheme.

Finally, it would seem that the importance of the fourth and the fifth to both the pentatonic structure itself and that structure's generation of chants and modes finds expression in the method of analysis used by medieval theorists. All eight modes (in the symmetrical systematization of Hermannus Contractus) were viewed as being founded on these two intervals.

> The system of the octave-species ... soon yielded ground in the analytical writings, being replaced in large part by consideration of what might be called the *modal nucleus* consisting of the notes immediately above the final, and of the various species of pentachords and tetrachords. The admissible pentachords were TSTT, STTT, TTTS and TTST; the admissible tetrachords were TST, STT and TTS; the diminished fifth and augmented fourth were inadmissible species. (Reese, 1940, p. 156)

This classification is linked with the designation of the octave, fifth and fourth as the only admissible consonances in medieval music, at least until the thirteenth century.

> The classified species of the Middle Ages are bounded solely by medieval consonances – the fourth, fifth and octave. To obtain a full complement of early medieval consonances one need add to these only the unison and such octave-compounds as the twelfth. The compass of the authentic modes is often extended downward by one degree ... but these modes, nevertheless, continued to be classified according to the species, not of their ninths, but, like the others, of their octaves. ... The sixths also, dissonances in the early Middle Ages, are among the intervals that never bound classified species: the hexachord, though used for purposes of classification, was not applied to the distinguishing of species. It could not have been, in its Guidonian form, since its TTSTT structure never varied. (Reese, 1940, pp. 156–7)

The exclusive use of the octave, fifth and fourth as consonances in early medieval music and as the distinguishing features of modal species provides parallels to the exclusive role of the fifth and fourth in generating a pentatonic structure. Given the exclusive use of these intervals as consonances and distinguishing features, it would be surprising to find that any other interval or intervals were fundamental to the structure of Gregorian chant. If the melodic formulae of the chant do articulate the fifth and the fourth as basic structural elements, then it is a small step to the externalization of these implicit elements as analytic tools.

The Articulation of an Ideal Feudal Structure through Pentatonicism

Unlike those of functional tonality, the fundamentals of pentatonicism are interlocking and mutually dependent; they do not point outside themselves. It is impossible and invalid to hear only one note of the structure as the one to which all others irrevocably and necessarily tend. Assuming that passing notes are not important structural elements in pentatonicism, six relationships only are possible for a pentatonic melody. The notes referred to are those of figure 1. Example 1 may also be consulted.

1   Any note can be heard as its own fundamental.
2   All the notes (except B flat) can be heard as the third harmonic relating to a second (perfect fifth).
3   All the notes (except D) can be heard as the fourth harmonic relating to a third (perfect fourth).
4   D can be heard as the fifth harmonic relating to a fourth (major third).
5   F and B flat can be heard as a sixth harmonic relating to a fifth (minor third).
6   C, D and G can be heard as an eighth harmonic relating to a seventh (whole tone).

Which of these relationships will be heard for any note will depend upon its position in any particular melody, with the preceding note (ignoring passing notes) being the most important factor. One can, of course, make a similar assertion for functional tonality. Any note of the major or minor scale may perform a number of different functions, all of which depend upon specific context. But whereas the function of notes in functional tonality depends upon a definite hierarchy in which certain relationships may be heard as more important or fundamental than others – giving rise to the oppositions of concord and discord, and the distancing of modulation – the relationships of pentatonicism have no hierarchy. Any one relationship is as important or fundamental as any other; it exists by and for itself, having no hierarchical function outside itself.

Yet, although no one note of a pentatonic melody can become a basic fundamental to which all others must resolve, many pentatonic and modal melodies give the feeling that one note is more important than others. This feeling is created by stressing one note (such as the tenor of a chant) more than others. This sense of importance, as Reti has indicated, is of a 'melodic' rather than a 'harmonic' nature. Reti demonstrates that a melody which possesses 'melodic' rather than 'harmonic' centrality can be brought to rest on the important note at any point in its duration. To attempt the same with a melody of 'harmonic' tonality would be to 'destroy the innermost sense of the whole line' (Reti, 1958, p. 16).

Feudal society was of a highly decentralized and localized type. The collapse of the Roman Empire, itself strongly centralized, created a situation favourable for the emergence of small social units whose population, at least in theory, were mutually dependent upon one another.

> To seek a protector, or to find satisfaction in being one – these things are common to all ages. But we seldom find them giving rise to new legal institutions save in civilizations where the rest of the social framework is giving way. Such was the case in Gaul after the collapse of the Roman Empire.
>
> Consider, for example, the society of the Merovingian period. Neither the State nor the family any longer provided adequate protection. The village community was barely strong enough to maintain order within its own boundaries; the urban community scarcely existed. Everywhere the weak man felt the need to be sheltered by someone more powerful. The powerful man, in his turn, could not maintain his prestige or his fortune or even ensure his own safety except by securing for himself, by persuasion or coercion, the support of subordinates bound to his service. On the one hand, there was the urgent quest for a protector; on the other, there were usurpations of authority, often by violent means. And as notions of weakness and strength are always relative, in many cases the same man occupied a dual role – as a dependent of a more powerful man and a protector of humbler ones. Thus there began to be built up a vast system of personal relationships whose intersecting threads ran from one level of the social structure to another. (Bloch, 1961, pp. 145–6)

In this fashion one became the 'man of another man' rather than an 'anonymous cog' within a strongly centralized and bureaucratic system.

In commenting upon the cross-fertilization of medieval sacred and secular music, Mellers has drawn an analogy between music and society:

> Not only had the religious art-music of the Middle Ages and the popular folk music many qualities, technical and spiritual, in common; there was a continual interaction between them which is of crucial importance from both a sociological and a musical point of view. There have been many learned arguments as to which came first, which influenced which, that seem to me irrelevant. If the feudal order meant anything (and one knows it nearly always failed to live up to its pretensions) it was an order in which cleric and peasant mutually succoured each other, one providing for the needs of the body, the other for the needs of the soul. They were complementary parts of a social organism, allied in their very differences, and their respective musical manifestations likewise complement one another. (Mellers, 1946, p. 26)

It is possible to go much further than this, however, for the pentatonic structure underlying much medieval music in itself serves to articulate the *ideal* feudal structure. The fundamentals of pentatonicism are complementary and mutually dependent. They are also centres without margins in the sense that the relationships they form are made *directly* with other fundamentals, something that is not the case with functional tonality. Insomuch as one note of the pentatonic structure may be stressed more than others, Bloch's statement that feudal society was 'unequal ... rather than ... hierarchical' (Bloch, 1961, p. 443) could equally be applied to the structure of pentatonicism as found in medieval music.

The structural articulations of medieval music are not restricted to the 'spatial' sphere alone. Both the 'spiritual' rhythm of plainchant and the 'corporeal' rhythm of folk-song conveyed a revelationary sense of becoming rather than an incarnate sense of being. Time was a product of becoming.

> To change was to pass from potentiality to actuality. But this transition had nothing about it necessarily temporal. By virtue of the Christian doctrine of omnipotence it could have a temporal quality only if there were some cause which did not allow the immediate transformation by divine action of the potentiality into the act. And this cause which required that time be involved in the change was a certain defect of matter. From this point of view,

matter was nothing other than a resistance which, manifesting itself in the substance of a thing, hindered that thing from assuming instantly the fullness of being which its form would confer upon it, a resistance which introduced distance and tardiness, multiplicity and delay, where everything, it seemed, should have happened simultaneously and at once. (Poulet, 1956, pp. 4–5)

Instaneity of oneness with God stands in stark opposition to the spatialized temporality of industrial societies. Both negate subjective flow: oneness with God implies a complete losing of the self, a solipsistic consciousness, whereas the conceptual control of spatialized time indicates an intense awareness of consciousness, together with a sense of history and progress. In negating the instaneity of oneness with God, the temporal flow of consciousness reveals time without making it incarnate as objective fact. The conceptual relationship medieval people have to the universe, therefore, remains slippery: 'these men, subjected both externally and internally to so many ungovernable forces, lived in a world in which the passage of time escaped their grasp all the more because they were so ill-equipped to measure it' (Bloch, 1961, p. 73). The lack of measurement (and measurement is so vital to the time of industrial societies) 'was but one of the symptoms . . . of a vast indifference to time,' (Bloch, 1961, p. 74) and so of the fact that medieval people existed largely *within* time.

The revelationary nature of becoming is related to medieval people's lack of self-contained margins. Medieval people seemed to feel more intimately involved with and affected by events than many people in industrial societies. Both the mutual dependency of the pentatonic fundamentals of medieval music and that music's spiritual and corporeal rhythms articulate this revelationary immediacy. From the standpoint of industrial societies, the music of medieval people seems to negate the individualism which is a dialectic correlate of those societies' dominant world sense. Mellers is of the opinion that the singer of plainchant 'is not interested in the "expression" of the individual' but in 'the medium through which the voice of God manifests itself' (Mellers, 1946, pp. 24–5). In noting certain similarities between plainsong and some secular songs, Mellers infers a link between musical structures and the structuring of medieval society and consciousness:

The rhythms are extremely flexible, flowing naturally from the spoken inflection . . . there is a tendency towards fluid pentatonic vocal figurations analogous to the plainsong tropes; there is an habitual avoidance of leading notes and implied full closes, the same insistence on conjunct motion and the absolute and perfect consonances. The impression still tends, that is, to the merging of the personality in something outside itself; for all the local details of the songs, the effect is not that of the incarnation of a 'personality', but of a creative act which is independent of any particular person made manifest through the human voice. (Mellers, 1946, p. 25)

Emergent Tonality

Accepting the notions of implicitness and explicitness, and the assertion that all musics articulate social structures, the difference between the *monody* of plainchant and the initial *harmony* which develops into functional tonality might not appear as fundamental as might be thought. The parallel fifths and fourths of organum make explicit in this first form of Western harmony the fifths and fourths of the underlying and implicit pentatonic structure of much early medieval music. Such externalization only represents a transient stage between the pure monody of pentatonicism and the fully developed harmony of functional tonality for pentatonicism, in becoming harmonically explicit, began to destroy its own implicit qualities. The only inequality between the fundamentals of pentatonicism resulted from stressing one note through repetition – a stressing which did not break up the mutual dependency (and therefore the ambiguity of relationships) existing between the fundamentals. The creation of the *vox principalis* and the derived *vox organalis* destroys this mutual dependency by creating a hierarchy. The *vox organalis* only exists insomuch as it is a function of the previously self-sufficient *vox principalis*. Although the *vox organalis* taken on its own (as in the *Musica Enchiriadis* – see example 2) could be a

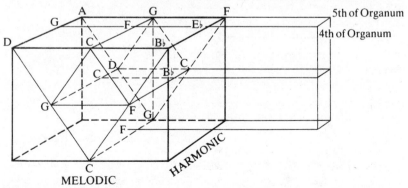

Figure 2

self-sufficient line of plainsong, the way in which it is conceived and heard by medieval people negates such a possibility. It is now possible to extend figure 1 to include these externalizations (see figure 2).

Organum may give notes which were previously *quilismas* a different hierarchical function, thus weakening their previous role as passing notes. In example 3 a note which is a passing note within the mode is now heard as a function of a fundamental. The process is clearer in example 4, where a piece of disjunct motion utilizes the note in a fashion that denies any possibility of its being heard as a passing note. Notes which were previously *quilismas* and, as such, were inessential, here become essential parts of the structure of organum. This is demonstrated in figure 3.

The role of organum in negating the very structure it is externalizing can be further explained by considering the increasing importance of *musica ficta* to the emerging polyphony of the late Middle Ages. The augmented fourth or diminished fifth, as approximated from the harmonic series, is a very unstable interval that falls roughly halfway both in an octave and between the intervals of the fourth and the fifth. Medieval theorists have labelled it *diabolus in musica* not only because of its

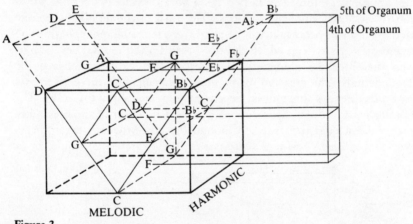

Figure 3

Example 3

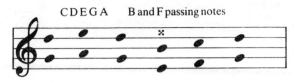

Example 4

Example 5

instability, but because any musical reference to it would tend to deny the function of fourths and fifths in halving the octave, *and so ultimately deny the underlying structure of pentatonicism.* There would consequently exist a negation of the feudal structure of medieval society. Further, the augmented fourth is the only interval that does not result naturally from the pentatonic structure and its passing notes. Fifths, fourths, major and minor thirds and whole tones can be derived from the pure pentatonic structure, and semitones occur as a result of *quilismas.* Augmented fourths can only occur in a pentatonic melody by a leap to or from a passing note. The fact that augmented fourths are not found in Gregorian chant not only supports the pentatonic theory, but shows, from a practical standpoint, how the admission of augmented fourths would undermine a pentatonic structure by giving passing notes an emphasis they do not possess.

The parallelism of organum is constrained to avoid the augmented fourths that would inevitably result (see example 5) by resorting to *musica ficta.* Notes which were not previously part of the natural gamut of a mode become an essential part of the structure of organum originating in that mode. In figure 3, for example, three natural gamuts may be derived from the pentatonic structure (C D F G Bb):

	C	D	E	F	G	A	Bb	
	C	D	Eb	F	G	A	Bb	
	C	D	Eb	F	G	Ab	Bb	
*	C	D	E	F	G	Ab	Bb	*

The starred shape is inadmissible, since it does not conform to a natural gamut. From the three admissible gamuts, two different gamuts with one *musica ficta* note may be derived:

```
C   D   Eb    F   G   A/Ab*   Bb
C   D   E/Eb* F   G   A       Bb
```

Figure 3 may thus be modified (see figure 4). This process, even more than that of making passing notes an essential part of the structure of organum, again seriously weakens the pentatonic structure being externalized.

Organum does not simply externalize the fifths and fourths of the

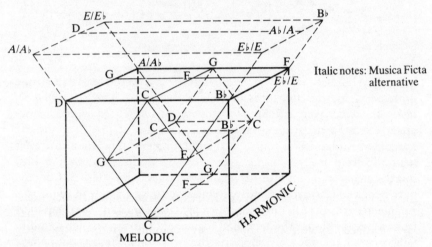

Figure 4

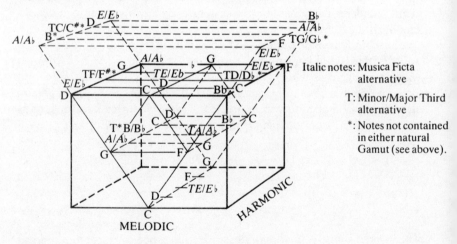

Figure 5

pentatonic structure but also, in free organum, the seconds and major and minor thirds. Since major and minor thirds do not follow each other in free organum, they will be given as alternatives in figure 5. For the reasons already discussed with reference to parallel organum, this procedure again negates the implicit qualities of the structure being externalized. A potential therefore exists in parallel and free organum for the articulation of an explicit 'three-dimensional' structure at the expense of the already existing implicit 'two-dimensional' structure.

Implicitness and Melody; Explicitness and Harmony

Before proceeding any further with this brief analysis, it is necessary to examine more closely the preconditions necessary for the development of functional tonality. Firstly, the possibility of externally stating or reproducing elements of music which before were only implicit results from the development of phonetic literacy and its concomitant concepts. However, it is not clear that the inception or creation of polyphony was coincidental with this 'conscious' externalization. Although Spiess is of the opinion that 'there is no scientific evidence to prove beyond question that there was a rudimentary polyphonic practice before the organum of the ninth century' (Spiess, 1957, p. 15), such practice is a possibility that can hardly be ruled out. The evidence relayed by Reese to the effect that an untrained congregation may sing 'organum' without apparently intending to would seem to suggest that an 'unintended polyphony' was not uncommon in the early Middle Ages.

It may be the case that the process of writing down harmony was partially engendered by the pre-existence of polyphonic forms which were not originally 'conscious' externalizations of implicit plainchant melodies. Without the growing distancing and objectivity of phonetic literacy people might not have been able to recede enough from the music to notice the implicitly structured and accidental or natural forms of polyphony (parallelism, heterophony and imitation). Further, without those forms, literacy might have been used for longer than was the case in encoding monophonic lines, whether implicit or explicit. It is a possibility that the development of an *explicit* musical structure might never have been *harmonically* mediated. There exists, in other words, a dialectic relationship between literacy and growing harmonic explicitness in which it is impossible to identify individual cause and effect. In the opinion of Stevens, then, the perpetuation and development of polyphony are linked with the importance of the book to the Carolingian Renaissance.

> The art of writing, of calligraphy, became wedded indissolubly to
> the art of music. Thus the polyphony of earlier times and distant
> nations, however well organised into parallel melodies, tunes-upon-
> drones, or thematic imitation, lacked the means to perpetuate itself
> unequivocally. It was the task of Western nations to transform
> sounds into symbols. (Stevens, 1960, p. 211)

It is crucial for an adequate understanding of developing functional
tonality that it is *not* viewed solely and simply as the result of the
harmonic externalization of a structure formerly implicit in the melodic
lines of another culture. Functional tonality is not *just* a 'three-
dimensional' version of pentatonicism. The phonetically literate concepts
which instigated and facilitated the creation of functional tonality were
themselves instrumental in changing the very structure of society and
consciousness. Evolving functional tonality represented a creative articulation and encoding of that change. The growth of a musical structure
where harmony represents an *initial* externalization of the structure as
implicit in melody is therefore part and parcel of a fundamental change in
the overall social structure. Thus, although harmony may be regarded as
the initial medium for growing explicitness, functional tonality as it
finally evolved displayed a total explicitness which transcends any
melodic or harmonic parameters. From this point of view it is incorrect
to hear the harmony of developed functional tonality *simply* as an
externalization of a structure formerly implicit in melody, or the melody
of developed harmony as simply containing structural or harmonic
implications that exist *only* because of the harmony. Any such line of
thought ultimately depends upon the assumptive equation of melody
with implicitness and harmony with explicitness. The validity of this
equation was brought into question earlier in the chapter.

Music does not possess its own internal laws. Functional tonality was
not generated *simply* from within previous musical forms, but was
constructed and created as part of a continually developing social
process. This process included other musical influences from sources such
as the folk musics of central Europe. It is not even possible, therefore, to
conceive of some internal and self-sufficient musical laws both giving rise
to functional tonality *and* paralleling wider social causation. 'Music' and
'society' cannot be legitimately thought of in this way as distinct and
separable entities. Further, social process knows no strict or prime
causation. Since creativity is an integral part of the social process, there
can be no ultimate and complete explanation for the particular form that
a symbol takes. Harmonic externalization cannot therefore be regarded
as a link in a causal chain which inexorably leads to the full development

of functional tonality. Rather, it was a symptom of creative and transcendent social change. Harmony might well *not* have been an absolute necessity for the development of an explicit musical language.

Functional Tonality Established

Two further developments were required before evolving functional tonality as set out in figure 5 could achieve full fruition. Firstly, the third was accepted as a consonance and replaced the fourth as an important structural element. Apart from the fact that the major and minor thirds are, respectively, the next intervals to be generated in the harmonic series after the perfect fourth (see example 1), the *preconditions* favouring the increasing importance of the third may be elucidated by considering the interplay between musical practice and theory in the Middle Ages. Crocker raises the question of why medieval theorists, given the legacy of the Greek Greater Perfect System, should bother with the construction of smaller theoretical units: 'What could be the purpose of articulating the scale into smaller units such as the tetrachord – as Hucbald did and as most other theorists did after him? Why, when early theorists had a complete scale – the Greater Perfect System – did they go through all this business with scale segments' (Crocker, 1972, p. 28)?

The probable answer, Crocker states,

> is ... that the Frankish musician started with the singing of the chant and worked his way toward theoretical constructions such as the scale, rather than the other way round. He was singer, teacher, theorist, in that order. *Cantus*, not *musica disciplina*, was his starting point; his curriculum was that of the monastic school of the 7th and 8th centuries, not the liberal arts curriculum of an earlier – or a later – time. The Greater Perfect System itself was not a basic assumption but rather a theoretical abstraction, relatively remote from practical experience. (Crocker, 1972, p. 29)

'In terms of that experience', Crocker continues, 'there was a clear need for a scalar module of manageable size, such as a fourth or fifth' (Crocker, 1972, p. 29). The octave did not provide a suitable scalar module.

> Nor was an octave module itself very appropriate; we are so accustomed to thinking of the octave as the basic scalar module that we do not immediately recognise the circumstances under

which it is inappropriate. From the Frankish point of view, the octave seemed too large a module . . . in considering any extended scalar construction, we have to remember that there was no handy mechanical embodiment – no keyboard – for a standard reference. . . . Any tonal structure referred to must be sung and held in the ear. Hence the obvious advantage of using repertory pieces of chant to illustrate, or rather to embody, tonal constructions. . . . This is a specific demonstration of the central importance of chant repertory in the development of medieval theory. (Crocker, 1972, p. 29)

It appears that the fifth was probably the important interval in this interplay between practice and theory. It is the first interval to be generated by the harmonic series after the octave (see example 1), and therefore the largest consonance to be of any great practical use to the medieval musician. Also, in being the interval of duplication between the disjunct tetrachords around which hexachords were constructed, it was a common element in medieval theory. Crocker intimates as much in his discussion of the *Musica Enchiriadis* scale.

Instead of octave duplication, the scale embodies consistent duplication at the fifth, comparable – but more consistent – to Guido's affinity at the fifth. As Handschin observed, Hermann's instructions, 'Take any tetrachord . . . add a tone at either end . . .' apply exactly to the constituent tetrachord of the *Musica Enchiriadis* scale, the tones added at either end corresponding to the tones of disjunction between successive tetrachords. (Crocker, 1972, p. 30)

The preservation of the fourth as a consonance in any developed polyphony having more than two parts would, through inversion at the fifth, produce the unacceptable dissonance of the major second. If medieval theorists could not accept the third as a consonance, there seems little reason why they should have accepted the second. As intervals which occur next in the harmonic series after the fourth, and which come midway between the second and the fourth, the major and minor third could be regarded as 'compromises'.

A preference for thirds rather than fourths in the harmonic dimension of figure 5 creates a situation favourable for the emergence of all the triads of the unified major-minor system. Before this could be achieved, it was necessary for one of the notes in each alternative situation indicated in figure 5 to be eliminated so that the resulting structure only utilized the seven notes of the major scale. This development is indicated in figure 6. The scale chosen in figure 6 is F major. It should be pointed out, however,

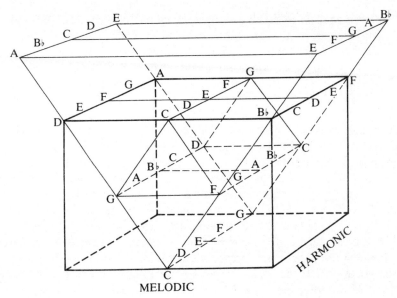

Figure 6

that two other scales, B flat major and E flat major, would have been equally possible, and that the particular development shown in figure 6 is thus only indicative of a wider and more significant change. For the possibility of deriving three scales from the same structure is symptomatic of the relationship obtaining between the keys of those scales, and so of the homogeneity and repeatability of the entire major-minor system. One major or minor triad of a key has relationships with other major or minor triads that may be precisely duplicated by those other triads if there is an appropriate key change. To put it in practical terms, a piece of functional tonal music involving modulation may be played in any one of twelve keys.

The homogeneity and repeatability of such interrelationships are not characteristic of the modal system. In this system each mode has a unique structure which is largely unrelated to the other modal shapes. When the modes were first classified according to their finals, there was no attempt to relate the finals on a common scale: 'It is essential ... to notice ... that the placement of the several finals on a common scale – so basic a step that we take it for granted – is actually distinct from the classification itself, which presumably came first as a separate step' (Crocker, 1972, p. 30). It is difficult for us, with our background of functional tonality, to imagine such a state of affairs.

it ... may require an effort to imagine the situation as it first presented itself to the chant singer: he would have perceived several autonomous groups of chants, each group with its own perceived set of tones and semi-tones, but he would not necessarily have been aware of any common scalar denominator that would relate the groups to each other. Indeed, there may have been no such denominator. (Crocker, 1972, p. 31)

Although there was no common scalar denominator which *related* the different groups of chant, it has been argued that there existed, in the form of the pentatonic structure, a common *generative* denominator. In this distinction lies the difference between explicit musical structuring, where the relationships between relata are made perfectly clear in the music itself, and a more implicit structuring, where the music does not obviously display its own underlying structure.

A crucial stage in the development of functional tonality is achieved when a scalar shape *itself* provides the module for relating the different shapes. A parallel development took place in medieval theory when the finals of different modes were placed on a common scale adapted and devised for that very purpose. This process explains the importance of the tetrachord to the scale of the *Musica Enchiriadis* and other medieval theoretical schemes. But it was a process whose implications were only understood with some difficulty, and this difficulty gives an insight into the fundamental difference between the modal and functional tonal systems.

The underlying moment in this process was ... to understand the extended pitch realm of the scale (i.e. the Greater Perfect System as adopted by medieval theorists) in terms of the relationship among the finals – that is, the relationships among any one final and the pitches above and below it and then the relationships among the finals *when they themselves were taken to be the pitches above and below each other*. This step led outside of and beyond any one final; to put it another way, the ultimate purpose of the tetrachord of the finals was not so much to understand a particular final in terms of a scalar construction as to understand a scalar construction in terms of the network of finals. For it was the scale, not the finals, that needed understanding. (Crocker, 1972, p. 33)

The difference between the development as it affected functional tonality and medieval theory is that whereas any medieval common scalar denominator was a theoretical concept having no *direct* musical expression, the tonal denominator was of *identical* shape with the scales being related. As such it had direct and explicit musical expression.

In order for the major scale shape to emerge from any of the modal shapes, it was necessary for the alternative notes of plainchant or organum to be eliminated according to a particular pattern (see figures 5 and 6). It is apparent that this pattern occurs as a dialectic correlate of the growing explicitness of evolving functional tonality, an explicitness which requires that the different modal shapes be syncretized into one homogeneous structure with a single unambiguous focal point. The minor scale emerges as a result of the homogeneous nature of functional tonal structures. If every note of the major scale (the scalar shape which provides the module for relating the 'different' shapes) generated a major triad or scale within the key of that scalar shape, then the structure would immediately lose its characteristics of homogeneity and repeatability. This may be observed by reference to figure 6.

This line of development (see also figures 1–6) is echoed by Reese in his discussion of the Notre Dame School. Pentatonic melody and 'tonal' harmony balance each other.

> The upper voices, in weaving about the tones of the triad often supplemented them by the second and sixth, thus producing a strong pentatonic effect. But the forcefulness with which the triad makes itself felt, also, and in addition, the increasing appearance of the third shows that the pentatonic and diatonic systems are poised in the balance. (Reese, 1940, p. 303)

The third, an interval originally regarded as needing resolution, gradually became a consonance, and superseded the fourth in its importance as a structural element.

> The feeling that thirds need resolution to perfect consonances is illustrated by Anonymous XIII ... who states ... that the major third should be followed by a fifth, and the minor third by a unison. ... Practical music in the 13th Century, however, gave greater liberty to the third in particular. ... While octaves and fifths predominate in the course of the pieces, the increasing recognition accorded to the third foreshadows the eventual downfall of a harmonic system based on unisons, octaves and fifths, and (originally) fourths – a system, that is betokening a pentatonic feeling for melody ... – and the approach of a harmonic system based on the triad. (Reese, 1940, p. 295)

Tonality's Encoding of the Industrial World Sense

With the full development of functional tonality, the interlocking fundamentals of pentatonicism become separated. In figure 6 it is perfectly clear whether C is heard as a fifth of F, as its own fundamental, as a third of A or a fourth of G, and, more importantly, at what level in the structure those relationships obtain. Functional tonality creates a hierarchy of fundamentals, all of which, through the various levels of the hierarchy, finally and ultimately relate back to one note.

The architectonicism of the functional tonal structure articulates the dominant world sense of industrial societies. It is a structure having one central viewpoint (that of the key-note) that is the focus of a single, unified sound sense involving a high degree of distancing. It is a centre-oriented structure with margins. But it is a further vital facet of the architectonicism of functional tonality that each note becomes a centre with margins. The more important structural notes relate to each other only insomuch as their precise function is defined by the less important notes belonging to higher architectonic levels, and these less important notes only relate to each other insomuch as *their* position is defined by their relationships to the more important structural notes.

The 'spatial' aspect of functional tonality is not the only one to articulate the social structures of industrial societies. As the simultaneously divergent viewpoints and time-spaces of medieval people snapped into a single three-dimensional focus whose adjunct was a spatialized time, so the syncretization of the different modal shapes into the unified structure of explicit functional tonality necessitated a precise vertical mensuration articulating a spatialized time. The correct vertical co-ordination of the notes of the different melodic lines leads to the possibility of making a 'spatial three-dimensional' cut along the 'time' axis of any functional tonal piece of music. The typification of such a cut is the bar-line. It is a dialectic correlate of the spatialized time articulated by functional tonality that many people in industrial societies, in becoming increasingly 'objective' and more intensely aware of their own consciousness, are able to stand back and objectify the passage of time. The revelationary nature of time as articulated by spiritual and corporeal rhythms is negated by a unified rhythmic structure which gains its effect from the pull of rhythmic patterns against pulse as contained in the strict metre essential to the three-dimensional cut already mentioned. By bringing the corporeal pulse of music into such *continual* high relief – and thereby altering and negating its original 'timeless' and hypnotic characteristics – the rhythmic structure of functional tonality maintains the intense and constant awareness that many people have, both of the passage of time and of their own consciousness.

The change in many people's orientation towards themselves and the environment that occurred during the Renaissance created the fiction, if not the fact, of progress. The classical and cyclical idea of historical degeneration and recovery

> lost its hold on the imaginations of men as a result of profound changes in the outward conditions of life which occurred in Western Europe from the fourteenth to the nineteenth century. Among these changes were the rise of ordered secular governments, the growth of towns and industry, the geographical discoveries and the extension of commerce which brought Western Europe into direct contact with alien customs and ideas, and above all the rise of an educated middle class whose interests were hampered by a form of society which supported the autocracy of kings and the privileges of a landed aristocracy. It was in this time of revolt against ecclesiastical and secular authority that the Christian doctrine of salvation gradually transformed into the modern idea of progress. (Becker, 1969, p. 12)

The central point upon which the social structures of industrial societies focus and from which the majority of power and influence is derived provides a goal towards which all other elements in the structures tend. The phonetic literacy and typography responsible for the growth of the social structures of industrial societies was also heavily instrumental in generating a class dialogue that took place *within* the framework of political and economic nationalism, and was overwhelmingly concerned with who (i.e. which men) should wield the centralized power of nationalism. Progress is concerned with impulsive movement towards the centres provided by the structures of industrial societies. The concept is also a product of the temporal aspect of industrial societies. The intense awareness of the passage of time concomitant with industrial societies' increased control over the environment leads such societies to conceive of manipulating and 'improving' the environment (social as well as physical) in specific stages which can be achieved within certain segments of spatialized time relevant to the life span of individual people. In being intensely aware of the passage of time and so of their own finite existence, many people in industrial societies tend to bring an urgency to their activities which medieval people, living within a revelationary time, would probably find hard to understand. The syncronization of events according to the clock which is so prevalent in industrial societies would not have taken place in medieval society.

The concept of progress through spatialized time towards culmination at a focal point finds expression in functional tonality through the spatial and temporal aspects already mentioned. However, the vital characteristic of functional tonality is its sense of *magnetic pull* towards the key-note. This sense provides the quintessential articulation of the concept of progress. Whereas the intrinsic nature of the relationships between the interlocking fundamentals of medieval music is partially responsible for its tendency towards temporal simultaneity, the sense of magnetic pull in functional tonality is achieved by utilizing the hierarchy of fundamentals in such a way that the fundamental of each chord – as used in relation to the other notes of that chord – plays an explicit and *retrospectively* predetermined part in the passage towards a final and irrevocable statement. Functional tonal music is about sequential cause and effect – a cause and effect which depends, in the fashion of materialism, upon the reduction of a phenomenon into 'indivisible' and discrete, but contiguous constituents that are viewed as affecting one another in a causal and linear manner. The analysis of functional tonal music often concerns itself with 'showing' how the final satisfying effect of stating the tonic chord is 'due' to previously created harmonic tension. It is no accident that completed and satisfying harmonic passages are frequently referred to as 'harmonic progressions'.

The sense of direction and resolution produced in functional tonal music is symbolized by one chord – the dominant seventh. The importance of this chord can be accounted for in two stages. Firstly, it remains true that the three most important notes in the structure of functional tonality, and the ones which ultimately define the feeling for any particular key-note, are the key-note, the fourth and the fifth. If movement between these fundamentals and the triads which are built upon them occurs, notes I and IV of the major scale are going to occur more often and so strike the ear as most important (see example 6). This phenomenon coincides with the fact that the perfect fifth is, apart from the octave, the most basic and therefore the strongest interval in the

I   IV   V

Example 6

harmonic series. As the two most important notes, and as an expression of an acoustical fact, these two notes, and, in consequence, the chords built upon them, are going to be heard as the most important factors in the establishing of a particular key.

Secondly, the next harmonic to produce a new note after the fifth harmonic is the seventh harmonic. This seventh harmonic produces the interval of a minor seventh above the fundamental, and so the chord of the dominant seventh. If this harmonic is added to the basic triads of the three fundamentals (I, IV and V), it becomes apparent that the one based on V is the only one to be included within the notes of the major scale derived from figure 6 (see example 7). The importance of the V – I movement just described is therefore reinforced by the legitimacy of this seventh chord, which contains the unstable tritone (formed by the fifth and seventh harmonies). If the seventh chord on the dominant is sounded, and the first degree of the scale is sounded, then the unstable tritone is going to be attracted to the harmonics produced by this latter note (e.g. in F:Bb – A, and E – F; the fifth degree of the dominant in this movement is strictly speaking redundant).

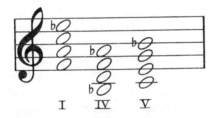

I   IV   V

Example 7

As well as reinforcing the V – I movement central for the establishing of a particular key, the dominant seventh further emphasizes the magnetic pull of functional tonality by being extremely important for the modulation without which any sense of progression in an extended piece would be lacking. The role played in modulation by the dominant seventh is related to the characteristics of the higher partials in the harmonic series – partials which, until the development of tonality, were not relevant as structural elements. Taking C as the fundamental and key-note, B flat and F sharp are stronger than B natural and F natural. Thus, when modulation is imminent, the introduction of these notes will not strike the ear as too unnatural. This is particularly true of the B flat, the seventh harmonic, which is audible to the ear.

It becomes apparent that the introduction of the B flat is the most natural manner of modulating. B flat is a relatively strong note in the harmonic series; it can be immediately inserted on top of the tonic chord to form a new dominant seventh; and it is slightly flat, thereby increasing its propensity to resolve to A. F sharp, on the other hand, is higher in the harmonic series than the B flat, and so relatively weaker. It is also flat, being almost halfway between F natural and F sharp, thereby weakening its tendency to move upwards to G. Finally, although its relative importance over F in the harmonic series allows it to be fairly easily introduced at a point when the overall feeling of tonality is C, it cannot be directly introduced with C as the fundamental. A new dominant chord, based on D as the secondary fundamental, has to be introduced. In this fashion the use of the dominant seventh emerges as the quintessential method of modulation in the functional tonal system, a state of affairs which is underlined by the immediate case of modulating flatwards.

The inherent instability of the augmented fourth, as underlined by the properties of the harmonic series, is in practice at the heart of a great deal of functional tonal movement and progression. Put another way, the functional tonal key system can be seen as the result of a conflict between the attempt to organize rationally (through the tempered scale) the properties of the harmonic series, and the properties themselves. This conflict again serves to illustrate that no music can be regarded as a closed system having internally sufficient laws. Both pentatonicism and functional tonality are grounded in the relationships of the harmonic series, but both structures are extended and directed in different ways as dialectic correlates of the social structures of the time.

A Question Answered

It now becomes possible to understand why the original pentatonic structure (see figure 1) was limited to three levels of notes and two generative intervals. In view of the creation of the structure represented in figure 6, it is apparent that the addition – in the structure as represented in figure 1 – of thirds to the original fourth and fifth (F and G), in probably encouraging a similar process with the fundamental (C), would have produced a structure involving a higher degree of distancing than was appropriate to the world sense of early medieval society. Furthermore, the addition of another level of fundamentals would have produced seven notes of relatively equal standing. In this situation the augmented fourth and semitone might well have been given more prominence than was the case. Extension of the structure along the lines suggested, therefore, would have produced a totally different structure having more in common with functional tonality than pentatonicism. The medieval world sense which pentatonicism at the same time mirrored and articulated would have been negated. Extension of the structure, in other words, could only occur as part of the continually developing social construction of knowledge and reality.

7 The Analysis of Popular Music: Class, Generation and Ethnicity

Introduction

Chapter 6 explored the social, cultural and intellectual messages implicated in the *emergence* of functional tonality. This chapter explores the continued hegemonic influence of functional tonal music in twentieth-century industrial societies, not only in terms of the social and ideological grip it maintains as the established (although not necessarily the *only*) music of powerful interests, but also in terms of the social and ideological influence it maintains outside the boundaries of 'strict' class interests through the harmonic-rhythmic framework it 'supplies' to most genres of popular music. In this sense, many genres of popular music may be understood as sites on which struggles relative to the acceptance or rejection of many features of capitalist social structures and ideologies have been played out.

This chapter extends the musical analyses of chapter 6 by describing the different technical characteristics of functional tonal and 'popular' musics. This analysis lays out a broad framework through which negotiations specific to the hegemonic influence of capitalist social structures and ideologies can be understood to be articulated through musical processes. Particular attention is paid to the 'oppositional' potential of male subcultural musics, as well as to the fracturing of capitalist social structures implicit, if never realized, in the musical articulations of punk cultures.

Musicological Premises

Afro-American musics (blues, rags, jazz, rock) came into being through the cross-fertilization of music which black slaves brought with them from central and western Africa with forms of functional tonal music to which they were exposed in North America. To understand the technical characteristics of most forms of Afro-American music, it becomes necessary to understand the technical characteristics of some central and western African musics, as well as those of functional tonality. An initial, *stereotypic* comparison between these two kinds of music will be made in terms of four categories: rhythm, melody, harmony and timbre.

African music and functional tonal music: a comparison

Rhythm   1   Metre in functional tonal music is 'divisive'. It starts with basic rhythmic units (usually 2: $1\ 2$, or 3: $1\ 2\ _3$) and builds up complex metres geometrically. Thus, the common time-signature 4\4 is, in fact, 2×2. This accounts for the typical stress pattern $1\ 2\ 3\ 4$, rather than $1\ 2\ 3\ _4$. Time-signatures of the complexity of 12/8 (4×3): $1\ _2\ _3\ 4\ _5\ _6\ 7\ _8\ _9\ 10\ _{11}\ _{12}$, are not uncommon. The metre of much African music is, on the other hand, additive. There is no regular metre or time-signature as we would understand it, and the duration of the beat appears to change. This is because the different rhythmic units, although repeated, are combined arithmetically and not geometrically.

  2   Given the nature of the metre in functional tonality, stress patterns have become highly stylized. The strongest stress is at the beginning of the bar and the weakest at the end. The relative stress of other beats is dictated by the time-signature. The stress patterns of much African music are not nearly so stylized, however, approximating more closely to the uneven stress patterning of everyday vocalization and language.

  3   The rhythms of functional tonality approximate to a mathematically strict sense of timing. In other words, the notes fall exactly 'on the beat' (or a geometrically calculated subdivision of the beat). Much African music, on the other hand, demonstrates a marked degree of rhythmic inflection, whereby notes are either 'anticipated' or 'delayed'.

  4   In functional tonal music there is strict vertical synchronization of notes. This is essential to the harmonic discussion (sequences of chords) which is the driving force of the music. There is, on the other hand, little importance placed on the strict vertical synchronization of notes in much African music. Interest here derives not from harmonic argument but from the rhythmic interplay between different, but simultaneously sounding lines of music with different metres. The superimposition of different additive metres (polymetres) gives rise to subtle cross-rhythms (polyrhythms).

Melody   1   The notes of functional tonal music *ideally* hold a discrete stable pitch before moving discontinuously to the next note. They are always strictly 'in tune'. Much African melody, on the other hand, indulges in melodic inflection, or the 'bending' of notes. Whereas the pattern of pitches in functional tonal music is highly stylized, in much African music it approximates more closely to the fluid, continually bending pitch patterns of day-to-day human speech and vocalization.

2   There is virtually no personal-spontaneous improvisation in the melodies of functional tonal music. The performer is in the position of reproducing the notationally frozen melodic line of the composer. Personal-spontaneous melodic improvisation is, however, fundamental to the articulation, re-creation and preservation of much African music (for the role of improvisation in preserving the cultures of oral-aural peoples, see Lord, 1964).

Harmony   1   Just as functional tonality starts with a very small number of simple, basic rhythmic units and builds outwards, it also starts with a basic harmonic framework (three chords: tonic, dominant and subdominant, I, V and IV, with various derivatives) and builds outwards in a complex, explicitly manipulative fashion. Functional tonality is about the creation and resolution of harmonic tensions – the articulation through harmonic progressions of explicit and complex arguments which come to a firm and satisfying conclusion on the key-note. Harmony in much African music, however, amounts to little more than a framework facilitating (and quite often deriving from) the subtle polymetric and polyrhythmic interplay of different lines which is the driving force of such music.

2   Much African music displays harmonic inflection, that is, the bending of otherwise stable chords, as well as a more continuous sliding of chords. While not unknown in functional tonal music, both are frowned upon.

Timbre   Tone qualities in functional tonal music approximate to ideal norms, and tend to be 'clean' and stable. Musicians studying in Western conservatories spend much time learning to coax the 'correct' tone from their instrument or voice. Much African music is marked not only by 'dirty' timbres (timbres which are much more rasping and nasal in character) but by timbres which have highly personal characteristics.

Afro-American musics

Rhythm   1   Rhythm in most Afro-American musics is contained within a framework of divisive metre derived from functional tonal music. The most usual time-signature is 4\4, followed by 3\4. It is significant that Afro-American musics do not usually indulge in the more complex time-signatures. Their metric frameworks cannot be said to be manipulated in such an explicit or 'outward' manner as those of functional tonality.

2   The stress patterns of Afro-American musics differ from those of functional tonal music. In more traditional forms of jazz, for example, the stress pattern in a bar of 4\4 is: 1 2 3 4. It is this stress pattern, typical also of a great deal of rock and Top 40 music, and resulting from the cross-fertilization of additive and divisive metrical principles, that is partially responsible for the feeling of 'swing' so characteristic of jazz. In many Afro-American styles, implicitly additive patterns (such as 1 2 3 1 2 3 1 2) are laid over the basic stress pattern. Often one gains the feeling that the legacy of additive metre is trying to break out of the constraining divisive metre derived from or imposed by functional tonality. This feeling is particularly strong in the middle of many blues choruses.

3   Afro-American musics indulge in rhythmic inflection derived from African musics. Jazz drummers, for example, can be classified by their tendency to play 'on top' of a beat (that is, to anticipate it slightly) or to 'lay back' behind it (to delay it slightly – see Keil, 1966). This again seems to be symptomatic of a desire to stretch or break out of a stylized rhythmic framework, and is also responsible for a feeling of 'swing' in jazz.

4   There is vertical synchronization in Afro-American musics, but it tends not to be strict. This looseness not only conforms to the constant tension between the legacy of additive metre and the containing framework of divisive metre, but also attests to the way harmony in Afro-American musics tends to provide a framework for implicit, internally directed inflectional development, rather than for explicit, outwardly directed argument.

Melody   1   Melodic inflection or 'bent' notes pervade all Afro-American musics.

2   Many Afro-American melodic lines seem to be pentatonic. This pentatonicism often appears to be in tension with the diatonicism of the functional tonal elements of Afro-American musics. In the rural blues, for example, the pentatonically generated, free-floating melodic line of the middle section of a twelve-bar chorus, uttered against a colouristic harmonic framework, is in contrast to the more diatonic lines of the opening and closing sections, these diatonic lines being harmonized functionally (for pentatonicism in blues melodies, see Wishart, 1977b).

3   The melodically improvisational nature of much blues, jazz and

rock hardly needs comment, except to note that it takes place around a 'standard' melody, and is contained within a harmonic-rhythmic framework (leading to a tension analogous to that observed in the field of rhythm).

Harmony 1   Afro-American musics tend to adopt the basic harmonic framework of functional tonality but, instead of manipulating it in an explicit, outward and complex fashion, use it as a 'given' within which to work out inflected and improvised personal statements. There is thus a conflict in harmonic usage similar to the rhythmic and melodic tension referred to. On some occasions harmony can work functionally: the individual notes of the harmonic framework then refer outside themselves in an explicit fashion to other notes in the development of a highly restricted harmonic-rhythmic argument. There is, in other words, some feeling for 'key'. On other occasions the individual notes of the harmonic framework function colouristically, confirming the partials inherent in the melodic note. Such colouristic use of notes is typical of the harmonic language of composers such as Debussy and Delius. Harmonies seem to float free, and there is little or no feeling for key. This conflict of usage can be heard in some rural blues, when bars 1–3 and 10–12 of a twelve-bar chorus seem to have some sense of functional progress and direction, while the harmonies of the middle bars of the sequence seem to float relatively free and unsecured. Concomitantly, the rhythmic framework of the outer bars is tighter and stricter, while that of the middle bars is more loose and inflected.

  2   There is much harmonic inflection in Afro-American musics. A good example is provided through the 'bottle-neck' technique of many rural blues guitarists.

Timbre   Afro-American musics are notable for highly personal 'dirty' timbres. The singing of Louis Armstrong provides a superlative example. Schuller elaborates on the significance of tone quality in jazz:

> The African quality of jazz sonority can be heard in the individuality and personal inflection of the jazz musician's tone. His is not basically the cultivated and studied tone of Western art music, nor a tone that is bought in the music store along with the instrument. Jazz's strength and communicative power lie in this individuality, which comes from inside the man; indeed a jazz musician without this individual quality is not a jazz musician in the strictest sense.
> (Schuller, 1968, p. 57)

The Musical Articulation of Social Reality

What, then, are the sociological implications of the technical characteristics of Afro-American musics? First of all, it is apparent that there is a harmonic-rhythmic framework *more or less* common to functional tonal music and Afro-American musics which derives from functional tonality. This framework, it can be argued, is structurally homologous to (and, through the articulation of specific musics, forms an integral part of) the symbolic environment of industrial societies, an environment which shapes the lives of most people on the planet. However, like other aspects of this symbolic environment, the harmonic-rhythmic framework at the same time becomes a symbolic code for the essential elements of the centralized social structures within which nearly everyone lives. Thus it works synchronically on two levels. Firstly, the entire framework is structurally homologous to the overall symbolic environment. The argument here is that as different groups and cultures relate differently to this environment, according to such variables as class, generation and ethnicity, so their musics articulate that relationship through the way they utilize and articulate the harmonic-rhythmic framework. At the same time, the framework is structurally homologous to the fundamental structures of industrial societies. On this second level the framework contains one element, the key-note, which is itself structurally homologous to the function of the symbolic environment *within* industrial societies. That function is one of centrally and distantly operated power.

The framework has one note, the key-note, which is more important than other notes. These other notes, in their turn, have an order of importance. This hierarchy of fundamental notes (or 'fundamentals') parallels the materially and intellectually hierarchical nature of industrial capitalist societies. All the other notes in the framework tend magnetically towards the key-note, this sense of magnetism being most intense in functional tonal music, and becoming weaker (almost to the point of non-existence in some cases) in different Afro-American musics. In any piece, the desire to end in a satisfying manner on the key-note *seems* to make that note the controlling factor in predetermining the placing of all other notes. It is as if the other notes are pre-existing atoms, to be placed at will in a piece in the same way that workers in capitalist societies tend to be seen as impersonal sources of labour to be placed at will in a predetermined economic system. As people in capitalist societies have difficulty in relating to one another except through the work-place and the market-place, so the individual notes of the harmonic-rhythmic framework can only relate directly, immediately and internally to one another in so far as their significance is mediated through the central, distanced control of the key-note. Notes do not relate directly, immediately and internally to one another, but externally and explicitly, in terms of centrally controlled and unambiguous functions. In this sense, they are no different from the discrete objects within a three-dimensional painting, whose ordering and significance are dictated through the central influence of the vanishing point.

Alienation of self by a central and remote controlling power finds musical expression through the alienation of the individual notes of the harmonic-rhythmic framework by the key-note. Typically, we do not listen to the inherent qualities of each note as it is sounded. We listen 'to an attempted realization of a conglomerate of ideal sound events' (Wishart, 1977a, p. 144) which constitute a piece of functional tonal music. We do not hear a note played on a trumpet at 440 hertz, with all the complexities of its intonation, envelope shape, interplay of partials, phasing and so on. We hear an 'A' that is defined as such quite independently of actual musical context. We do not hear a sound gestalt in all its complexity, but the relevance of an idealized and stylized sound gestalt to other idealized and stylized sound gestalts and through them, to the controlling idealized and stylized sound gestalt we call the key-note (which is thus equally alienated). Notes do not speak on their own behalf. They cannot realize their full potential upon the musical world. Their inherent sonic qualities are repressed so that they can fit homogeneously into seemingly predetermined musical relationships with other such musical slots. The dirty timbres and inflected notes articulated *within* the harmonic-rhythmic frameworks of much Afro-American music, on the other hand, speak of a less alienated, more intimate relationship both to self and others. Notes seem more able to speak on their own behalf, albeit within an imposed and containing framework.

The different ways in which Afro-American and 'serious' musicians utilize and relate to the harmonic-rhythmic framework mirror and articulate the different ways in which the social groups these musicians represent relate to the social world in which they live. People situated differently in the social structures of industrial capitalism experience and articulate reality in different ways.

Social theorists have long been aware that participation in the ownership and control of material or intellectual property creates a different relationship to the world and a different interest from the non-participation of people who can only sell their labour power. The profit-motivated 'efficient' division of labour had 'rationally' separated functional communities according to the dictates of an industrial technology and market. Schematically, there are those whose habitual practice is theoretical, whose function is ownership and control, and an intellectual, abstract operation upon the world; and there are those dispossessed from their material products and from their own potential of consciousness and decision, who labour according to the dictates of those with authority over them. (Virden, 1977, p. 157)

Those whose function is ownership and control (as against those whose function is labour) are charged with the intellectual and abstract maintenance not only of the symbolic environment which orders our lives, but, through that, of the social, political and economic framework within which most people live. They think while others do. Their role is one of impersonal manipulation at a distance over relatively extended time periods. So it is musically. The music of those with power is concerned with the impersonal and abstract manipulation of a relatively simple harmonic-rhythmic framework at a distance (functional tonal music is concerned with philosophical discourse rather than immediate, personal statement) and over relatively long time periods. It starts with simple materials and builds outwards in increasingly complex fashions.

As the 'controlling factor' in functional tonal music, the key-note provides the distanced and central focal point for complex and extended harmonic argument. Such extended harmonic argument could not take place without the possibility of modulation from one key to another, and such modulation, in turn, could not take place unless functional tonality were a finite and closed musical system displaying characteristics of homogeneity and repeatability. There is a closed and finite circle of related keys from which escape is impossible without radically rewriting the system (as Schoenberg did). The finite and homogeneous character of functional tonality is in turn predicated upon the notion of spatialized time so vital to the organization of life and work in industrial capitalist societies (for the different conceptions of time in pre-industrial and industrial society, see Thompson, 1967).

Spatialized time, homogeneity and finiteness underpin and give expression to the centralized control and the alienation which results from such control. Unless the alienated notes of functional tonality were capable of fitting into slots 'predetermined' by the key-note, complex and extended harmonic argument would not be possible. An 'A' played on a trumpet has to be capable of fulfilling many different, harmonically defined functions regardless of its own inherent sonic qualities. Like people in industrial capitalist societies who, as Erving Goffman puts it, have to engage in a 'certain bureaucratization of the spirit' (Goffman,

1959, p. 64) in order to meet the demands of the work-place and the market-place, notes in functional tonal music suppress themselves for the sake of a homogeneous system. A note's function is not directly related to its inherent sonic qualities but is externally defined. In the same way that the advent of mass consumerism ensured that there was only one externally defined way of living (the capitalist), so the syncretization of different modal shapes into the unified major-minor scale system ensured that there was, for individual notes, only one, externally defined way of being musical (at least until the turn of the century, when Afro-American and serious modernist and avant-garde musics both made a significant impact). Uniformity became a prized social-musical value in terms of which to control and manipulate the world.

For the materially and intellectually dispossessed such abstract, outward manipulation is less possible. Those in the lower reaches of the social order have little choice but to live within a social, political and economic framework over which they have little influence, and which they cannot hope to manipulate. Their utterances, musical or otherwise, tend to be personal and immediate rather than global and abstract, and to have minimal effect on the contextual, social-musical framework. This has become the situation of a surprisingly high percentage of people in the industrialized world. In much Afro-American music, the harmonic-rhythmic framework drawn from functional tonality becomes little more than a given conceptual scheme within which to make personal, immediate statements. Such individuality and immediacy is expressed through inflectional devices (reminiscent of the immediacy, individuality and power of the human voice in day-to-day discourse), improvisation (which can only genuinely occur in the immediacy of the here and now) and dirty timbres (which clearly mark off one performer from another), as well as through other devices such as pentatonicism and colouristic harmony. The individual, personal statements of Afro-American musicians do not, however, reflect the open-ended, isolated individualism of 'middle-class' intellection, but the individuality of those enclosed with other individuals in a shared and imposed, social, political and economic environment. This individuality-in-community is noted by Mellers in connection with the rural blues.

> The rigidity of form was a part of the Negro's act of acceptance: a part, therefore, of the reality from which, without sentimental evasion, or even religious hope, he started. That is why, though the blues are intensely personal in so far as each man sings alone, of his sorrow, they are also . . . impersonal in so far as each man's sorrow is a common lot. (Mellers, 1964, p. 267)

When the social, political and economic environment is given, unchange-able and experienced by all in much the same way, there is no need to spell it out and explicitly discuss it. One simply reproduces it, and communicates personally and intuitively within it. The communication is from within the person, and is in continual tension with the superim-posed abstract framework, whether social or musical.

A Reassessment of Value and Greatness in Music: Ideology

In his famous article, 'Some Remarks on Value and Greatness in Music', Meyer argues that the success of a piece of music is related to the extent to which the composer or performer can delay gratification of tendencies created as the piece progresses. At the beginning of a piece of music the sounding of a certain sequence of notes leads to certain expectations (or probabilities) as to what might follow. If the most obvious expectation is immediately gratified then, Meyer argues, the melody will seem banal and the piece of music will not convey a sense of overall coherent argument. If, however, the composer or performer indulges in low probability gratifications, which in turn set up other expectations that can likewise be manipulated, then final gratification can be delayed until the end of the piece. By continually diverting the attention of the listener from the totally expected, tension can be increased until a dénouement and resolution are achieved through the sounding of the final tonic chord.

Meyer sees the delay of tendency gratification as a sign of both individual and cultural maturity.

> One aspect of maturity both of the individual and of the culture within which a style arises consists ... in the willingness to forgo immediate, and perhaps lesser, gratification for the sake of future ultimate gratification. Understood generally, not with reference to any specific musical work, self-imposed tendency inhibition and the willingness to bear uncertainty are indications of maturity. They are signs, that is that the animal is becoming a man. (Meyer, 1959, p. 494)

An alternative interpretation is possible. When people struggle purposely and competitively to overcome the difficulties and obstacles they encoun-ter 'on the road to success', we might say they are forgoing immediate gratification 'for the sake of future ultimate gratification'. By saving money or going to school at night they are sacrificing 'smaller', immediate pleasures for the 'greater' pleasure that will result when they climb the social ladder and come to exercise greater control and power. Such people are acting in accordance with capitalist ideology. In so doing they are altering the nature and condition of their alienation. They are acting, not in a way which allows them to put as much of themselves *as society will allow* into their actions, but in a way which results in their actions being defined for them to an even greater extent so that they may paradoxically gain more control over their own lives and those of others. So long as dispossessed people act in accordance with the dictates of the work-place and the market-place, any behaviour which does not directly affect the logic of industrial capitalism becomes permissible. It is, in other words, acceptable for those who are alienated intellectually and materially to lead more immediate and richer emotional lives, because they are unlikely to grasp the social and historical roots of their intuitive sense of frustration and insecurity, or to possess the material basis to do anything meaningful about it. The social, political and economic framework will remain untouched and unharmed. It is also acceptable for those who are increasingly alienated from their experiential and emotional roots to develop 'higher' intellectual capacities, and gain the material benefits that result, because such development, through a *literately* based education, acts to filter out the efficacy of strong emotion, directly and powerfully experienced as the result of fundamentally oral, face-to-face social interaction. As members of the class charged with the maintenance and preservation of the social, political and economic framework, such people will tend to act on the basis of *a priori*, literately encapsulated abstract principles, rather than on the basis of internal drives resulting from the polemical flux of direct social interaction. There is external definition rather than internal feeling. 'Social climbing' is to be encouraged, not only because it gives spurious credibility to the spectacle of social change (spurious because as some go up, others go down), but because it represents little challenge to the overall social system. Nothing is therefore more threatening to the established social order than people capable of fulfilling themselves in both an experiential and intellectual sense.

It is the behaviour involved in moving from a position of 'dispossession' to one of 'possession' which Meyer values, because, in suppressing the immediacy of the emotional self, one may later experience pleasure related to the conquest of difficulties and to the achievement of control and power. At first, says Meyer, in discussing criteria for making cross-cultural value judgements between different styles of music it seems that we do in fact distinguish between what is *pleasurable* and what is *good*. Indeed the difference between them seems to parallel the distinction ... between immediate gratification and delayed gratification. But as we state it, the distinction breaks down, even linguistically. For delayed gratification too is pleasurable, not only in the sense that it does culminate in ultimate and increased satisfaction, but also in the sense that it involves pleasure related the conquest of difficulties – to control and power. (Meyer, 1959, p. 494)

It was argued in chapter 2 that pre-literate people tend not to make the fundamental distinctions between the objective and the subjective, the intellectual and the emotional, upon which the double-edged alienation of industrial societies rests. There is little way in these societies in which 'literate' values and life-styles can be hived off from oral values and life-styles, and people put through a re-orientation of alienation in 'climbing' from one to the other. Any alienation that occurs in pre-literate societies, it can be argued, will be at the same time emotional, 'intellectual' and material. It will not occur in a distanced, impersonal fashion, but in a manner displaying personal immediacy. The orality of pre-literate society suggests a social organization in which social control, however legitimated ideologically, must to a very considerable degree be exercised in the here and now. There is little room for teleology, because the basis for social power is located in the 'emotional rationality' of the here and now, and not in a future, or even 'past rationality'.

Similarly (though not without differences), there are many people in industrial societies (perhaps the majority) who attempt to fulfil themselves as fully as society will allow within a preconceived social, political and economic framework. Subscribing *not* to the literately encoded and mediated values of the materially and intellectually powerful, the people of fundamentally oral cultures within industrial capitalism relate to their world with an 'emotional rationality' not totally unrelated to that of pre-literate cultures. Although the mass culture of the overall society may have engendered a significant degree of distrust and incipient competition between the individual members of working-class and ethnic cultures, and although a significant degree of 'false consciousness' may be present, the social control and alienation which is *specific* and *internal* to these cultures (rather than imposed from outside) is nevertheless mediated in a more immediate and personal way. If the 'rational' is hived off and people choose not to pursue it, then, as far as is possible in the context of a rationally superimposed, all-encompassing social structure, people will think, act and behave 'emotionally'.

With its extended harmonic-philosophical argument, its sense of harmonic tension and conflict to be resolved in the future on the final satisfying statement of the tonic chord, functional tonal music articulates the ideologies of industrial capitalist societies. It articulates a sense of personal individuated struggle against the forces of the world, culminating in eventual success. The attainment of the key-note is the final attainment of power and control. It signifies a squeezing out of direct emotion, a loss of experiential roots, that equate with the mathematical precision of rhythms, evenness of pitch and ideal purity of timbres. Emotion in functional tonal music can only be dealt with indirectly, through a distanced commenting on the framework in terms of musical concepts drawn from the framework. There can be little breaking through to direct, unfettered experience. Functional tonal music is the music of those 'alienated from the possibilities of an immediate life of the unselfconscious body' (Virden, 1977, p. 157). The key-note in functional tonal music thus articulates a false sense of freedom and 'democracy', because the attainment of the final key-note can *only* be achieved by controlling others and alienating them from *their* full power to exist in the world.

According to the analysis being put forward, the music of those who do not act teleologically, who do not climb the social ladder, but who fulfil themselves as fully as society will allow within a preconceived social, political and economic framework, should not display a strong sense of tension with the framework on the one hand, nor a strong sense of tonal purpose on the other. So it would seem to be. It can be argued that such people tend to listen to Top 40/AM music and easy listening-light classical music. Such music is made up of a straightforward functional tonal *framework* with either mild inflectional-timbre development or mild explicit elaboration. Top 40/AM music speaks of a straightforward and relatively uncritical acquiescence in the political, economic and social framework. There appears to be an investment in the dominant themes of love and courtship propagated by such music through highly stylized inflections and individualistic timbres that are nonetheless soft, pleasing and essentially unchallenging.

It is hardly surprising that Meyer values functional tonal music (the music of the 'ruling' elements in industrial societies) over pre-literate musics and those musics (usually labelled as 'popular') associated with those who largely ignore more global political, social and economic questions in order to live as pleasant a life as possible. Meyer's judgements fail to take into account the vastly differing social realities of pre-literate people, or the reality of the majority of people in industrial societies who live in relatively dispossessed situations, the social and historical roots of which are mystified through ideological devices. Judgements as to the 'value' of 'greatness' of music, which are made on 'purely musical criteria' and ignore social context are inadmissible because they tend to misunderstand the music in question (as well as, often, being based on the wrong criteria for that music). In terms of musical criteria drawn from the Top 40/AM tradition, some Top 40/AM music is 'good' and effective, while some is not so good and rather banal. So it is with any musical tradition. Meyer's application of concepts drawn from information theory to questions involving the effectiveness of different kinds of music *may* be highly illuminating. High redundancy *within* a particular tradition may well equate with the banal, and high non-redundancy (as long as it does not approach an archaic loss of *any* formal principles) may well equate with highly effective and interesting communication. However, redundancy and non-redundancy must be understood and judged in terms of culture-specific musical criteria and not in an absolute cross-cultural fashion. Non-redundancy can be mediated immediately, in the here and now, as well as in an extended fashion over relatively lengthy, spatialized time periods. In this sense it is interesting to speculate that within different Afro-American-influenced musical traditions such non-redundancy is handled in an almost totally inflectional manner. That, however, remains a matter to be explored at some future date.

The Music of Subcultures and Counter-cultures: Reactions to Social Realities and Ideologies

Meyer has observed that 'popular music can be distinguished from real jazz [in terms of speed of tendency gratification]. For while "pop" music ... makes use of a fairly large repertory of tones, it operates with such conventional cliches that gratification is almost immediate and uncertainty is minimized' (Meyer, 1959, p. 494). What is meant by 'real jazz' has never been clarified, but the drawing of this kind of distinction raises questions concerning the social messages of Afro-American and Afro-American-influenced musics perceived as being in tension with the prevailing social-musical order. The discussion of these questions will be split into two, considering black forms of music first, and then white forms.

It would appear that the more helpless black people have been to counter the framework with which they were in tension, the less close and constraining is the framework in musical terms. Thus, in the early

Delta blues, which grew up in the Mississippi valley among black people who were thoroughly subjugated and kept separate from white people, the musical framework drawn from functional tonality was not always obviously apparent. This does not mean that the framework was not present. Nor does it mean that the framework did not *contain* the highly inflectional elements which were very much to the fore in the Delta blues. It means that the framework was geographically and therefore culturally distant, and that there was consequently little possibility of, or point in, engaging it.

The Texas blues, on the other hand, grew up among black people who were more integrated with whites and less severely subjugated, and the framework was more apparent. It can be argued that the relative closeness of the framework was symptomatic of a situation in which black people were in a closer relationship to whites; further, that being in a *relatively* stronger position to take on the framework, black people faced the framework in a more immediately antagonistic manner; finally, that in order to overthrow the framework, black people must ultimately, in their music, take on some of the global and intellectually abstract qualities of that framework.

This line of thought may include more recent black forms such as rhythm-and-blues and avant-garde jazz. With the move of blacks to urban areas, their relative increase in political power and their increasingly overt aggressiveness towards white culture, the framework drawn from functional tonality became closer and more oppressive. Blacks were face-to-face with whites and the inflectional elements of rhythm-and-blues came face-to-face with the framework. Indeed, the word 'rhythm' in the rather generalized label of 'rhythm-and-blues' does little more than signify the increasing tightness of the framework. Tension becomes electric, not only in a political and social sense, but also musically.

At this point black people faced a dilemma, socially, culturally and musically. In order to contest the framework, it was necessary to take on some of its elements. That is why those blacks who could see little point in contesting the predominant social system, and who were resigned to living within it, had a music that was 'dirtier', 'less structured' and more symptomatic of an emotionally rich relationship to the here and now. But as black people gained a stronger sense of an ability to contest their dispossessed situation, and a stronger sense of the possibility of gaining more power, their music became less 'dirty', more 'cool' and 'laid back', and teleological. However, to eliminate all that was inflectional and 'dirty' would have been to espouse entirely the values of white society and ensure the destruction of black culture.

In order to provide a musical *alternative* as powerful as prevailing social realities and ideologies, it becomes necessary to develop musical languages capable of mediating the world in as global and extended a fashion as functional tonality, but without the centrally distanced control and alienation articulated through functional tonal music. It is perhaps for this reason that black rhythm-and-blues did not develop significantly as a musical *language* beyond the music of B. B. King. However, there is one form of black music where it is possible to argue for a development beyond the stage of confrontation with the framework derived from functional tonality. Black jazz developed an affinity with 'classical' forms of music during its 'cool' period. The reaction to this was 'hard bop' which then gave rise to black avant-garde jazz. It would be difficult to claim that a sense of framework is *totally* absent from the music of performers such as Cecil Taylor and Archie Shepp, but it is very weak.

Without a more detailed analysis it is difficult to make the case incontrovertibly. However, it can be argued that (a) it is first necessary for radical black (and, indeed, black-inspired) forms of music to develop a sense of the explicit in order to contest prevailing social-musical realities and ideologies; (b) in order to avoid being totally assimilated into the prevailing power structure, it is then necessary to infuse a strong sense of the explicit with an equally strong sense of the inflectional, so that extended formal principles grow out of the intuitional, the inflectional, the personal, immediate and spontaneous instead of these qualities being contained within pre-existing formal principles. Such music need not be anarchic in the sense of developing untrammelled non-redundancy. Formal principles grow out of musical characteristics inherent in the inflectional and become an extension of them.

The situation of white Afro-American-influenced music is different in the sense that although many white people have suffered considerable material and intellectual (and, to some extent, emotional) dispossession, they have never been outside the social system in the same way as black people. White people have never had a cultural and musical reality situated (in one way or another) solidly outside the social structures of industrial capitalism in terms of which to formulate disaffection towards that social structure. The social location of different forms of white Afro-American-influenced music has been at the margin of the structure rather than outside it. This is as true of 1920s white jazz as of the various forms of rock music that have grown up since World War II. World War II gave rise to substantial social upheaval which led a new, young generation to see the world in a different light from its parents. The marginal status of young people that has been a symptom of industrial capitalist societies received an additional emphasis from the increased youth spending power resulting from a capitalist system operating in full gear. For American, mostly working-class young people, the new cultural markets were filled musically by Elvis Presley, and for British, mostly middle-class young people, by the Beatles. Both Elvis Presley and the Beatles drew on the one hand from the music of their parent culture (country and western for Presley, and, it can be argued, music of the mainstream white ballad tradition for the Beatles) and, on the other, from a form of black music that would give sufficient expression to the marginal status of the cultures for whom they were performing (black rhythm-and-blues in both cases – mediated, for early British rock, to a significant extent through early rock 'n' roll).

Only once since World War II has there emerged a white culture whose degree of material, intellectual and, indeed, emotional dispossession remotely approached that of some black cultures. British punk grew up in the late 1970s among young working-class people (and young, 'avant-garde', middle-class youth) at a time when the country faced serious economic problems, and was entering a period of significant political realignment. Coming from a parent culture which had, since the late 1930s, experienced at least some reasonable expectations in life, these young people faced rampant unemployment and lacked the neces- sary skills to avoid the fate of an apparently pointless existence. Since, unlike the blacks of early, southern rural America, young British working-class whites of the late 1970s *did* come from a parent culture that had experienced reasonable expectations, their reaction was one, not of resignation and of spiritual survival based on an already established and vibrant culture, but of hostility and aggression towards a social structure that had deprived them of their very basis for being in world. Although punk drew to a limited extent on black British reggae, this was hardly a culture in which white working-class young people could take wholehearted refuge. Experiencing a nothingness imposed by a greater social structure, punk culture had little alternative, as Hebdige (1979) has pointed out, but to take the established symbols of the greater social structure and, schizophrenic-like, throw them back in its face in a manner incomprehensible to those living securely within that structure. The symbols of capitalist society were used as a means of spiritual defence against the cultural annihilation threatened by that same society. The meaning of punk culture did not go beyond shock, raw aggression and sheer survival.

It is not difficult to draw structural homologies between the three kinds of white subculture referred to above – 1950s American working class, 1960s British middle class, 1970s punk – and their musics, although, once again, without more detailed analysis, it is not possible to do more than establish the main lines of argument.

In *Profane Culture* Willis argues that rock 'n' roll 'has opened up "new" possibilities because it has avoided being trapped by the received conventions concerning rhythm, tonality and melody' (Willis, 1978, p. 76). While it is possible to agree with Willis that the continuous pulse of much early rock music articulates a temporal flow of consciousness, an emphasis on the ever-unfolding immediacy of the here and now essentially denied through the spatialized time of functional tonality, and that earlier rock music 'was not caught up in the end of the possibilities of harmony' (Willis, 1978, pp. 76–7) or, for that matter, in the harmonic teleology of extended emotional structures, it is not possible to agree that the rhythms of early rock music 'escaped from the determinations of the classic bar structure' to 'subvert the bar form' (Willis, 1978, p. 76) or that 'the normal rules of progression, and forms of cadence, are replaced in rock 'n' roll by a kind of anarchy . . .' (Willis, 1978, p. 77). It would be fairer to say that while early rock's *more* even pulse (as compared to some jazz and blues, as well as to functional tonal music) and its 'simple' chord structures allow for a strong emphasis on the temporal flow of the subjective here and now, they at the same time constitute a largely neutral and apolitical reproduction of the musical framework derived from functional tonality. There is, to be sure, a 'timelessness' in early rock music, but it is the 'timelessness' (so-called: representing the abnegation simply of a spatialized sense of time, which itself squeezes out the true flow of temporality) of a social-musical framework that is taken for granted and largely unquestioned. This essential tension is caught in Willis's description of the time sense of one of the subcultures to espouse early rock music, the bikeboys.

> In one way, and concentrating on its oppositional aspects, the whole motorbike culture was an attempt to stop or subvert bourgeois, industrial, capitalist notions of time – the basic experiential discipline its members faced *in the work they still took so seriously.* The culture did not attempt to impute causality or locigal progression to things. It was about living and experiencing in a concrete, essentially timeless, world – certainly timeless in the sense of refusing to accept ordered, rational sequences. (Willis, 1978, p. 78, my italics)

There is a sense in which this kind of tension is characteristic of much working-class culture, albeit in a milder form. Although working-class people are subjugated (as are most people in the Western world) to the mechanical time of the work-place, they tend to concentrate outside the work-place on the enjoyment of the here and now. The crucial and more obvious tension within rock music would seem to come between the musical framework (itself containing tension) and the strong personalities revealed through the vocal lines. The singing of Presley and Buddy Holly reveals a marked innuendo of virile, individualistic masculine sexuality eminently successful in flouting the propriety of middle-class sensibilities. Early rock music subscribes to the traditional reality ('false consciousness') of working-class culture with the one exception of taking the rugged individuality of capitalist ideology and overblowing it to the point where it concentrates solely on the sheer hedonistic joy of being alive. This is what makes teddy boy, bikeboy and greaser subcultures marginal as against their parent culture.

What, then, are the musical correlates of cheeks pierced with safety pins and electric kettles used as handbags? It has been observed that punk rock represented a return to grass-roots rock 'n' roll. In one sense this is true. As with early rock music there is the same insistence on a straightforward framework drawn (originally) from functional tonality and an overblown vocal line in tension with that framework. But with punk rock these elements are handled in a different way. The insistence in punk culture on the qualities of the experiential moment derive not from an overblown, confident emphasis on the sensuality of immediate subjective experience, but from the difficulties of eking out an identity in a cultural and mental space that is constraining and repressive. Punk culture draws attention *away* from its *true* self (weak, unfashioned and unformed) by focusing the gaze of society on symbols taken from that society. This is achieved by stripping the symbols of their accepted and unexceptionable meanings and, Warhol-like, imbuing them with exceptional meanings which make people question what, indeed, they are perceiving. One can almost feel the safety pin going through the otherwise inviolable cheek or the shiny hardness of the electric kettle which throws into sharp relief the normally muted softness of most handbags. The same process occurs musically. The framework, which is unexceptionable and taken for granted in much rock music, is in punk rock twisted and distorted (whether by amateurish accident or professional intent is immaterial) so as to make people question, in an almost Cage-like manner, what, indeed, they are listening to. Such distortion represents a moment of alienated musical dealienation. Society is being asked to focus its attention on the inherent qualities of the elements and forces which control and maintain that society. Punk rock holds a musical mirror up to capitalist societies so that they cannot escape the image of their own structures. It presents those societies with a distortion it can appreciate in its own distorted terms.

Similarly, the strident, nasal, throwaway lines that threaten to destroy the containing influence of the distorted framework focus the attention of that framework on the alienated, quasi-schizoid individuals it has produced – individuals who have been told they are so worthless they might as well not bother investing their singing with any great sense of self. The strident vocal line is a scream of aggression and a scream for help. It holds the world at a distance and asks the world to come in. It represents the essential dilemma of the schizophrenic who fears to obtain help from the only source they can, the world which is the source of the problem.

British rock music of the middle 1960s and the progressive rock it spawned came from a class background very different from that of either rock 'n' roll or punk rock. Rather than representing an attempt to present a working-class challenge to the framework from beneath, early British and progressive rock seems in most cases to represent an attempt to drop out from the framework within which the parent culture lives so comfortably, and to search for alternative cognitive and social modes beneath and outside that framework. This in some ways explains the attraction for hippie counter-cultures of the world views of dispossessed subcultural groups, as well as the musical eclecticism of the Beatles. The search is for the 'lost' emotional and experiential roots of white middle-class culture, and, at least in the early stages, it did not seem to matter where the search led so long as it provided a platform from which to concentrate on the immediacy of the experiential here and now. That concentration does not take the form of an overblown and inverted individuality, or of a reflective and distortive *bricolage*, but of a more leisurely and extended form of consciousness. With one foot securely inside the parent culture, middle-class counter-cultures have been able to take a step outside onto different platforms from which to gaze unswervingly at the inherent qualities of the parent culture. What results is not the urgent and stridently distorted counter-thrusts of punk culture, but a straighter, more heightened awareness, often drug-triggered (but not necessarily drug-induced), of the world of industrial capitalism.

However, middle-class counter-cultures have not been able to provide an alternative to the structures of industrial capitalist societies. In some ways this is not surprising, since the motivation for the counter-cultures' marginal status has been escape from the intellectual rationality of the parent culture which squeezed out awareness of the essentially experiential in the first place. Concentrated awareness of the experiential here and now of industrial capitalist societies has thus tended to filter out a more intellectual awareness of the social and historical roots of that social system and the counter-cultures it has given rise to. However, although eschewing intellectual rationality, these counter-cultures have usually managed to preserve a sense of the global, the abstract and the extended which is co-extensive with intellectual rationality. At the same time this sense of the global, abstract and extended is co-extensive with the leisured and 'timeless' nature of heightened awareness, and it is at this point that counter-culture and parent culture paradoxically link, for the extended, abstract nature of the counter-culture's heightened awareness contains within it the seeds for an alternative order to that of industrial capitalism.

In *Profane Culture* Willis offers us a musicological account of progressive rock. Once again it is not possible to agree with Willis's stronger claims for this music, which would seem to suggest that progressive rock had succeeded in overthrowing or replacing the framework originally derived from functional tonality, and was thus offering us a musical model for an alternative society. It is, however, possible to agree with Willis that 'whereas rock 'n' roll ignores the received conventions, "progressive" pop inverts them, plays with them ironically, disrupts them, or produces shadows of them in new and unexpected forms' (Willis, 1978, p. 167). From their heightened awareness of the social-musical order, counter-cultures have been able to take different aspects of the framework and experiment with them. But the framework still remains as an ultimate containing presence. However, the potential for eventual reordering is equally present in the sense of the musical extension of the here and now immanent in all progressive rock. As Willis observes,

'Progressive' music had a commitment to larger forms, oppositions and variations in a way which rock 'n' roll did not, and which is shown most clearly in the development of the 'concept album'. It exploited the break-up in convention accomplished by rock 'n' roll to combine both traditional and new elements in original and creative forms. At the same time, however, it maintained the essential rock 'n' roll gain of timelessness and subversion of sequential form. (Willis, 1978, p. 168)

In many ways, the progressive rock of the late 1970s and early 1980s seemed to be moving in a direction similar to that of the black avant-garde jazz of the 1960s. But instead of a 'thrusting up from below', there seemed to be a 'reaching down from above', a desire to rediscover 'lost' emotional and experiential roots and from those roots to evolve an alternative abstract and extended order that could challenge the order of industrial capitalism. Progressive rock, too, has had its love affair with classical forms, yet, like avant-garde jazz, it has refused to be taken over.

However, in assessing the radical potential of progressive rock, both musically and socially, it is essential to remember that the possibility of searching for emotional and experiential roots from a marginal social position, as well as the potential for evolving a reordered reality, would not be possible without rock 'n' roll. As Willis says, 'we must never be in doubt that "progressive" music followed rock 'n' roll, and that it could not have been any other way' (Willis, 1978, p. 166). Equally, rock 'n' roll would have been impossible without black rhythm-and-blues. In assessing the impact of capitalist social relations, Braverman observes that 'the unity of thought and action, conception and execution, hand and mind, which capitalism threatened from its beginnings, is now attacked by a systematic dissolution employing all the resources of science and the various engineering disciplines based upon it' (Braverman, 1974, p. 171). The potential for avant-garde jazz and progressive rock to collapse the literate and oral worlds, to collapse intellect and emotion, thought and action, into one another, and so evolve a new social-musical reality would not exist but for the ability of past black cultures to turn a white mask to white society and preserve an inviolate sense of that which was essentially spiritual and cultural.

Conclusion

The purpose of this chapter has been to lay out a theoretical model in terms of which to grasp the musical articulations of different cultural realities existing within industrial capitalist societies. Early in the chapter it was argued that the reality structures typical of people located differentially within industrial capitalist societies were social in their very essense. In reflecting and giving expression to these different structures, music as a socially constructed symbolic medium therefore speaks immediately, concretely and globally to the experiential world of different individuals. There is in other words little or no disjunction between people and music. Within a particular cultural context, both are in intense dialectical relationship with the same social structure. It is possible to understand, therefore, how functionally tonal music speaks to the experience of those charged with manipulating, in an emotionally distanced, explicit, abstract and teleological fashion, the social structure within which most people live; how early rock 'n' roll speaks to the experience of those lodged securely enough within their own parent culture and thus the overall social structure, that expression of marginal status is located in an optimistic exaggeration of a feature important to the ideology of the overall social structure; how punk rock speaks to the experience of those whose only salvation from extreme alienation comes from the social structure which caused the alienation in the first place; finally, how progressive rock speaks to the experience of those who dropped out (to differing extents) from white middle-class reality in order to attempt a more humane understanding and reordering of that reality. What is common to the social-musical reality of these kinds of rock music is an emphasis on the experiential richness of the here and now, on the inherent potential of people to exist fully in the world, which is essentially denied by the social-musical reality of functional tonal music.

This chapter has dealt with only one dimension of meaning in popular music, although an important one. Once a piece of popular music has been created, there remains the all-important question of its distribution and marketing. Modes of consumption all too often neutralize what may be taken as the inherent social meaning of a piece of popular music to ensure that meaning fits prevailing patterns of social reality and ideology. As Frith has observed, in the context of progressive rock music,

> If its creative breakthroughs are the musical expressions of needs and changes in real communities, it does not take the industry long to control and corrupt the results. Indeed, the record companies' task has been made easier by the confusion of counter-cultural ideology with the ideology of the teenager. Counter-cultural musicians can legitimate their acquisition of star status by reference to their importance for youth in general, while the rebellious youth groups themselves are diverted by the commercial success of the counter-cultural stars. (Frith, 1978, p. 200)

The machinery of mass marketing takes the ideological deviance of some rock musicians and their music, and utilizes it to create for the musicians a star status. The musicians are different, so the implication goes, not because of their radical life-styles and musical utterances, but because of the hard work which has enabled them to escape the condition of the masses and succeed. Their difference lies in the nature of their success. Many youth groups are in this way being fed the spectacle rather than the actuality of social change. Rather than acting as a catalyst for social change, much rock music comes to act as an agent of social control. Through rock music, youth groups are fed many of the major elements of capitalist ideologies, and, depressingly enough, some rock stars aid the process through their own statements and actions. Cliff Richard, for example, emphasizes the Protestant work ethic in the following way:

People have some crazy idea that *star status* is a wonderful life of sleeping late in the morning and dining off caviar and champagne. Apart from never having tasted the first and not liking the second, I can tell you star status is hard work – hard work in the most glamorous and exciting profession in the world but nevertheless hard work. (quoted, Frith, 1978, p. 159)

Strong individuality is a value frequently espoused by rock stars in their contempt for mainstream bourgeois and proletarian life. As Frith notes, 'individualism is dominant, and it is not much of a move from hipster to tax exile, as Mick Jagger takes his place with Tom Jones, Tony Jacklin, and the rest' (Frith, 1978, p. 171). Rock stars are subverted by wealth, and, in their leisure time, members of different youth groups are subverted into accepting values that will fit them for their role in the work-place. The ability of industrial capitalism to maintain itself in the face of ideological challenge is daunting.

8 Music and Male Hegemony

Introduction

One of the central themes of this book has been that the media of communication predominant in any society can have considerable consequences both for the organization of that society and its dominant modes of thought. This theme was based on the premise that media can be more than just enabling devices, themselves constituting dialectic and active moments in processes of social and cultural reproduction. In chapter 1 it was suggested that this more active role of media can result from the playing out of the vested interests of certain classes or groups within a particular society. That is, it may be in the interests of a class or group to exploit the inherent characteristics of a medium as a means of furthering and entrenching its own political power and influence. It was further suggested in chapter 1 – a suggestion reiterated in subsequent chapters – that the influence of analytic phonetic literacy and movable type printing on the development and establishing of certain, dominant ways of thinking within the 'modern' industrial world has been an influence exercised essentially by 'educated' men as a means of furthering and entrenching their own political power.

To this point in the book, it has not been necessary to explore this connection in any detail, simply to note it. What has been at issue is the consequence of the power of certain media, not how those media came to have power in the first place. However, as suggested in chapter 5, it is not possible to understand the way in which music *as sound* speaks to the logics through which individual subjectivities are constructed without reference to processes of gender as they are fundamentally implicated in the construction of subjectivities. This chapter seeks to explore that connection. However, in so doing, it raises issues which strike at the heart of many of the discussions so far undertaken in this book.

In 1980 Angela McRobbie published a seminal article that was heavily yet sympathetically critical of much subcultural analysis carried out within the 'Birmingham school'. McRobbie's criticism, essentially, was that the work of scholars such as Willis and Hebdige was silent on the subject of women. This silence meant not only that girls were seldom, if ever, studied in terms of their own cultural activities. It also meant that the roles played by women (mothers and girlfriends) in servicing the lives of young working-class men were almost completely hidden from view. The focus, in such analyses, was almost exclusively on the public acting out of political contests between men, not on the domestic and personal realities which make such acting out possible in the first place. The 'oppositional' values of male subcultures and their musics have thus been values grounded in particularly traditional and conservative notions of gender roles and relations.

What McRobbie's article demonstrates is that, in the same way that it is not possible to study social processes independently of issues of gender, it is not possible to study gender issues independently of wider social processes. Rectifying a silence involves not only contextualizing a new body of knowledge (or, more accurately, a new, *public* body of knowledge) within the pre-existing intellectual terrain. It also involves renegotiating the pre-existing intellectual terrain in such a way that the new body of knowledge can be accommodated appropriately. The study of gender does not simply involve the study of women. Neither does it simply involve the addition of the study of women to the study of men. It involves a reconceptualization of the study of humanity so that the rectification of this particular silence (itself a consequence of a particular political agenda) results in a different understanding of the social world. To study the situation of women is, in other words, to challenge the political domination of men.

As moments of sociality, music and its study have been shot through with the consequences of this dominance. This chapter argues that in occupying a position within the structures of industrial societies not totally dissimilar to that traditionally occupied by women, music has been subject to similar processes of control and domination. There are also curious ways in which music has been rendered silent. Is it not strange, for example, that historical musicology and music theory – disciplines dedicated to the understanding of music as a form of human expression in sound – have been almost completely successful in avoiding any discussion of sound itself. The parameters of music predominantly discussed are those of harmony and melody (constituted through abstract relations *between* sounds) and rhythm (constituted through patterns of arbitrary decisions concerning the *duration* of particular sounds). The study of timbre, described in chapter 5 as 'the nature of sound itself', is notably absent from the academic study of music.

In beginning to move the discussion of part II from the general to the particular, this chapter also broadens and recontextualizes musical analyses which have hitherto concentrated upon 'masculine' parameters in 'masculine' ways. Through linking the dual issues of timbre and gender, it seeks to move the discussion in this book closer to a point where it is possible to begin to understand what music has to tell us about the conditions of our own sociality. In so doing, it also broadens and recontextualizes the basis of the analyses carried out in part I concerning media, social processes and music.

Gender Relations and Cultural Reproduction

The premise underpinning the arguments presented in this chapter with regard to timbre and gender is that the worlds of culture and nature are inextricably linked through processes of social interaction. Such linking should not, however, obscure the mapping or notational function of the material world, or the different possibilities the material world presents in this regard. One of the most obvious and immediate differences presented to people by the material world is that of their own biological differences. Since the species is reproduced at the biological level through the coming together of women and men, there exists a predisposition to map processes of cultural reproduction onto processes of biological reproduction. In many societies, therefore, modes of sexual behaviour and relatedness come to stand for modes of social relatedness. That which makes social life and reproduction possible may be the fertile coming together of differentiated and *totally abstract* epistemological categories which are variously mapped or notated on aspects of the material world – such as the biological differences of women and men.

This possibility may be explored in the context of contemporary capitalist societies. Dorothy Dinnerstein has argued that the development of child-rearing in our society as an essentially female occupation has had far-reaching consequences for the creation and maintenance of traditional gender-typing. Children of both sexes, she argues, first experience their world as being almost totally constituted by a woman: 'for the girl as well as the boy a woman is the first human centre of bodily comfort and pleasure, and the first being to provide the vital delight of social intercourse' (Dinnerstein, 1976, p. 28). But whereas girls tend to internalize this relationship with the female source of social and emotional life as being a relationship with a member of their own sex, boys do not. Boys, if one can put it this way, *tend* to internalize a relationship which is comparatively negative and vacuous. When, therefore, the boy, as an adult, finds delight in heterosexual lovemaking, 'he finds it outside himself, as before, in a female body.' The girl, however, 'now lives in the female body that was once the vital source of nourishment, entertainment, reassurance.' As a consequence, Dinnerstein concludes, 'the mother-raised woman is likely to feel, more deeply than the mother-raised man, that she carries within herself a source of the magic early parental richness. In this sense ... she is more self-sufficient than the mother-raised man: what is inside oneself cannot be directly taken by a rival' (Dinnerstein, 1976, pp. 41–2). There is a sense, therefore, in which the male adolescent enters his particular stage of life with a certain inbuilt insecurity. The source of life is always external to him, and, 'to be sure of reliable access to it he must have exclusive access to a woman' (Dinnerstein, 1976, p. 43).

Dinnerstein argues the classic solution to this problem is control over women. Women are necessary as the source of life, as well as potentially dangerous in their power to withdraw it. Given the necessity of leaving the warmth of the woman's world and encountering the cold reality of the 'real world', the need for women becomes that much greater and their presence that much more tenuous. The growing male adolescent consequently discovers 'that authority over a woman or women is a mark of status, respected by men' (Dinnerstein, 1976, p. 49). So long as women do not engage in the 'real world', but are kept safe at home or in traditional 'female' occupations, male supremacy in the 'real world' will go unchallenged, and women will remain a reliable source of emotional sustenance that men can draw on for their 'real world' struggles. As a consequence, women typically experience the public world vicariously, as presented and brought to them by men. Both women and men, concludes Dinnerstein, become diminished as a people: men because they are undernourished as sentient beings, women because they are undernourished as people of the world.

In contemporary capitalist societies, the processes of biological reproduction – in which men figure only momentarily – come to be controlled conceptually through the processes of cultural reproduction which are mapped onto them. Women, as emotional nurturers, as the first people to 'provide the vital delights of social intercourse' for very young children, come to stand for the very process – social relatedness – through which people and societies are created, maintained and reproduced. Men, on the other hand, in controlling women as necessary adjuncts both of their identity development and their forays into the 'real world', are led to deny symbolically the process responsible for their creation as people. The male desire to control women therefore parallels their desire to control the world.

There is, of course, a paradox here, which is that men cannot ultimately deny the relational and emotional because they have a very real need of it. As a result, the relational and emotional is downgraded to a second-class status – something vaguely undesirable and intimately associated with women – to be controlled by superior, 'rational' men. To be sure, social relatedness implies negotiability of political power. Yet as reflections of male desire to control the world, women themselves must be controlled and manipulated. This is accomplished by means of their isolation and objectification. The conceptualization of people as objects decontextualized from social relations implies the possibility for uncontested, unilateral control. The objectification of women thus becomes a crucial step in the mystification of social relatedness. If women symbolize the source of life, the social interactions that are the source of our being as people, and if sexual relatedness provides a biological code for these same processes, then women tend to become equated with sex. In order to be 'successful' in a male-dominated society, they must package themselves (or be packaged, as in advertising images) as objects amenable to control by men.

Male-defined culture is projected back onto nature; women *as objects* are in turn equated with a natural or material world thus susceptible to unilateral control by men. Control of cultural reproduction compensates for a lack of centrality in biological reproduction, and nowhere is this control more effectively exercised than on the mapping and notational procedures – among which music figures prominently – which both facilitate and constrain processes of cultural reproduction. It is no accident that the vast majority of noetic and scribal elites have been male, for by this means men preserve themselves paradoxically as independent and in control of the very social relations which produce them.

Male hegemony is essentially a *visual hegemony*. Touch reminds us constantly of our relatedness to the world, and, as argued in chapter 2, sound brings the world to us both circumambiently and circumjacently. Vision by contrast is the silent and inert sensory channel which allows us not only to distance ourselves from the phenomena of the world but also to interject ourselves into the world from a distance. It is the sensory channel which allows us, from a single point of view, to order discrete objects into their uniquely structured locations in space.

The consequences of the supremacy of vision are explored by Geraldine Finn. And while her immediate concern is with the effect on the male viewer of the pornographic image, the implications of her assessment carry well beyond the specificity of her topic.

A subjectivity which is external to its world, as the observer-subject is, deprives itself of nourishment which only the world can supply;

and as a result becomes increasingly impoverished and isolated, and estranged from itself, from others and from the reality of the world it aspires to know and control merely by looking. Sights, appearances pried away from their meaning (their contexts and their history) are silent. Dead objects are mute. In the world of the voyeur, therefore, there is no dialogue, no relationship no speech and no response, and therefore no understanding, neither of the self nor of the objects 'known'. (Finn, 1985, pp. 89–90)

Male hegemony is constituted through strategies whereby men render silent and inert a social world that is bubbling, evanescent and constantly rubbing up against us. Conceptually, this requires that life must not be allowed to originate above the level of the material, where it can be seen and controlled. By locating prime causation for social processes ultimately and exclusively within material productive forces, therefore, *traditional* Marxist analyses eradicate knowledge both of subjects and dialogue between subjects. Moreover, the above observations suggest that *traditional* notions of human sexuality as 'natural' or 'given', and the consequent 'freezing' and projection of women as sexual objects, constitute little more than a *cultural* construct representing male dominance in the world.

A result of these observations is that the omissions noted by McRobbie (1980) where the work of Willis (1977) and Hebdige (1979) is concerned – that their analyses of 'spectacular' British subcultures are silent on the question of women – begin to speak volumes. Each of these studies, in their different ways, is concerned with the issues of class (and ethnicity) and thus revolves around the question as to which *men* should exercise political power. This question now appears peripheral to understanding processes of cultural reproduction and resistance: the seeds of cultural reproduction are not sown in the public world of men, but, as Dinnerstein has so persuasively demonstrated, in the home.

The position being adopted here is that social stratification, with its differentiated cultural realities and modes of alienation, is more likely to be a projection of the logic of gender relations than gender relations a projection of the logic of social stratification. The emphases placed on questions of social stratification, both by the general public and by different schools of social analysis, can themselves be viewed as a consequence of the particular forms of male hegemony that developed during and after the Renaissance.

The capacity for unilateral control implied through male conceptualizations of people as objects decontextualized from social relations is powerfully realized through the social structures of industrial capitalism.

As argued in chapter 3 the *centralized* control and consequent patterns of alienation which characterize these structures could not have come into being without a stress on an overall uniformity of social existence. As Braverman argues, the habituation of workers to capitalist modes of production was achieved through the destruction of '*all other forms of the organization of labour, and with them, all alternatives for the working population*' (Braverman, 1974, p. 149). Relations of consumption and self-identity soon followed suit (Ewen, 1976), so that capitalist social relations soon appeared not only simply as the *only* kind possible, but as given, natural and unquestionable. As McLuhan has argued, such homogeneity of social relatedness – not to mention of thought and perception – could arise only if relatedness between people was ultimately filtered through one channel of communication to the relative exclusion of all others. The emphasis on the visual, resulting from the increasing importance in the lives of 'educated' post-Renaissance men of analytic phonetic literacy and movable-type printing, gave rise to a whole series of interrelated concepts (for example, objectivity, spatialized time, straight-line cause-and-effect analysis, deterministic rationality and control) which were eminently successful as tools of organization and as means for manipulating the physical environments (Lowe, 1982).

As argued in chapter 3, 'educated' men came to be seduced by these concepts. They quickly thought themselves into the entirely mythical position of being separate from the world, of being able analytically to pin down physical, human and social existence as a unidimensional, static display having relevance only for the gaze of the beholder. The individual became supreme. But precisely because such an approach to the world is mythical, precisely because people can only become people and remain people through an interaction with others (which necessarily implies a creative and dialectical relationship with the physical environment), this fiction of unilateral physical and social control implied a control over self that is both unconscious and invisible. In surrendering to the seductive possibility that post-Renaissance culture was a culture without myth, post-Renaissance men surrendered their birthright and, through that, the birthright of all others in society under their sway. At worst, European and European-derived societies have tended to become reifications without people: perfect but mythical bureaucratic systems where essentially human values could only survive among the powerless in cracks and margins. The comparative experiential and emotional richness of proletarianized and minority ethnic cultures can in this sense be viewed as a projection through social stratification of values more fundamentally associated with the world of women.

Music, Gender and Social Stratification

The argument to be developed here is that the visual stress on controlling and structuring the public world has had certain consequences for the development both of 'classical' and 'popular' musics. These consequences can best be approached by understanding first that *the very fact of music*, based as it is on the physical phenomenon of sound, constitutes a serious threat to the visually mediated hegemony of scribal elites.

To reiterate: vision, smooth and silent, stresses separation at a distance. It is the sense that allows us to inject ourselves into the world, to operate on the world over time and space, rather than simply having the world come in on us circumambiently and circumjacently. Touch is the sense basic not only to activating an awareness of ourselves, but also to making the fundamental distinction between us and not-us. Sound, by contrast to both vision and touch, stresses the integrative and relational. It tells us that there is a world of depth surrounding us, approaching us simultaneously from all directions, totally fluid in its evanescence, a world which is active and constantly prodding us for a reaction. Similarly, the voice, which is the paradigm of sound for people, is fundamental to the particular form of communication, language, which both facilitates and gives rise to that which is essentially human in people. The orality of *face-to-face* communication cannot help, in other words, but emphasize the social relatedness of individual and cultural existence.

If timbre, as 'the nature of sound itself', is the very vibratory essence that puts the world of sound in motion and reminds us that, as individuals, we are alive, sentient and experiencing, then, as the essence of individual sonic events, it can be said to speak to the central nexus of experience that ultimately constitutes us all as individuals. If timbre is the texture, the grain and the tactile quality of sound which brings the world into us and reminds us of the social relatedness of humanity, then in touching us and stroking us it makes us aware of our very existence. Symbolically, it *is* our existence.

The existence of music, like the existence of women, is *potentially* threatening to men to the extent that it sonically insists on the social relatedness of human worlds and as a consequence implicitly demands that individuals respond. When this happens music reminds men of the fragile and atrophied nature of their control over the world. Expressed in terms already outlined with regard to gender relations, the male fear of women is mirrored in 'the threat posed by uncontrollable musical experience to the "moral fibre" of the rationalistic scribe-state' (Wishart,

1977a, p. 128). But since music cannot ultimately be 'denied' any more than social relatedness, the answer to music's 'threat' for post-Renaissance men has been to isolate those components, pitch and rhythm, which can be objectified and frozen through a 'fully analytic' notation (Wishart, 1977a). Pitch and rhythm, as spatial and temporal extensions of timbre, are thus distanced from the core of musical articulation precisely in order to decontextualize articulation through transfer to the written or printed page, and so to control and 'silence' timbre as a central component of music. This parallels the way in which a material and notational control is exercised over processes fundamental to the creation of people and the reproduction of culture in general.

It is in these terms that the arguments presented in chapters 6 and 7 with regard to the social significance of 'classical' and 'popular' musics now need to be approached in understanding the role of timbre in articulating and reproducing gender identities. The argument to be pursued is that the sounds essential to meaning within the 'classical' tradition have been stripped down as far as is possible to a small number of basic and homogeneous units or atoms *susceptible to the exigencies of control through an analytic music notation*, and have in this way come to constitute a fundamental harmonic-rhythmic framework that is elaborated into individual pieces of music through complex and extended developments according to principles intrinsic to the framework itself. Notes stripped of much of their inherent sonic possibilities thus form the basis for a musical 'code' or realization of the brand of individualism characteristic of industrial capitalist societies. However, as noted in chapter 7, the individualism of those with power and influence is not at all the same as the rich, emotive, individuality-in-community of proletarianized cultures. It may be an individualism necessarily capable of initiative and a singular point of view, but it is, at the same time, an individualism that is standardized by imperatives of social acceptability and demonstrated loyalty. Individualism among those with power and influence must be underpinned and controlled through a structured homogeneity. As this homogeneity has been generated, maintained and controlled by an all-inclusive stress on visual channels of communication, so it has been in the generation, maintenance and control of sounds admissible to the tradition of 'classical' music.

Such standardization of musical components does not however mean that people are 'excluded' from musical processes in the tradition of 'classical' music. The ideal of *perfect* intonation and mathematically *precise* rhythms that derives from analytic music notation (that is, a notation that is 'fully analytic' of the pitches and rhythms essential to musical significance) is just as mythical as the ideal of a perfectly bureaucratic social system. Good performances in the 'classical' tradition *depend* on subtle deviations from the notational norms of pitch and rhythm, and many instruments are either tuned slightly out of tune (as with the three strings for each note on a piano) or played with an appreciable degree of vibrato so that a certain brilliance of sound is generated. Without such brilliance, the sounds of instruments would become dead, and they would lose much of their power to communicate. However, in the same way that personal initiative in the 'social' realm must be constrained through imperatives of social acceptability and demonstrated loyalty to bureaucratic ideals, so individual musical initiative as expressed in performances through deviations from notational norms of pitch and rhythm must be constrained through relatively tight adherence to those norms.

A similar observation may be made with respect to composition in the 'classical' tradition. One could argue that the music of many 'great' composers attempts to compensate for the loss of spirituality implicit in the harmonic-rhythmic framework of 'classical' music precisely through the creation of extended and architectonically complex pieces of music according to principles intrinsic to the framework. It may be the *ultimate* futility of this exercise that guarantees much music in the 'classical' tradition its very considerable power in speaking to the politically personal in people. Nevertheless, both musical interpretation and musical creativity in the 'classical' tradition render themselves safe, harmless and ultimately subservient to the dictates of a bureaucratized norm through *a priori* adherence to sounds which are *initially* admissible to musical practice (Vulliamy and Shepherd, 1984b).

It is, indeed, the ideal homogeneity of pitches, rhythms and timbres that enables 'classical' music to be exclusively articulated through a finite, closed and infinitely repeatable musical system echoing and giving expression to the closed, finite and infinitely repeatable nature of capitalist social relations. In the same way that the management of capitalist social relations as uniform and 'all-pervasive' requires that contexts always be made clear, that meanings and terms be explicitly spelled out and that logical connections always be made apparent (Bernstein, 1972), so, as we have seen in chapter 6, 'classical' music is articulated through a musical system where ambiguity of function is ultimately not permitted.

Capitalist social relations are not only thought of as given, natural and unquestionable because they are the only ones possible, but because their logic of bureaucratic rationality is made manifest in their very articulation. There *seems* to be no mystery to existence. Everything *seems* clear and transparent. So it is with 'classical' music. Its logic, its underlying rationale is made manifest in its very articulation. The scale that relates adjacent keys is, as we have seen in chapter 6, articulated in the here-and-now of any musical utterance. As Crocker argued, this crucial step towards the development of 'classical' music was taken when the finals of previously autonomous medieval modes were themselves conceived as being related on a scale. As a consequence, previously autonomous melodic shapes eventually became subservient to a unified harmonic scheme. It was not sonic events themselves which were henceforth important, but the various functions that could be visited on them. As homogeneous building blocks facilitating the construction of extended and complex architectonic structures, notes directed the ear not to their internal qualities, but outwards and away to their unambiguous relationship with other notes. Typically, people hear only the external surface of notes in the 'classical' tradition, not the interior richness that remains even after analytic notation has done its work. 'Classical' music is, then, yet another justification of the ideology whereby people become objects and systems dominate individuals.

With 'classical' music, processes of classifying and marking out relations can be heard directly because they are immanent in the music itself. That is why traditional analyses of pieces of 'classical' music usually *seem* self-evident in their significance. The basis of the analysis is contained in the music itself. It is for this reason that 'classical' music has *appeared* to many to approach the condition of music itself, a self-sufficient and purely formal mode of aesthetic expression essentially divorced in its processes of signification from the social and cultural contexts of its creation and consumption.

In this sense it is no different from what Barthes has termed *écriture classique* (Barthes, 1967), the style of writing pre-eminent in France from the mid-seventeenth to the mid-nineteenth centuries which appeared not as a style at all, but as inevitable, right and suitable for all times and places. However, as Barthes has pointed out, there is no such thing as 'white writing', writing which in its clarity seems to constitute an innocent reflection of reality. Just as there is no society, no reality that is not mythical (despite the myths of post-Renaissance 'rational' men), so there is no writing and indeed no music that is not opaque, structuring the world in one way rather than in any other. All writing, all music is style and, as such, 'clarity is a purely rhetorical attribute, not a quality in general which is possible at all times and in all places' (Barthes, 1967, p. 64).

The particular structuring of the world implicit in 'classical' music can only be properly penetrated, deconstructed, when it is realized that the dominant myth of post-Renaissance 'educated' Western culture is that it is the culture without myth. Reality seems really real, essentially divorced from human volition, ultimately discoverable and therefore communicable through the passive, inconsequential media of *écriture classique*, three-dimensional, representational oil painting, and, by implication, 'classical' music (although, clearly, there have been problems in this area, as expressed through debates in music aesthetics, because music is essentially a non-denotative medium). In music, art literature and, indeed, science, post-Renaissance 'educated' culture has worn its logic on its sleeve. It not only appears transparent, clear, lucid and self-evident, but also, therefore, self-sufficient. It is a culture that one either takes or leaves. To use Walter Benjamin's terminology, it does not absorb the spectator, it can only be absorbed by the spectator. In Barthes's terms it is 'readerly' (Barthes, 1975). It does not allow the spectator in to complete the meaning.

'Classical' music thus reproduces the experiential alienation of those with power and influence. As with 'readerly' texts, there is little *jouissance* (Barthes, 1976), little possibility for a meaningful dialectic between music and listener, little opportunity for an appreciable assertion of subjectivity through an active role in meaning construction. Much 'classical' music appears as inscrutable and impenetrable because there is a myth of vacuousness, of a complex and rich interiority that no longer exists because its logic, its rationale has been seemingly devolved onto a smooth and urbane exterior for all to hear. More often than not 'classical' music simply confronts the brilliant, reflective surface of its own logic and builds outwards and away in increasingly complex fashions. It is, however, through a very '*real*' elasticity in its technical characteristics, through the silences behind its inscrutable exterior, that 'classical' music allows for the simultaneous expression of a social reality and the mythical, contradictory ideology that supports it.

Some 'popular' forms of music, on the other hand, do know a certain *jouissance*, do assert an appreciable degree of subjectivity, and do subvert, *if only partially*, the bureaucratized norms of 'classical' music. As argued in chapter 7, the structures of many Afro-American and Afro-American-influenced 'popular' musics reflect the situation of proletarianized peoples contained by social institutions that they cannot influence or affect in any consequential fashion. Expressive musical statements are made within the sharply defined harmonic-rhythmic framework derived from 'classical music' through devices such as inflection of pitch, rhythm and timbre, individuated 'dirty' timbres and improvisation. People who are dispossessed instrumentally thus reproduce the social-musical framework which contains them and communicate personally within it. But in so doing, they create a tension, not only between their inflectionally and timbrelly individuated musical utterances and the harmonic-rhythmic framework which contains them, but within the framework itself. Experiencing considerable alienation, proletarianized peoples attempt to win back what cultural space they can, whether on the shop floor in terms of soldiering, sabotage and horseplay (Rinehart, 1975, pp. 78–81), or musically, by altering harmonic sequences (for example, I7, V7, IV7 instead of I, IV, V) and metric stress patterns (for examle, 1 2 3 **4** instead of **1** 2 3 4). Such reordering and re-contextualization, as well as the expressive devices which are in tension with the reordered and re-contextualized framework, have as their origin the musics of black Africa, the Caribbean and Latin America.

It is important to understand, however, that there are limits to such reordering and re-contextualization. Like those with power and influence, proletarianized peoples seem to recognize the inscrutability and 'naturalness' of capitalist social relations, to internalize them as such and then to reproduce them, externalizing them in a form consistent with their own image of their own material and intellectual dispossession. This, perhaps, goes some way to explaining the traditional conservatism of many proletarianized cultures. People in these cultures have no more secure a basis than do those with power and influence to get behind the apparently seamless logic of the industrial capitalist world. So it is musically. However much the harmonic-rhythmic framework is stretched, suspended, reordered and dismembered as part of a creative, interpretive act, Afro-American and Afro-American-influenced musics seldom approach a true transcendence and dissolution of that framework. It is nearly always there, a seemingly inevitable coathanger on which to place more immediate and significant personal statements.

Timbre and Gender

In both 'classical' and 'popular' musics, timbre, the core of sound, is in different ways constrained by the same harmonic-rhythmic framework. In the case of 'classical' music this constraining takes the form of an insistence on standardized purity (which students are carefully taught to achieve) which compensates for timbre's insusceptibility to being fully notated and thereby being *visually* controlled *a priori* to its actual realization in time. This insistence has in turn resulted in the unexamined assumption that timbre in 'classical' music is a neutral and largely unimportant element, having little to do with the expressive quality of the music. But perhaps the assumption of timbral innocence is unfounded. Perhaps the purity of timbre in 'classical' music is no more neutral and innocent than the supposed naturalness of *écriture classique* or 'white writing'. If there can be no 'white writing' – or at least if the colour of such writing does not designate purity and innocence – then, equally, white or pure timbres are not as neutral and innocent as supposed. For like white writing, pure timbres are not simply the open route through which intended meanings pass: they are themselves intended meanings. White writing and readerly texts seem to make all connections apparent, all logic visible. In the same way, pure timbres, within the technological limitations of each instrument and voice, *seem* to reveal all there is to be known about the inherent sonic qualities of each instrument and voice, precisely by their inclusion of (again, ideally) all possible harmonics. Pure timbres – like explicit musical languages, readerly texts and the impenetrability of traditional, representational visual images (Berger, 1972) – are all highly alienating, in that in their apparent 'completeness' they admit of little participation: they seem to 'say it all'.

The manner in which timbres in 'popular' musics are constrained is rather more complex. 'Dirty' or 'un-pure' timbres as heard in various genres of 'popular' musics (apart from those electronically generated) only use some of the harmonics inherent in the ideally pure sound of the voice or instrument. This, it can be argued, renders such timbres immediately implicit or 'writerly' because they invite completion from the outside. In this sense, it may be suggestive that the vast majority of the world's music does *not* display pure timbres. If people can only become people through interaction with other people, then modes of musical utterance and timbrel qualities must leave the door open for immediate interaction unmediated by a centralized or standardized bureaucratic norm. Only in highly industrialized cultures does there appear to exist a hegemonic bureaucratic rationality that attempts to squeeze the spiritual and personal out of itself, thus giving rise to a music in which conversation, call-and-response and 'incomplete' timbres are inadmissible.

It is now possible to lay out this argument against the mediations brought on by gender. If the timbres of 'popular' musics seem, through their 'incompleteness', to offer the possibility for meaningful dialogue between subjects, then such a possibility, at the cultural level of gender relations, is rendered extremely difficult because of the nature of male hegemony. This thesis can be explored by reference to two kinds of 'popular' music, hard or 'cock' rock and 'soft' rock or Top 40/AM ballads, the particular gender identities with which they are traditionally associated, and the vocal timbres that they typically spawn.

'Cock' rock, as Frith and McRobbie have noted, tends to be 'an explicit, crude and often aggressive expression of male sexuality' (Frith and McRobbie, 1979, p. 5). Archetypal examples of 'cock' rock are provided not only by performers such as Mick Jagger, Rod Stewart and Bruce Springsteen, but also by 'Heavy Metal' groups such as Iron Maiden, Mötley Crüe and Twisted Sister. 'Cock' rock performers tend to be 'aggressive, dominating, boastful and constantly seeking to remind their audience of their powers, their control' (Frith and McRobbie, 1979, p. 5). But at the same time, they may also be reminding themselves, and their *male* audience, that these are traditional male characteristics that need to be adopted and internalized. And the reminder is all the more necessary because of the precariousness of the male gender identity, particularly during adolescence: 'Numerous cock rock songs . . . express a deep fear of women, and in some cases . . . this fear seems pathological, which reflects the fact that the macho stance of cock rockers is . . . a fantasy for men. . . . Rock, in other words, carries messages of male self-doubt and self-pity to accompany its . . . confidence and aggression' (Frith and McRobbie, 1979, p. 13).

The traditional bastion of male security (from fear of female fickleness) is male solidarity. It is no surprise, then, that such solidarity is reflected in the rock world, where women's role is essentially peripheral and over-determined by men: 'The male-ness of the world of rock is reflected in its lyrics, with their assertions of male supremacy, narcissism, and self-pity; but, for musicians, what is most significant is women's exclusion from the heart of their lives: exclusion from their friendships and work together as comrade craftsmen in the studio, on the road, in performance' (Frith, 1983, p. 85).

The reverse side of 'cock' rock is 'soft' rock or Top 40 pop. This latter music is based traditionally on the sentimentality of the ballad form, which is infused, to a greater or lesser extent, with elements drawn from mainstream rock music. 'Soft' rock speaks in various ways, to three different gender locations. Through songs of artists such as Anne Murray, it speaks first of all to the young girl or housewife who uses her source of life to attract and nurture the vulnerable male. Secondly, through the songs of artists such as the younger Donny Osmond and David Essex (not to mention some of the early Beatles' songs, and Frank Sinatra in his earlier incarnation), it describes the situation of the young and vulnerable male: 'the image is of the boy next door: sad, thoughtful, pretty and puppy like' (Frith and McRobbie, 1979, p. 7). The gender symbiosis is here complete, for what the strident, aggressive male needs in his weaker moments of self-doubt 'is not so much someone to screw as a sensitive and sympathetic soulmate, someone to support and nourish the incompetent male adolescent as he grows up' (Frith and McRobbie, 1979, p. 7). Finally, through the songs of artists such as Shirley Bassey and Sheena Easton, 'soft' rock and Top 40 ballads speak to the woman as sex object, attracting men through an initial visual 'come-on'. In these three different ways, 'soft' rock and Top 40 pop therefore speak to the structural position of young girls as they discover the 'freedom' 'to be individual wives, mothers, lovers ... to be glamorous, desirable sex objects for men' (Frith and McRobbie, 1979, p. 12).

Both 'cock' rock and 'soft' rock seem to have archetypal timbres associated with them. The typical 'cock' rock vocal sound is hard and rasping (for example, Mick Jagger singing 'Have You Seen Your Mother, Baby, Standing in the Shadow?'), produced overwhelmingly in the throat and mouth, with a minimum of recourse to the resonating chambers of the chest and head. Its origins seem to lie in what is regarded as the typical Delta blues sound of performers such as Willie Brown, which then found its way north to Chicago and into various forms of rhythm-and-blues and rock music. The sound relies on a highly constricted use of the vocal chords, presumably reproducing physiologically the tension and experiential repression encountered as males engage with the public world.

The typical vocal sound as woman-as-nurturer (for example, Anne Murray singing 'Snowbird'), on the other hand, is very different. It is soft and warm, based on much more relaxed use of the vocal chords and using the resonating chambers of the chest in particular in producing a rich, resonating sound. The physiology of sound production in this case seems to speak to a person more fully aware of her inner, experiential being in offering herself as a source of emotional nourishment. The typical sound of 'the boy next door' (for example, Paul McCartney singing 'Yesterday') is also soft and warm by comparison with the hard and rasping 'cock' rock sound, but the softness and warmth here depends not so much on the use of resonating chambers in the chest as it does on the use of head tones. The sound is consequently much more open than that of the typical 'macho' voice. However, the physiology of the sound production still reflects an experiential emptiness in avoiding the resonating chambers of the chest cavity, and for this reason the sound is typically light and thin compared to the dark, rich tones of the woman-as-nurturer. The music of the vulnerable male is thus essentially 'head' music, an appeal for emotional nurturance that does not, however, abdicate the supposed supremacy of traditional rationality. The typical sound of woman-as-sex-object involves a similar comparison. The softer, warmer hollower tones of the woman singer as emotional nurturer become closed off with a certain edge, a certain vocal sheen that is quite different from the male-appropriated, hard core of timbre typical of 'cock' rock. Tones such as those produced by Shirley Bassey in 'Big

Spender', for example, are essentially head tones, and it could in this sense be argued that the transition from woman the nurturer to woman the sex object represents a shift, physiologically coded, from the 'feminine heart' to the 'masculine head', with its stress on a cerebral, intellectual, controlled *view* of the world.

It would appear to be the case that the harmonics produced in articulating the hard, rasping timbres of 'cock' rock are typically not those produced in articulating the sounds more characteristic of Top 40 pop (and vice versa). The production process are, in the case of 'macho' and 'female nurturer' timbres in particular, mutually exclusive to an appreciable degree. From the perspective of culturally constituted gender relations, it might seem as though there exists the potential for two essentially different and opposed timbrel components to come together to form something that is greater than the sum of its parts.

However, this potential does not seem to be fulfilled in the case of 'cock' rock, especially in its more recent manifestations. Soft timbres, if heard at all, address male vulnerability rather than the warm nurturing of female receptiveness. 'Cock' rockers establish their personality against a bureaucratic norm by leaving themselves timbrelly open. But they do not let anyone in for completion. Their vision is inward looking and narcissistic (Taylor and Laing, 1979). They attempt to complete themselves, and in this sense the masturbatory symbolism of guitar playing is not without significance. It is hardly surprising that the ideal-typical male identity displays an element of self-doubt and self-pity. It seeks, at least timbrelly, fulfilment through self-denial: male reproduction attempts to be 'homosexual' or 'homosocial' (Kanter, 1977, p. 48). The rasping timbres of 'cock' rock in particular can thus be interpreted as an attempt, through the exclusion of typically female timbres (whether these be the timbres of woman-as-nurturer, the 'masculinized' tones of woman-as-sex-object, or the 'feminized' tones of the 'boy next door') to control the female world, to keep women external to the man's life and 'in their place'.

The relationship of 'macho' timbres to the timbres of 'classical' music is, however, a little more complex. On the one hand, male timbres expunge the femininity symbolic in industrial capitalist societies for social process. Moreover, male timbres are in tension with the harmonic-rhythmic framework whose logical timbrel expression is that of an explicit purity. On the other hand, although the timbres of 'cock' rock are in a sense atrophied and those of 'classical' music, *through their 'completeness'*, contain both the male and female elements of the timbre-gender equation, it seems that the timbres of 'cock' rock speak to a greater sense of individuality than those permitted in the tradition of 'classical' music.

The point is that the timbres of 'classical' music, although containing both male and female elements of the timbre-gender equation, do not speak to the full personal and social constructiveness that would result from unfettered male-female relationships. The 'completeness' of timbres in 'classical' music results not from the fertility of relatively unfettered male-female *gender* relationships, but from being a reflection, presumed white, innocent and neutral, of the rationality of the harmonic-rhythmic framework of 'classical' music. It is this framework which encodes musically the desire of post-Renaissance 'educated' man visually to pin down and control the material world en route to the control of processes of cultural reproduction and resistance. Social male-female fertility is thus both contained and *aurally* denied through the timbrel completeness of 'classical' music. To use Barthes's terminology, the grain of the voice is flattened to filter out *jouissance*, thrill, erotic ecstasy (Barthes, 1977). In reflecting the essentially male, bourgeois, bureaucratic explicitness of harmonies in 'classical' music, 'classical' timbres render fertility unimportant, transparent and androgynous – just as in the aural and visual image portrayed by Julie Andrews in *The Sound of Music*. And that, in a world deemed susceptible to frozen, explicit control, is how it should be. The fertility of social relatedness becomes redundant, and gender relations are rendered safe and non-threatening. Gender relations are heard through male, bourgeois ears, thus making irrelevant Henry Higgins's gnawing question: 'Why can't a woman be more like a man?'

Such androgyny, such bourgeois male dominance and recontextualization of gender relations can only occur through a rejection of what the female gender could in actuality offer were this offering not downgraded to a second-class status or even to a status of non-knowledge. Male culture attempts to be self-sufficient, although the attempt is ultimately doomed to failure because that which is fundamental to human existence can never ultimately be denied. However, the *attempt* at closure on the part of traditional male culture implies the necessity for an attempt at closure on the part of traditional female culture. The logic of the gender symbiosis of industrial capitalist societies is, to put it briefly, that if men are hard, women are soft. That is the way that *potentially* constructive gender relations are set up in an essentially male, bureaucratic world.

However, masculine hardness rarely calls out feminine softness precisely because the generation of hardness denies softness at the same time as implying it. The assertive, successful male has little need of female nurturing, traditionally choosing to demonstrate his power and influence, *inter alia*, through the presentation of a masculinized version of femininity. The woman-as-sex-object, as Berger has argued (Berger, 1972, pp. 46–7, 51–64), subscribes 'to the vision that man has of her'. So masculine hardness calls out feminine hardness, the women-as-sex-object whose airbrushed fleshtones speak to an explicit exterior sheen that hides and denies the person within. Equally, if masculine hardness calls out a potentially depersonalizing hardness in women, then male softness calls out female softness, the self-doubt, self-pity and vulnerability of warmer male timbres requiring the interiority of the person rather than the exteriority of a sex object. Softness and hardness in gender relations, it can be argued, oscillate in a never-ending circle.

If the rasping timbres of 'cock' rock are symptomatic of a control of women through an exclusion of other, frequently softer timbres, then they represent equally an attempt to deny and contest an urbane, bourgeois 'asexuality' through the assertion of an *individualized*, aggressive and essentially male constituted 'sexuality'. But although denial is possible, a successful contest is not. If rock 'n' roll and other forms of 'cock' rock are 'screw and smash' music (i.e. 'screw the girls and smash the opposition') (Brake, 1980, p. 147), then it has to be conceded that while one is possible, the other is not. So if the timbres of 'cock' rock attempt to smash the urbane 'asexuality' implied in 'classical' timbres, then the attempt is doomed from the beginning precisely because it is couched in technical musical characteristics that confirm the very logic of that 'asexuality'.

The same observation may be made with respect to female timbres. Soft female timbres (as well, it may be added, as soft male timbres) are usually acceptable to male-dominated culture, because they variously represent what is left behind when the male first moves into the world. 'Macho' vocal sounds are, in a manner of speaking, 'all mouth', all projection into the public world with little behind them. The timbres of woman-as-sex-object are also acceptable, if a little more challenging, because they speak to a male image of femininity. However, the vocal sheen of woman as sex object changes perceptibly when women singers actually begin to occupy male locations in the social structure. It is interesting, for example, that the vocal timbres of many female classic blues singers are harder than those of many white women singers who portray stereotypic 'sexual' images. This may be because the 'sexual' aura so powerfully projected by singers such as Ma Rainey and Bessie Smith translated, for many black women, into unstable and frequently ephemeral relationships with men. Black women (both Ma Rainey and Bessie Smith personified this in their lives) frequently needed to develop a 'masculine' assertiveness and independence to survive while, at the same time, remaining 'women'. While, therefore, a song like 'A Good Man is Hard to Find' reveals many head tones in Bessie Smith's singing, there seems to be greater evidence of throat constriction and of emphasis on the mouth as a formant. This tendency becomes even more interesting with a figure such as Memphis Minnie. There is, for example, in a song like 'Give it to Me in My Hand' (performed with Kansas Joe McCoy), a striking similarity between the voice tones of female and male singer. The relentlessly hard voice quality of women singers such as Memphis Minnie who worked outside the classic blues tradition speaks, in the opinion of Paul Oliver, to their social location. To a considerable extent, he says: '... the aggressiveness of the woman singers is directly related to their position in Northern black society in the years between the wars. In the main the women were more able to get jobs than men, and for this reason found themselves in the position of the family "head",' (Oliver, 1969, p. 111).

The vocal sheen and vocal hardness that characterizes the woman-as-sex-object and the women moving towards a male location in the social structure can become exaggerated to stridency when the woman singer as rock artist attempts to carve out a niche for herself. Although the stridency of female rockers such as Janis Joplin has represented a clear challenge to the status quo, this stridency as a form of cultural resistance is also doomed to failure because it derives from the same splintered notions of 'sexuality' that also give rise to the rasping timbres of 'cock' rock. The 'cock' rocker finds it difficult to *communicate* with the feminine underside of his masculinity, seeking rather to possess it, absorb it wholesale through an externalized, objectified form. In the same way, by invoking closure of her 'intrinsic' femininity to provide that same objectified form, the woman-(singer)-as-sex-object runs the risk of losing touch with her already atrophied self, of being taken over by a masculine image of her 'own' inner nature. The initial inscrutability and un-approachability of the woman-as-sex-object that represents an initial 'come-on' for the male and holds out the promise of eventual 'sexual' and personal encounter, can become with the female rocker a total closure that prevents any such encounter. The masculinity appropriated in the processes of actively generating a 'sexually desirable' female image steps over into the masculinity adopted in actively becoming 'one of the boys' (Frith and McRobbie, 1979, p. 9).

Conclusion

In view of the above analysis, it can be suggested that the vast majority of music consumed in the Western world is concerned with articulating, in a variety of different ways, male hegemonic processes. 'Classical' music is founded on a notational control of pitch and rhythm which in turn implies an androgynized sense of self as expressed through pure and standardized timbres. The 'incomplete' or 'dirty' timbres of much 'popular' music speak to a greater sense of subjectivity, and they are, in many cases, in clear tension with the harmonic-rhythmic framework which contains them. But the logic of the individualized masculine identity, as expressed through the archetypal timbres of various forms of 'cock' rock, ensures that, at the cultural level, there is little meaningful dialogue between different gender identities as thus over-determined. The qualities of sound which speak so strongly in various 'popular' music genres to a sense of individual identity therefore achieve little but a reinforcement of the traditional gender types that both result from and serve to reproduce an essentially masculine view of the world.

It should not be imagined, however, that the voice types described above are the only ones possible within an over-determined male hegemony. There is, for example, the 'pure virgin' voice of Annie Lennox, the 'little girl' voice of early Kate Bush, not to mention what can only be described as the highly self-conscious and clearly ironic 'virgin/slut' voice of Madonna. Equally, it should not be supposed that individual singers use only one voice type. It is more usual for individual singers to move between voice types in performing a song in order to keep an audience interested.

In 'A Good Man is Hard to Find', for example, Bessie Smith frequently begins a vocal phrase with a growl of 'sexual' aggressiveness appropriated from the traditional 'macho' timbre, then moves to her standard, hard, 'woman-as-sex-object' timbre for the majority of the phrase, and then lets the phrase fall away with a hint of the softer 'woman-as-nurturer' timbre. Such changes in voice tone imply a dialogue with the unseen male as voyeur, initial aggressiveness and closure moving to the openness of personal encounter. The undeviating hardness of Memphis Minnie's voice, by comparison, seems to give notice that there is no such intention to enter into any such dialogue. In this sense it is quite possible for women singers to engage in a kind of 'vocal striptease', the 'revelations' of the striptease as a visual act translating into the 'revelations' made possible through an oscillation between traditional female voice types. Perhaps one of the more remarkable examples of this kind of vocal performance is to be found in the live recording of Aretha Franklin singing 'Amazing Grace'. It may seem out of place to hear the vocal achievements of women gospel singers in this way. However, if it is accepted that religion in black America has served as an important reservoir of cultural identity, cultural survival and cultural opposition, then perhaps it is not so inappropriate to think of women gospel singers – women traditionally being the source of life and cultural reproduction – as on many occasions revealing the wide variety of ways of being-in-the-world possible under white male hegemony. The woman gospel singer charges her audience by offering the opportunity for the fullest of dialogues as constrained and over-determined by white male hegemony.

Finally, and most significant, it is important to emphasize that traditional notions of gender and 'sexuality' are not phenomena that are 'given' or 'natural', phenomena that 'popular' music either expresses or controls (Frith, 1985). If, as was suggested above, traditional notions of gender and 'sexuality' have essentially been constructed by men in the interstices between culture and nature in order to control culture through nature, then they are notions that remain eminently negotiable. 'Popular' musicians do not as a consequence inevitably find themselves in a position of relating to something over which they have no influence in giving expression to senses of individual identity. Traditional notions of gender and 'sexuality' can be renegotiated by 'popular' musicians, and this, as Frith (1985) has pointed out, is a process that became increasingly common during the 1970s.

Negotiation is the key concept in understanding how the politically personal is articulated from within the internal process of music. There is nothing technically immanent about the meanings and relevancies analysed in this book as being articulated from within the qualities and relationships of pitch, rhythm and timbre. As material phenomena the various technical characteristics of music may both favour and constrain the articulation of certain cultural and social messages, but they cannot determine them. The technical characteristics of music in this sense represent little more than sites over and through which power may be mediated textually. The *theoretical models* elaborated in this book for the socially sensitized analysis of music remain nothing more than that: a basic and partial map of *what*, stereotypically, is being negotiated by performers *and* consumers alike, over and through the different technical characteristics of music. No performers, not even the ones mentioned here as being associated with traditional gender-timbre types, simply and passively reflect a given gender type or notion of sexuality any more than individuals simply and passively consume them. As Frith concludes: 'Teenybop culture . . . is as much made by the girls who buy the records and magazines as by the boys who play the music and pose for the pin-ups, and once we start asking how pop produces pleasure then notions of passivity/activity cease to make much sense' (Frith, 1985, p. 23). The deconstruction of meaning in music requires not only a catholicity of theories and methodologies, but also a variety of entry points. However, *without the elaboration of some initial theoretical models*, it is difficult to conceive a way into understanding the technical characteristics of music as sites for the textual mediation of politically personal power.

9 Music, Text and Subjectivity (with Jennifer Giles-Davis)

Introduction

If negotiation is the key concept in understanding how the politically personal is articulated from within the internal processes of music, then it is necessary to move from the elaboration of theoretical models as a way into understanding the technical characteristics of music as sites for the textual mediation of power to the elaboration of theoretical models for understanding this textual mediation of power as but one moment in the socio-cultural formation as a whole. There is a difference, in other words, between understanding the presence in and articulation through music of contextual forces and processes, and the negotiation of meaning as immanent in and articulated through music in relation to those contextual forces and processes.

This chapter concerns itself primarily with a consideration of how to develop the second set of models referred to. It does this through a discussion of some fieldwork which explores the consumption and use of music by middle-class English-speaking teenage girls in Montreal (Giles, 1987). This discussion points back to the importance of understanding sound as the central component of musical expression and comprehension, as well as to the necessity of considering in more detail than hitherto the relationship between processes of subjectivity and text. As will be argued in part III, a principal difficulty in understanding music as a social form lies not, in fact, in the presumed lack of musicological competence on the part of some analysts, but in a resistance to accepting that the central sonic manifestations of musical expression are socially constructed and therefore in need of theoretical protocols capable of teasing out this sociality *at the same time* as respecting the specificity of music as a social form.

Theoretical Protocols: Some Considerations

In developing such protocols a number of considerations are paramount.

1   (a) meaning is not immanent to the musical text itself. Here the musical text is defined as 'the aural combination of music *and* words' (Frith, 1983, p. 63), but separating out the hard, literal content of the words.

(b) conversely, meaning is not completely arbitrary in its relationship to the musical text as defined. It is not something that is externally visited upon the text regardless of the text's inherent qualities. There are, it could be argued, powerful iconicities between meaning and musical texts.

Meaning, in any situation, is thus a consequence of an intense dialectical interaction between text, other adjacent texts (lyrics, images, movement) and social, cultural and biographical contexts.

2   In approaching this dialectic, there is no privileged point of meaning – no privileged moment in the process of production of consumption when meanings can be definitely read. There is an absence of a privileged point of meaning for two, principal reasons:

(a) the different intentionalities that producers and consumers bring to bear on musical practices are specific to concrete conjunctures of social, cultural and biographical processes. Intentionalities are in other words socially located in a differential and variegated manner.

(b) a 'piece' of music, even if it can be assigned some kind of 'centre of gravity' with respect to meaning, also has a biography of its own during which this supposed 'critical mass' can shift. It is arguable, for example, that music of the 1960s as currently featured on North American A.M. radio's 'nostalgic' formatting of 'music of the 1960s, 1970s and 1980s' now carries a significantly different 'meaning' for the generation that grew up with it than it did in the 1960s.

However, the moment of consumption is the moment on which producers and consumers alike tend to focus, and, for this reason, that moment has been chosen as the point of analysis for this chapter. Such prioritization of the moment of consumption for purposes of analysis should not, however, be interpreted as conferring on that moment a privileged status in terms of the location and negotiation of meaning.

3   In the consumption of music, there is clearly an interplay between major structural forces, the formation and reproduction of specific

cultural realities in relation to those forces, and the way those forces and identities are negotiated as a consequence of individual biographical processes, processes themselves which are intensely social in their mediation. Such negotiation can be reproductive or non-reproductive in its consequences. The interplay between structures, cultures and biographies presupposes a theorization of processes of negotiation. The most successful attempt at such a theorization, which takes into account the full force of social structures at the same time as remaining sensitive to the ability of individuals to strategically engage the lived consequences of such structures, occurs in the work of Bourdieu in the form of his concept of the habitus. The habitus, according to Bourdieu, is

> the strategy-generating principle enabling agents to cope with unforeseen and ever-changing situations ... a system of lasting, transposable dispositions which, integrating past experiences, functions at every moment as a matrix of perceptions, appreciations and actions and makes possible the achievement of infinitely diversified tasks, thanks to the analogical transfer of schemes permitting the solution of similarly shaped problems. (Bourdieu, 1977, p. 72)

This habitus operates according to a coherent logic, a logic of practice deriving from the internalization of objective social conditions through successive processes of socialization. The analysis of this 'cockpit' or 'nerve centre' of human action and response, in relation to the consumption of music as to any other arena of human activity, begs the question of appropriate methodologies. It has been argued (Shepherd, 1986), in the context of the analysis of people's use of music, that a combination of quantitative and qualitative methods is appropriate:

(a) the play of major structural forces and related cultural identities can be discerned through quantitative and statistical methods. It is possible, in other words, to obtain a reasonably reliable map of who listens to what without, however, obtaining much reliable information as to why these listening habits occur and how they relate to major structural forces and related cultural identities.

(b) this latter information can be teased out through qualitative methods such as in-depth interviews. These methods can also reveal non-reproductive moments and some of the reasons that lie behind them.

4 The consumption of music is rich and complex in an intertextual sense. It can be argued that there are four, textual channels of meaning with music: sound, words (the 'content' of lyrics), images and movement. In relation to the 'same piece of music' these channels may be contradic-

tory in terms of the intentionalities with which they are implicated (Frith and McRobbie, 1979). The consumption of some channels by individuals may be reproductive while the consumption of others may not. This means, in terms of hegemonic theory, that the negotiation of hegemony through popular music may be complex in an intertextual sense.

5   Finally, the nature of the interplay of textual processes and processes of subjectivity is important, and has been insufficiently examined. These processes are not extrinsic to one another. An analysis of consumption processes in popular music demonstrates that, in the same way as contextual, intertextual and textual processes are interpenetrative (that is, the meaning of music is simultaneously extrinsic and intrinsic), so are processes of textuality and subjectivity.

All five of these considerations dictate that the development of theoretical protocols take into account the expressed intentionalities of actors without, however, eliding the dialectical presence of the technical features of music implicated in processes of meaning construction. Indeed, it is instructive that the expressed intentionalities of actors themselves bring into play the question of the *specificity* of musical texts. Some insight as to this dual importance of the expressed intentionalities of actors in constructing theoretical protocols *which have specific reference to music as text* can be gained by reference to fieldwork undertaken in Montreal in 1986 and 1987. This fieldwork examined moments of individual music consumption as experienced and interpreted by four English-speaking, middle-class girls.

The Research

The research was undertaken against the background of a statistical consumption study undertaken in Montreal during 1985 and 1986 (Shepherd, 1986). According to the findings of this study, it could be expected that English-speaking, middle-class teenage girls would favour middle-of-the-road ballads as well as soul, funk and disco in terms of both their gender and ethnic affiliation, and most forms of rock music (mainstream, hard and alternative) in terms of their age and occupation as students. These tendencies were, in general, borne out by the fieldwork (Giles, 1987). It could be argued (an argument also borne out by the fieldwork) that the second set of preferences had less to do with the internal subjective sense of individuals within this social group than it did with an investment by these individuals in the musical tastes of their boyfriends. Indeed, it became apparent from the clarity of the statistics relating directly to gender as an independent variable, and from the qualitative evidence of the fieldwork, that questions of gender constituted the most important influence on the girls' musical tastes, consumption patterns and use of music.

Firstly, they all hated Heavy Metal with a vengeance. There was, on the part of the girls, an almost total lack of comprehension with regard both to the music and its implicated meanings. This aversion was probably reinforced by the girls' class membership. Secondly, the girls' consumption and use of music was universally active in terms of singing along. This active form of consumption, it can be reasoned, represents a powerful personal investment in and ownership of the music, which is thus, at the same time, a putative rejection of an encompassing masculine identity from whose formation the girls are in any case excluded. These common responses on the part of the girls can, as a consequence, be argued to represent two sides of the same coin in the sense that the exclusion of a foreign, encompassing and potentially threatening musical reality is matched by an active affirmation of self through the 'other' of music.

The arguments in relation to investment, ownership and affirmation are significant in that vocal responses are reflexive. Unlike all other musical instruments, which in some way are manipulated externally, the larynx responds reflexively to a thought, conscious or unconscious, which indicates that in vocalizing an individual is responding to something which is heard internally. This means that the girls really 'know' the songs they sing whether they are aware of the knowledge or not. Often when they are singing, the words and the melody just seem to come to them out of nowhere. It is a habit for them to sing, and it is a dominant factor in the formation of their musical tastes which is guided from both a physical and an emotional base. The physical considerations have to do with the individual vocal instrument, its range and capacity, and the individual's access to it. The emotional considerations have to do with the particular musical expression involved and how the individual reacts to it. These factors combine into a sensation of elation which is an integrated physical and emotional experience not unlike the experience of alcohol, drugs or sex. The experience is thus an extremely powerful one.

The conservatism of this group concerning typical gender identities is revealed through their 'lack of desire' to play popular music on an instrument. There were a few girls who half-heartedly expressed a wish to play an instrument, but not one of them felt strongly enough to act on these feelings. Instrumentalists in rock music have always been predominantly male, and even though there are now more females, very few of them appear to come from this particular social group. This tendency is consistent with the theory that a strong masculine desire to control the world is demonstrated through a control of the material sphere, and therefore technology. Boys seem to be attracted to musical instruments (in particular, saxophones, horns and percussion) because instruments represent technology. Girls, on the other hand, seem to present themselves in a more revealing and personal way in that what they are attracted to is the voice, which is intrinsic to their bodies. But this does not mean that it is really 'natural' for these girls not to be as interested in technology as boys. Rather, their 'lack of interest' in technology results from a structured exclusion and, as such, constitutes an important aspect of the social construction of gender identities.

This interest in the voice, and concomitant 'lack of interest' in musical instruments, is consistent with the view that women typically develop an internal, experiential security not typically reflected in the subjective constitution of men (Dinnerstein, 1976). In making these connections, it is also interesting to make reference to the idea developed in chapter 8 that there may exist a structural equivalence with respect to the construction and reproduction of epistemological categories (or, at least, a tendency for there to be a structural equivalence) in industrial capitalist, as well as in some socialist and third-world societies, between 'women', 'sexuality', 'women as the symbols of social reproduction', 'sound' and 'music'. Sound (and therefore music as text) is the only major channel of communication that actively vibrates inside the body. The sound of the voice could not be amplified and projected were it not for chambers or resonators of air inside the human body (the lungs, the sinus passages, the mouth) that vibrate in sympathy with the frequencies of the vocal chords. Equally, the human experience of sound involves, in addition to the sympathetic vibration of the eardrums, the sympathetic vibration of the resonators of the body. Sound is thus *felt* in addition to being 'heard'. As a consequence it transcends *actual* tactile sensations in the sense that interpersonal tactile awareness and the *particular* form of erotic experience that flows from it is generally an awareness at the surface of the body which then finds internal resonance. Sound, however, is in the body and enters the body. It is, in the form of popular music, a way in which we possess others and are possessed by others (see, for example, Frith, 1987, pp. 143–4). It is interesting that the four girls interviewed were aware, some quite consciously, some less consciously, of these empowering and possessive qualities of music.

The relationship of two of the girls to the music they consume will be discussed here. 'Cathy' is the only child of a single mother. She is very

close to her mother and has tried, mostly in vain, to be close to her father.
His rejection of her has been a constant source of problems, and she has
difficulty making and keeping friends. Cathy is a solitary listener. She
prefers male, folk artists and is very much involved with the lyrics of their
music. The meanings of the lyrics are important to her and she takes
them literally. She responds to images in much the same way. Cathy
values sincerity and responds negatively to commercialization, fame or
success, which for her degrade the music. She has photos of artists on her
bedroom wall. It is not simply the music to which she is attracted, but the
whole person.

> See Leonard Cohen and David Bowie are not there for their music.
> . . . I love their music but they're there because I like them. See if the
> person who is singing it, if I like that person a lot, more than for just
> their song, but I like what's going on in their head which I can tell
> by the lyrics to their song, or I'll listen to all their songs and I'll
> figure what their head space is like, and if I like them, and they have
> a neat sort of vibe, and they seem like really neat people, then I'll
> become, like a fan. But I don't go . . . I don't read stuff about them, I
> just put a picture of them on my wall, it's as simple as that. . . . Or I
> write, 'Leonard Cohen lives' on bathroom walls. Nobody knows
> who he is.

Although she claims her keenest interest lies in the lyrics, her most
passionate descriptions are reserved for the sound.

> It drives you into it, and it sort of flows through you . . . you'll hear
> one note and then you'll be waiting for another note, and you'll go
> – now – please do this note NOW – and it'll make me feel good.
> And if they don't do it, then you sort of go – oh – oh well – it would
> have sounded better if he'd gone this way. And then, if the music
> does do what you're anticipating, then it becomes part of you, and
> you just, you know, it moves you.

The sound is the channel of interpersonal communication in which
sexuality has a balanced place for Cathy, and she prefers the sound of the
male voice: 'I like the sound of a male's voice better than I like the sound
of a female's voice, no matter how good she can sing. I find it just nicer to
have around, to listen to.' Also, she is not averse to sexuality in songs as
such.

> A person should be able to write songs about it [sex] and then other

songs that have absolutely nothing to do with it. I think it's good if you can be in touch with it enough to be able to write something, put it in your song, because it's so much a part of human beings. And if you've come to grips with that, then that's when you find it in the song. Or if you're going through something, that's when it comes out, which I respect. . . . Just as long as it's not completely about that . . . see, I like it poetically put. I don't like it too blunt. If it's blunt then it's just silliness. . . . The way Bob Dylan writes about it . . . it's just sort of mentioning it here and there, you just make the association.

With Cathy, the development and expression of her personal involvement with music, the way she says it becomes 'part' of her, her possessiveness in making it her own by making it her choice, are especially important in that it provides a link between her and the social world of teenagers where she has difficulty in finding an identity with which she is comfortable. She actually replaces social contact with musical contact, and to some extent lives her own life vicariously through it.

Diana's mother left a failing marriage in the southern USA when 'Diana' was two years old, and came to Montreal to make a home for them. They lived in a hippie culture, and Diana grew up surrounded by musicians and a very active social environment. She is a bright, talented girl who is popular with her peers. She is hard working and knows how to take care of herself in an urban environment. She has broad but somewhat conservative musical tastes. Her singing is the most developed of all the girls in that she has performed frequently in public, and aspires to a professional performance career as an actress. However, Diana has difficulty describing the sound of music and seems to derive most of her conscious meaning from visual images. There is an interesting set of alliances here.

I started singing on my own, singing *a capella* stuff, I guess at the end of Grade 10. Because I'd always been singing and suddenly I was faced with a choice of having to do something for a drama exam . . . I'd never sung in front of people before, I got such an incredible reaction, I was floored by the reaction I got. . . . So I started. Whenever I had the chance I'd sing for an exam. It was like easy marks. And I had fun, and I was exposing myself, you know?

Here it is evident that Diana is conscious of 'exposing herself', yet she needs to have total control of the situation in which this happens.

Consequently, she does not like performing in groups.

> I've jammed with some friends, who have a group, and they always want me to come and sing with them, but I'm always like, you know – uhhhhhh – because it takes me so long to get into it with so many people around, when there's like four other people around. If I'm on stage, by myself or with some other people, and there's a hundred people in the audience, I can sing. ... I'm one of those people, when I get on stage, inhibitions, well not inhibitions necessarily, but you know, I can *sing*. I'm a performer, but I'm not a show-off. ... I think there's a big difference.

Diana is aware of the 'poses' of music making as well as the real and authentic feelings that lie behind the understanding of something that is to be performed. On stage she is able to find the right combination of both these elements, but she has always performed *a capella*. Rehearsal situations with a group are difficult for her because, in practising with others, the balance between the poses and the authentic feeling is not under her control, and the revelation of either in excess, she feels, could potentially be witnessed by all. It is very difficult for her to talk about the sexual suggestiveness rampant in the music she does like.

> I don't like most of the bands that talk about sex constantly. And, uh, I don't like bands that use certain words. I mean there's 'Nazi Punks Fuck Off', and then there's another way of using the word which I don't appreciate very much. I don't know if I get offended so much – well, yeah, I think I do. Because Heavy Metal bands, you say Heavy Metal to me – three things come to mind – sex, drugs and alcohol. And probably not much talent or imagination either. When a Heavy Metal band is going to talk about those things that's because it's the only thing that they know how to talk about. When all you do is talk about sex in a song, when it's sex, says to me that you don't think that you're going to be able to sell unless you talk about sex, or, you don't know much else, other than your frustrations about sex, you don't care about anything else, and you basically don't have much intelligence.

Chapter 8 discussed the ways in which rock as a mucial genre is explicitly concerned with sexual expression, not only in terms of lyrics but also through the techniques of sound manipulation. It was argued that the expression of sexuality through rock constitutes a predominantly male discourse. Diana is not really aware of this integral alliance between music and sexuality, and tries to separate the sexuality from the music. This attempt at separation may explain why she seems unable to talk about the sound. It may also explain why she is so embarrassed in a rehearsal situation, and why she is so free when performing *a capella*. As long as she is dealing with 'Rock against Reagan' or 'Children for Peace' she feels free in the music. She is not, however, willing to deal consciously with sexual intimacy as a public display on stage.

Diana is, however, consciously aware of gender issues. She has a strong desire to be appreciated as a performer on a professional level, not because she is beautiful, but because she is sincere about her craft and is good at it. When she watches women performing she sees what is required for her to attain their position. And because she knows about 'poses', knows that they are infrequently 'real', she is unwilling to participate in the standard commercial presentation of women by the music industry. In her words: 'The thing with women, they're not real. They're not real at all. And that's really hard to accept, and I don't think that I should have to accept it. Definitely in my field!'

Subjectivities and Musical Texts

In the case of both girls there appear to be intense relationships with the sound of music. In the case of Cathy the relationship seems relatively conscious and active; in the case of Diana, relatively less conscious and 'through omission'. There are two ways in which these relationships have to be understood. Firstly, they can only be grasped in the light of intentionalities themselves grounded in individual biographical processes. In turn, these biographical processes and their expression through a certain kind of investment (or non-investment) in the inherent textual properties of music (as well as in other, intertextual, dimensions of music), have to be understood in terms of their specific potentials for the reproduction and non-reproduction of the wider social and cultural processes in which they are implicated. The musical behaviour of both Cathy and Diana could, for example, be judged, in different ways, as displaying distinctly reproductive and non-reproductive moments. The point, however, is not whether individual aspects of the use of music and the individual's relationship to the various intertextual dimensions of music are reproductive or non-reproductive. It is that the complex relationship of the individual to their use and consumption of music in ways that may be judged reproductive or non-reproductive, active or passive, conscious or unconscious, is both constitutive and reflective of a coherent *logic*, a logic of practice rooted in processes of biography and their differentiated and variegated internalization of sets of objective social conditions and associated cultural identities.

This theorization of music's use brings into play Bourdieu's concept of the habitus. However, insightful though this concept is, the way in which it is located within the broader context of Bourdieu's work remains problematic. As John Frow (1987) has argued, there exists in Bourdieu's work an essentialist connection between class position and taste formation. Bourdieu's empirical work is overwhelmingly statistical, and for this reason alone there is a tendency for him to conceive of the habitus as largely expressive of internalized class predispositions, with symbolic systems acting predominantly as producers, within the ambit of the habitus, of subjectivities and consciousnesses. Indeed, it is difficult for Bourdieu to theorize his position as a politically engaged sociologist cognizant of these processes of social and cultural reproduction precisely because there is no firm basis within his work for the theorization of resistance.

It is at this point that an awareness of musicology's albeit idealist emphasis on autonomously creative and individualizing musical processes becomes instructive. Resistance can only be satisfactorily theorized if processes of subjectivity, that which Garofalo has so pertinently referred to as 'the motor of history' (Garofalo, 1987, p. 91), are seen to be driven, in their encapsulation of the phenomenological, by a 'formless but dynamic potential for integration' (Shepherd, 1982, p. 9). Resistance is driven by a desire to explore blockages as well as openings, and it is not always the case that the lived consequences of social structures, together with their associated cultural identities, can hegemonically buy off the inbuilt urge to subvert and evade these blockages. In the last instance, and albeit under massive social, cultural and biographical pressures, subjectivities construct themselves, and they construct themselves through the articulation of an internal logic which finds expression, *inter alia*, in specific uses of music. It is the subjectively affirming, empowering and possessive power of music which helps to keep alive the notion of an integrated subjectivity in the face of the flattening, determining influence of 'structural causalities'.

Secondly, the relationship of the girls to the sound of music has to be understood in terms of the specificities of music as text, those very specificities which help to keep alive the notion of the relative autonomy of subjective processes. The interpretive moves of the girls themselves point to the need to theorize the way in which the abstract yet concrete patterns, rhythms and textures of music can speak iconically to the internal logic through which the boundaries, structures, rhythms and textures of subjectivities are maintained and reproduced. They point to

music departments will of necessity involve musicologists in a fundamental reorientation in the manner in which they study music in the 'serious' tradition, it is necessary, as Richard Middleton (1984) has argued, not just to include popular music studies alongside serious music studies as an adjunct to already existing curricula, but to develop a '"*critical musicology*", which implants popular music within the study of the whole musical field, thereby subverting received musicological assumptions'. Middleton sees two principal lines of development within his suggested 'critical musicology'. First, there should be initiatives within '*semiology*, broadly defined and stressing the social situation of signifying practice: this should take over from traditional formal analysis.' Secondly, there should be an '*historical sociology* of the whole musical field, stressing critical comparison of divergent sub-codes of the "common musical competence": this should take over from liberal social histories of music.'

The value of the global nature of Middleton's suggestions where the discipline of musicology is concerned can be grasped in the light of experiences in introducing the study and practice of popular music into the secondary school curriculum. The radical criticism of the 'new sociology of education' perspective which underpinned Vulliamy's arguments for the inclusion of popular music in the secondary school curriculum was that it overvalued questions of curriculum, culture and knowledge within the classroom to the detriment of more general questions to do with fundamental and pervasive social and economic processes outside the classroom. Marxist accounts of social processes implicit in education have highlighted a naive optimism on the part of the 'new sociology of education' in assuming that curriculum changes alone would result in radical educational practices. With its background in phenomenology and symbolic interactionism, the 'new sociology of education' has tended, according to Marxist critics, to overestimate the autonomy of the individual in effecting educational change. Marxist criticisms of scholars associated with the 'new sociology of education' may be summarized as follows:

> They have done valuable work, but if its value is to be realised and not distorted, it must be 'contextualized'. The 'autonomy of the individual' is important to interactionists, and they sometimes make great play of upgrading the individual in contrast to apparently monolithic deterministic approaches which see him as a kind of puppet at the mercy of massive societal forces. Action is re-sited within the individual. However, without a context, without addressing the objective grounds for their own existence, the

historic grounds constraining their production, they have the ironic
effect of reproducing the alienative, reified relations which they
themselves denounce. (Woods and Hammersley, 1977, p. 15)

The ability of individual teachers to effect radical educational practices
through curriculum changes will thus be compromised to the extent that
such changes are not accompanied by parallel reforms in important
social and economic processes situated outside the classroom. It is not so
important *what* is taught, runs the criticism, but *how* it is taught. If a
curriculum change *aimed* at valorizing student culture is not accompanied by a more egalitarian power relationship between teacher and
students that weakens traditional authority structures implicit in the
world outside education, then the student culture will effectively be
devalorized and any oppositional potential it possessed neutralized. In
order to maintain traditional authority structures inside the classroom,
teachers are under subtle but persuasive pressures to apply to alternative
forms of knowledge associated with student culture criteria drawn from
a knowledge base which is essentially theirs and *not* the preserve of
students. I observed such practices occurring in the music classrooms of
one Ontario schoolboard (Shepherd, 1983). Compromises centring on
tensions between the 'overt' and 'hidden' curriculum have also accompanied the introduction of popular music studies in some British schools
(Vulliamy and Shepherd, 1984b).

Lessons learnt at the secondary level may be valuable in developing the
kind of 'critical musicology' envisaged by Middleton. Not only is it
important that a critical pedagogy of popular music as historical and
cultural process incorporate categories of analysis appropriate to the
object of study. It is also necessary that the practical theory components
of undergraduate music degrees are adjusted to include the wide range of
technical characteristics which are specific to different genres of popular
music and not often to be found within the tradition of 'serious' music. A
positive feature of many undergraduate degree programmes in historical
musicology is a reluctance to allow students to graduate without
achieving a respectable level of competence as a practising musician.
There is a feeling that although Literature and Art History departments
typically allow students to graduate without being required to experience
at first hand processes of creative writing and painting, such an approach
would be ill-advised with 'music' since, as a form of signification, its
embodiment in dynamic and abstract sound patterns and textures is so
much at odds with the static and reified, visual and literate categories
prevalent within Western academic discourse. In studying and *writing*
about music within an academic setting, it is thus important to be

reminded constantly about what 'music' *feels* like as a creative act. This principle is especially pertinent in the case of popular music. As a cultural form which is essentially non-notated and therefore nonvisual in its mediation, popular music more than 'serious' music makes its impact as 'raw sound' that 'rubs up' against the recipients and constantly reminds them that they are alive and sentient beings. Some kind of musical *practice* relevant to the technical characteristics of different popular music genres is therefore essential if these genres are not to fall uncritical prey to the inscrutable and silent categories of semiological and structuralist analyses. As Pelinski (1984) has pointed out, semiological analysis is not helpful at getting at the cultural signification implicit in the way in which tango singers seem to 'taste' words before giving them to the world.

Given the present distance that exists between cultural theory and musicology, it is difficult to be more specific concerning pedagogies for the critical study of popular music. Clearly, students will need to be exposed to existing bodies of knowledge within social and cultural theory as well as to much knowledge and practice currently available within departments of music. Although the study of popular music is inadequate *purely* in terms of categories drawn from the 'common practice' of 'classical' music, such categories nonetheless remain applicable and appropriate to the more syntactical elements of the many popular music genres that have in their histories some kind of cross-fertilization between non-Western and 'classical' music. The labels 'popular' and 'classical' are, indeed, inherently inadequate. Although 'popular' music genres *do* display technical and cultural characteristics specific to themselves, there is no one set of musical, cultural and social criteria appropriate for subsuming all 'popular' music genres and excluding all 'serious' music genres. The label 'popular' emerges as little more than a catchall in terms of which to refer to all those kinds of music developed or consumed in relation to people's daily lives which are not customarily assumed to constitute 'classical' or 'traditional' forms of music. The inadequacy of such labels underlines the importance of developing a critical musicology as opposed to simply including certain popular music genres within the curriculum in the hope that their putative oppositional qualities will magically result in alternative, radical educational practices (Shepherd, 1985). As Middleton concludes:

If we don't study popular music in such a way that we transform musicology, we shall not only misunderstand popular music but also we shall be *marginalized* in terms of intellectual and institutional politics – placed in a half-forgotten, half-patronised 'homeland'. (Middleton, 1984)

If a knowledge base for the critical study of popular music is to be developed and made available to students, then it is important that these kinds of initiatives are themselves constantly monitored. As Papagiannis has argued (Papagiannis et al., 1982), it is to be expected that where innovations in education are proposed, those that threaten the *status quo* most will be the most difficult to implement. For reasons explored in this book, the introduction of critical, popular music studies into the university curriculum will not only require a re-evaluation of the problematics of major, host disciplines. They will also strike at many beliefs and assumptions dear to the heart of Western academia. There is much to learn from the work of American curriculum scholars (Anyon 1980 and 1981; Apple 1979, 1982a and 1982b; Giroux, 1981a, 1981b, 1981c and 1983; McNeil, 1981; Wexler 1982) in their advocacy of a constant, critical, theoretical *and* empirical assessment of pedagogies themselves intended to be critical.

11 Towards a Musicology of Society

The Specificity of the Musical Text

In a well-taken criticism of my work, Swanwick has argued that:

> The 'meaning' of music while arising in a social context, cannot be linked ultimately to social significance. It were so, then it becomes impossible to see how anyone can respond to the music of other cultures or other times and find it significant, powerful, disturbing, moving ... the deviations from normality, the particular personal gestures of a composer or performer. It is these things to which we are able to relate across historical time and cultural difference, and it is this which accounts for the fact that it is possible to be responsive to music from a quite alien social structure and in almost total ignorance of that structure. (Swanwick, 1984a, p. 53)

At the time, Graham Vulliamy and I replied to this criticism in the following way:

> It is not to be denied that we can respond to the music of other cultures. The crucial question, however, is whether the response is true to the culture and the music. Even within our own society there is ample evidence of the way in which the members of one culture can misinterpret the music of another, even when the interpretation is well-intended and sympathetic. ... Such misinterpretations can only be avoided by examining the musics of other cultures as integral aspects of the societies in which they are created and performed. To hive off individual creativity from social process and then approach musical significance predominantly in terms of that creativity in a cross-cultural fashion is to allow idealism and

ethnocentrism to creep in through the back door. (Vulliamy and
Shepherd, 1984a, p. 63)

While I would still stand by this reply, I feel that Swanwick was
pointing in his criticism to something important that neither Vulliamy
nor I had *explicitly* recognized. While neither Vulliamy nor I have ever
subscribed to a view of music as socially determined, I think it would be
fair to say that we have tended to reproduce the often unexamined
assumption of British subcultural analyses (see, for example, Willis,
1978) that, in the final instance, significance in specific musical processes
has to be understood by being grounded in the social reality that is *both*
extrinsic and intrinsic to them. What this assumption misses is the
distinct possibility that, because all areas of social process are *relatively*
autonomous (at least in theory), there can exist musical-social articulations which are *purely* intrinsic to musical processes in the sense that any
extrinsic significance can result only from such articulations being
subsequently recognized as of relevance to other areas of social process.
In other words, significance in music does not depend, ultimately, on the
existence of echoes in other areas of social process of articulations yet to
be uttered musically. To this extent, it remains possible for people to
both create and know about aspects of their world which may not be
available to them initially through any other medium than 'music'.

The importance of this point magnifies when it is realized that no
social reality to which music contributes has firm and fixed boundaries.
To the extent that the music of a culture may say something to that
culture that the culture itself does not wish to hear or recognize, the
music may be thought of as only existing within the cracks and margins
or beyond the boundaries of what passes for 'reality' in that particular
culture. In a significant number of cultures music seems to act as a form
of mediation between the known and the unknown, the acceptable and
unacceptable, that which is powerful and that which is dangerous. It may
then be asked what the difference in status is between a music which is
'intrinsic' to a culture and one which is 'extrinsic' to it where the
potential for knowledge and learning is concerned. If there is one,
perhaps it is of degree rather than kind in the sense that some musics are
initially closer than others to the particular 'social reality' they are to
address.

It is thus possible to agree with Swanwick that 'the musics of other
cultures or other times [can be] significant, powerful, disturbing, moving . . .', not because there is an element of individual creativity that exists
on a cross-cultural basis independently of specific social contexts, and
not because all that is involved in the cross-cultural communication of

music is distortive readings (although the reading of a music of one culture by another certainly involves complex and difficult questions). The musics of other cultures and other times can be significant, powerful, disturbing and moving because they have something of relevance to say. And nowhere is this more true, perhaps, than in the cultures of industrial capitalism, whose own social realities have in one way or another relegated music to their cracks and margins as 'cultural capital', 'leisure' and 'entertainment'.

Indeed, it is possible to argue that a certain deafness has arisen in the cultures of industrial capitalism in relation to what our music can tell us about ourselves because music is generally used to escape the everyday consequences of the 'real world'. If popular music 'provides an experience that transcends the mundane, that takes us "out of ourselves" ... [and] ... frees us from everyday routines and expectations that encumber our social identities' (Frith, 1987, p. 144), then transcendence through the reception of 'serious' music occurs through a special emphasis on the ideology of autonomy, as Leppert and McClary testify. 'The ideology of autonomy', they say, 'informs the ... conventional musical reception of the "music lover" who listens to music precisely in order to withdraw from the real world and to experience what is taken to be authentic subjectivity' (Leppert and McClary, 1987a, p. xiii).

Another form of the intensification of self in relation to society through music has, however, been claimed for the Venda of South Africa by John Blacking. Blacking makes the following observation on the relationship between work and music in Venda society:

> If the Venda perform communal music chiefly when their stomachs are full, it is not simply to kill time ... the Venda make music when their stomachs are full because, consciously or unconsciously, they sense the forces of separation inherent in the satisfaction of self-preservation, and they are driven to restore the balance with exceptionally cooperative and exploratory behaviour. Thus forces in culture and society would be expressed in humanly organised sound, because the chief function of music in society and culture is to promote soundly organised humanity by enhancing human consciousness. (Blacking, 1973, p. 101)

The comparison being made here is that in Western cultures everyday reality, the 'really real', is traditionally taken to be constituted primarily through those processes fundamental to the material reproduction of society and humanity. In this view of 'reality', music is not seen as central to social processes, as being of any 'real' importance. It is, in the case of both 'serious' and 'popular' music, seen as a marginal phenomenon: either cultural capital, the realm of the independent, autonomous subject; or leisure and entertainment, a peripheral diversion from more weighty matters that, perhaps because of this position vis-à-vis 'reality', allows individuals to experience a greater sense of self.

In societies such as that of the Venda, however, the claim can be made that what is seen as important and central to the culture is the continued reproduction of society as a cohesive and integrated unit. Processes of material reproduction are essential to processes of cultural reproduction, but it appears to be recognized that what is 'really real' to the society is located within processes of cultural reproduction and that processes of material reproduction can be potentially divisive. Music, as a medium of communication that mediates so powerfully and directly between the individual and society, is understood, certainly intuitively and maybe even consciously, to be a force of fundamental importance to society. In manifesting and giving back to society in a concrete, perceptible and recognizable form its own textures, motions and rhythms it makes possible for the individual, through an emphasis on integration, a greater sense of self. This fulfilled sense of self acts, in turn, as the prime seat of cultural reproduction. While music in Western culture seems, on the whole, to be used as a mechanism of withdrawal in order to gain a respite from the consequences of everyday reality, there are a number of traditional societies where music seems to be used as a mechanism of collective contemplation in order to reaffirm the 'proper' nature of everyday reality.

There remains the distinct possibility, then, that the musics of our own cultures (as well as those of others) have things to tell us which we frequently do not hear because of the way in which we categorize and locate music socially. It is at this point that the specificities of music as text become relevant, because it is these specificities which have been largely silenced, either through the way in which music has been traditionally categorized and located in our cultures, or through the often unexamined assumption that if, indeed, 'music' is 'social', then it must in some way reflect society rather than contribute in distinctive ways to its reproduction. The ability of music to be transcendent in socially constructive ways, to speak to us about ourselves in ways which relate powerfully to its specificities as text, are issues which have been taken up by Catherine Ellis. Ellis's basic premise is that 'through music we can shift to a different vantage point in which cultural opposites [for example, those of Aboriginal and white society] can be merged in a larger whole' (Ellis, 1985, pp. 3–4). This is possible, says Ellis, because music:

... can bridge various thought processes; it is concerned with the education of the whole person; it can stimulate inter-cultural understanding at a deeply personal level, with the result that a person is no longer a member solely of one culture. The student must break through the limits of his own culture – often painfully – and learn to see all situations from many points of view. This type of cross-cultural learning is available to any person who chooses to study seriously under musicians of high calibre whose culture is different from that of the student. By being open-minded, a student can become at one with the thought processes of his teacher, irrespective of the cultural barrier which may exist in all other spheres of interaction between the pupil and his master. (Ellis, 1985, p. 15)

To summarize Ellis's argument, such cross-cultural learning can occur because music is capable of transcending individual cultures, *not* by constituting some kind of culture-free, universal language, as is often claimed in the West, but by constituting, informing and reflecting culture-specific realities in a way that escapes the prison of denotative and referential modes of signification. If it is difficult to experience the different logic of French culture because we cannot crack the code of the language, then we *may* experience the logic of French culture in an immediate, unfettered and direct manner through the abstract and relational dimensions of music.

The case that is being made here is that through their abstract and dynamic dimensions of syntax, process and texture, all kinds of music can speak to the socially informed and socially constituted nexus of symbolic experience that constitutes us all at the existential level (Shepherd, 1982). Music, as sound, cannot help but stress the integrative and relational in human life, that is, the way in which we are all in constant and dynamic touch with the world. Music thus enables people *in the West* to feel the world as well as knowing it.

Music is therefore privileged in a very particular and narrow sense of facilitating transcendent cross-cultural consciousness. But why should we need such consciousness? The answer lies in the grounds of our own socialization. The seduction of the discrete, the particular and the referential in the thinking of our cultures precludes, although it does not ultimately prevent, a move in which one becomes more intently aware of the grounds of one's own socialization and develops the ability to examine and creatively expand them. Traditional modes of thinking in Western cultures concentrate consciousness on the surface level of concrete and discrete particulars, drawing it away from deeper, more abstract, structural and relational levels specific to processes of socialization. These modes of thinking become dominant and attempt to be exclusive as a by-product of the maintenance and reproduction of male, bourgeois hegemony through materially and visually mediated modes of control. Those who are encompassed by and operate such modes do not typically wish to examine their social grounding because the intensified awareness of the integrative and relational in the human world would explode as myth the pretended *exclusiveness* of systems of thought based on the discrete, the particular and the referential.

According to Ellis, Aboriginal thought, life and music seem to encourage access to the grounds of socialization *because* of the way in which boundaries are not maintained in a rigid way, but are constantly susceptible to negotiated change, and *because* of the way that boundaries, once agreed upon and defined, can accommodate different expansions of content. Such a cultural system – which seems to allow access to the grounds of its socialization for those who are old (at least over forty) and wise, and who can be relied upon to use such power constructively and not destructively – can thus contemplate and accommodate some of the premises of other cultural systems. This access can be, and frequently is through music. Music, through its abstract and dynamic syntactical, processual and textural dimensions, seems, among all media of communication, most able to speak directly and globally to the abstract processes which give people the grounds of their socialization. Music, it can be argued, is ideally suited for the gathering up of the grounds of socialization and so the production of a most powerful experience because it does not have to rely, ultimately, on specifics and particulars. However, there are two dangers for Aboriginal society in thus opening themselves to the grounds of their own cultural system and those of others. Firstly, there is always the danger that people will use the secret power of song in the wrong way.

> The close sanctions that apply to the teaching of secret songs and to the use of the power these contain is the statement of a fixed boundary which, if traversed by the wrong person, can cause the system to disintegrate from within. Once a knowledgeable person has been admitted to such realms of power, he cannot subsequently be excluded. (Ellis, 1985, p. 87)

Secondly, there is the danger of incursion of an unwelcome nature from outside.

In such a system, where inclusion is always possible, it is necessary to have strong barriers preventing unhealthy penetration in the first place. Otherwise, too much non-traditional interference may force the system to a point beyond which it cannot recover its boundaries of limitation intact. This unrecognized potential for over-incorporation in tribal/white contact often leads to a total break-down of the tribal system. (Ellis, 1985, p. 85)

We, in the West, do not typically put ourselves in either of these dangerous positions. We have either lost the ability to gather up *fully integrated* social power through music, or we do not or do not want to recognize it for what it is when we experience it. Either way, we do not seem to be able to benefit from such power in a fully transcendental manner.

Conclusion: Musicology

It is now possible to return to the issue raised over twenty years ago in the exchange between Harrison and Kerman referred to in chapter 10. The distinction made by Kerman in arguing that people in society should be studied as a means of furthering the comprehension of works of art rather than works of art being studied as a means of furthering the comprehension of people in society is crucial for musicology in the sense that musicology should never become a projection of sociology, providing sociology with information and evidence for its understanding of social processes in terms dictated by the various problematics of that discipline.

It may be that, in the context of the kind of criticism made by Swanwick where my own work is concerned, Frith's continued insistence that 'aesthetic questions' should be approached from a 'sociological' base is well taken (Frith, 1987, p. 144). All discussions of music should be sociologically informed. Yet, to assert, as Kerman does, that, in the enterprise of musicological criticism, all sociological and, indeed, musicological analyses of a technical nature should be subservient to the critical undertaking should not of necessity imply that, approached in a sociologically grounded fashion, musicological criticism could not in turn provide considerable insights into the conditions of our own, and other, cultures. It is perhaps in this sense that Harrison's claim that musicology should become the study of people in society 'insofar as they express themselves through the medium of music' is well made. Critical musicology should remain open to the possibility that, rather than becoming a projection of sociology (or, for that matter, anthropology), or simply remaining an ungrounded enterprise in itself, it could fulfil a *distinct* and *specific* role in expanding our understanding of different cultures and societies.

Recently, Kerman lamented that:

> What I would call serious music criticism – academic music criticism, if you prefer – does not exist as a discipline on a par with musicology and music theory on the one hand, or literary and art criticism on the other. We do not have the musical Arnolds or Eliots, Blackmurs or Kermodes, Ruskins or Schapiros. In the circumstances it is idle to complain or lament that critical thought in music lags conceptually far behind that in other arts. In fact, nearly all musical thinkers travel at a respectful distance behind the latest chariots (or bandwagons) of intellectual life in general. ... Semiotics, hermeneutics, and phenomenology are being drawn upon only by some of the boldest of musical studies today. Post-structuralism, deconstruction, and serious feminism have yet to make their debuts in musicology or music theory. (Kerman, 1985, p. 17)

Remaining open to the possibility that musicology could make a distinct and specific contribution to the understanding of different cultures and societies would surely enable musicology as a discipline to take its proper place in the academy alongside other disciplines whose critical awareness is rather more developed. The question no longer remains that of how to understand music and individuals in terms of society, therefore. The crucial question has become that of how to understand societies and individuals in terms of music. What needs to be developed is no longer a sociology and aesthetics of music, but a musicology of aesthetics and society.

Ellis thus presents a timely and important message concerning the importance and proper use of music. This message suggests a framework for advancing the criticism and evaluation of music beyond that envisaged by either Kerman (1985) or Frith (1987). However, for that framework to be further developed it is necessary to fully situate Ellis's lines of argument and possible criticisms of them in the social and historical circumstances of late capitalism. The proper recuperation of music is particularly important to our society because of what it can tell us about ourselves and our future. If musicology as a discipline does not recognize this, then it will continue, like its object of study, to occupy a marginal and peripheral position in the world, responding always to the intellectual initiatives of others. It will, to use Arthur Mendel's words, remain a 'young science' (Mendel, 1962, p. 14). Musicologists not only need to analyse, to deconstruct, to dig beneath the surface of common-sense reality in helping to understand the musical and cultural reproduction of our own world. Musicologists need also to look beyond as well as underneath our commonsense reality to devise strategies for changes in modes of consciousness and how we relate to one another through a greater understanding of what music can tell us about ourselves and our society. Ellis provides the spur for these initiatives and thus reminds us that, like any other human activity, musicology is an essentially political undertaking.

Conclusion: Cultural Theory

To return to the problems of the sociological analyses of popular music raised in chapter 10, it is not a great distance from Frith's homily that 'the meaning of popular music is the result of a process in which the significance of the text itself, the particular organization of sounds ... is neither static nor determinant but involves a number of con-textual questions' (Frith, 1983, p. 63) to the adoption of a position in practice (and thereby through omission) that the inherent sonic qualities of music are of little or no consequence to the articulation of meaning. This position seems to deny considerable evidence in support of music's powerful iconicities. A related position (again arrived at through a combination of practice and omission) is that popular music is so complex in an intertextual sense that it is impossible in practice to isolate the role of abstract, concrete sound in the articulation of meaning. Yet to the extent that cultural theory engages in the analysis of cultural events, it cannot avoid, at some stage and at some level, 'reading texts'. It is to be questioned whether some channels of communication are privileged over others. There are, for example, analyses of films which ignore the rich intertextual dimensions of the musical soundtrack. Few film scholars seem disquieted by this omission.

If, as Andrew Goodwin (1986, p. 259) comments: 'the field [of popular music studies] remains undeveloped theoretically [compared to] film and television studies', then it could be because it is simply easier to discuss music from already existing cultural theoretical perspectives without reference to music's central, abstract, concrete, sonic channel, and its ability unswervingly to profile processes of subjectivity and individualization. This observation may be more closely related to popular music studies 'lack of status' in cultural theory than statements about musicological competence. One reason why musicology has been slow, as Kerman has pointed out (Kerman, 1985), to embrace cultural theory is that there are no theoretical protocols which can force a radicalization of its subject matter in a manner analogous to the way a partial radicalization has been achieved in some other disciplines. If theory is grounded, ultimately, at the level of discrete particulars, then it becomes difficult to engage phenomena which do not *have* to embrace that level in order to articulate meaning. It is for this reason that music theory and music analysis in particular are still able to analyse music in some remarkably sophisticated, technical ways, as a self-referring system completely decontextualized from social and cultural processes. Conversely, it has been difficult for analysts of music to elaborate theoretical perspectives specific to some of music's intrinsic qualities in such a way as to force an interrogation of the cultural theory presently applied to the analysis of music.

The purpose of chapter 9 was to spell out some of the considerations to be taken into account if the affective power of music is to be adequately understood as a phenomenon that contributes in distinctive ways to the interactional complexities of social, cultural and biographical processes. These considerations point frequently to a biological materialist account of musical experience. It is important, however, to distinguish two positions in relation to music's corporeal realities. According to the first, music is initially experienced in a raw visceral fashion which is then interpreted by the individual in relation to the complex interactions of social, cultural and biographical contexts. This position, it could be argued, essentially drops the musical experience out of the realm of social discourse. It is the interpretive moves which are understood to be socially, culturally and biographically relevant, not the initial musical experience which forms the basis for those interpretations. According to the second position, the visceral realities of musical experience are themselves socially, culturally and biographically relevant. Since it can be argued that biological materiality itself forms a dialectically efficacious pathway of social, cultural and biographical mediation, they can be understood as constituting just as integral a part of the complex web of social, cultural and biographical processes as any other form of experience. To argue for a clean distinction between musical experience and interpretation, with only the latter being admissible to the realm of social discourse and therefore susceptible to cultural analysis, would seem either to make a second-class citizen of music or to draw the enterprise of cultural analysis dangerously close to a behaviourist position.

It is to be admitted that people appear more articulate when discussing forms of communication which invoke narrative and vision than they do when discussing forms of communication which invoke to a significant degree the sonic channel of music. This lack of articulateness with respect to music, as Feld (1984) has argued, may well have to do with music's capacity to speak simultaneously on many levels at once: social, cultural and biographical; or, as Feld describes it, locational, categorical, associational, reflective and evaluative. If the 'simultaneous multiplicity and generality of what is being communicated' (Feld, 1984, p. 14) leads people to become inarticulate, then it should not be concluded either that musical experience is something special, something apart in the sense of lying outside the realm of social constitution, or that it is only the *interpretation* of experience that can be analysed socially, not the experience itself. Musical experience should not become the victim of a failure to problematize categories of understanding and analysis as they might apply to that experience. Allowing the musical text a relatively autonomous position in the field of cultural theory may lead to an understanding of what music, in its abstract and concrete dimensions, can tell us about ourselves and the cultures in which we live.

Bibliography

Anyon, J. (1980) 'Social Class and the Hidden Curriculum of Work', *Journal of Education*, vol. 162, no. 1, pp. 67–92
——(1981) 'Social Class and School Knowledge', *Curriculum Inquiry*, vol. 11, no. 1, pp. 3–42
Apple, M. W. (1979) *Ideology and Curriculum* (London: Routledge and Kegan Paul)
——(1982a) 'Curricular Reform and the Logic of Technical Control: Building the Possessive Individual', in Apple (1982b), pp. 247–74
——(ed.) (1982b) *Cultural and Economic Reproduction: Essays on Class, Ideology and the State* (London: Routledge and Kegan Paul)
Baily, J. (1984) 'The Soul of Mbira', *Popular Music*, vol. 4, pp. 301–6
Barthes, R. (1967) *Writing Degree Zero* (trs Annette Lavers and Colin Smith) (London: Jonathan Cape)
——(1975) *S/Z* (tr. Richard Miller) (London: Jonathan Cape)
——(1976) *The Pleasure of the Text* (tr. Richard Miller) (London: Jonathan Cape)
——(1977) 'The Grain of the Voice', in *Image-Music-Text* (tr. Stephen Heath) (New York: Hill and Wang), pp. 179–89
Barzun, J. (1943) *Classic, Romantic and Modern* (New York: Doubleday)
Bateson, G. (1973) *Steps to an Ecology of Mind* (St Albans: Granada)
Becker, C. L. (1969) 'Progress' in W. W. Wagner (ed.), *The Idea of Progress since the Renaissance* (New York: John Wiley and Sons), pp. 9–18
Berger, P. L. and Luckmann, T. (1967) *The Social Construction of Reality* (Harmondsworth: Penguin)
Berger, J. (1972) *Ways of Seeing* (London: BBC)
Bernstein, B. (1972) 'Social Class, Language and Socialization', in P P. Giglioli (ed.), *Language and Social Context* (Harmondsworth: Penguin), pp. 157–78
Blacking, J. (1973) *How Music is Man?* (Seattle: University of Washington Press)
Bloch, M. (1961) *Feudal Society* (London: Routledge and Kegan Paul)
Bourdieu, P. (1977) *Outline of a Theory of Practice* (tr. Richard Nice) (Cambridge: Cambridge University Press)
Brake, M. (1980) *The Sociology of Youth Culture and Youth Subcultures* (London: Routledge and Kegan Paul)
Braverman, H. (1974) *Labor and Monopoly Capital* (New York: Monthly Review Press)

Capek, M. (1961) *Philosophical Impact of Contemporary Physics* (Princeton, N.J.: Van Nostrand)

Carey, J. W. (1967) 'Harold Adams Innis and Marshall McLuhan', *The Antioch Review*, vol. XXVII, pp. 5–39

Carothers, J. C. (1959) 'Culture, Psychiatry and the Written Word', *Psychiatry*, vol. XXII, pp. 307–20

Carpenter, E. and McLuhan, M. (1970a) 'Acoustic Space', in Carpenter and McLuhan (1970b), pp. 65–70

——(1970b) *Explorations in Communication* (London: Jonathan Cape)

Chailley, J. (1966) 'Essai analytique sur la formation de l'octéchos latin', in Westrup, J. (ed.), *Essays Presented to Egon Wellesz* (Oxford: Clarendon Press), pp. 84–93

——(1970) 'Une nouvelle méthode d'approche pour l'analyse modale du chant grégorien', in Becker, H. and Gerlach, R. (eds), *Speculum Musicae Artis – Festgable fur Heinrich Husmann* (Munich: Wilhelm Fink Verlag), pp. 85–92

Chaytor, H. J. (1970) 'Reading and Writing', in Carpenter and McLuhan (1970b), pp. 117–24

Cohen, G. A. (1978) *Karl Marx's Theory of History: A Defence* (Princeton, N.J.: Princeton University Press)

Crocker, R. L. (1972) 'Hermann's Major Sixth', *Journal of the American Musicological Society*, vol. XXV, no. 1, pp. 19–37

Crossley-Holland, P. (1960) 'Non-Western Music', in Robertson, A. and Stevens, D. (eds), *The Pelican History of Music*, vol. I (Harmondsworth: Penguin Books), pp. 11–135

DiMaggio, P. and Useem, M. (1982) 'The Arts in Class Reproduction', in Apple (1982b), pp. 181–201

Dinnerstein, D. (1976) *The Mermaid and the Minotaur* (New York: Harper Row)

Douglas, M. (1970) *Purity and Danger* (Harmondsworth: Penguin)

Duncan, H. D. (1968) *Symbols in Society* (Oxford: Oxford University Press)

Eliot, T. S. (1948) *Notes towards the Definition of Culture* (London: Faber and Faber)

Ellis, C. (1985) *Aboriginal Music: Education for Living* (St Lucia: University of Queensland Press)

Ewen, S. (1976) *Captains of Consciousness* (New York: McGraw Hill)

Feld, S. (1982) *Sound and Sentiment: Birds, Weeping, Poetics and Song in Kaluli Expression* (Philadelphia: University of Pennsylvania Press)

——(1984) 'Communication, Music, and Speech about Music', *Yearbook for Traditional Music*, vol. 16, pp. 1–18

Finn, G. (1985) 'Patriarchy and Pleasure: The Pornographic Eye/I', *Canadian Journal of Political and Social Theory*, vol. IX, nos. 1–2, pp. 81–95

Flew, A. (1976) *Sociology, Equality and Education* (London: Macmillan)

Frith, S. (1978) *The Sociology of Rock* (London: Constable)

——(1983) *Sound Effects: Youth, Leisure and the Politics of Rock 'n' Roll* (London: Constable)

——(1984) 'Popular Music in Non-Music Departments', oral presentation at a one-day colloquium: 'Popular Music in Higher Education', Department of Music, Dartington College of Arts, UK

——(1985) 'Confessions of a Rock Critic', *New Statesman*, vol. 110, no. 2840, pp. 21–3

——(1987) 'Towards an Aestheic of Popular Music', in Leppert and McClary (1987b), pp. 133–49

Frith, S. and McRobbie, A. (1979) 'Rock and Sexuality', *Screen Education*, no. 29, pp. 3–19

Frow, J. (1987) 'Accounting for Tastes: Some Problems in Bourdieu's Sociology of Culture', *Cultural Studies*, vol. I, pp. 59–73

Garofalo, R. (1987) 'How Autonomous Is Relative: Popular Music, the Social Formation and Cultural Struggle', *Popular Music*, vol. VII, no. 1, pp. 77–92

Giedion, S. (1970) 'Space Conception in Prehistoric Art', in Carpenter and McLuhan (1970b), pp. 71–89

Giles, J. (1987) 'Music Consumption among English Speaking Teenage Girls in the City of Montreal', M.A. research paper, Institute of Canadian Studies, Carleton University, Ottawa

Gipps, R. (1975) 'A Personal Credo', *Composer*, no. 54, pp. 13–14

Giroux, H. A. (1981a) *Ideology, Culture and the Process of Schooling* (Lewes: The Falmer Press)

——(1981b) 'Hegemony, Resistance and the Paradox of Educational Reform', *Interchange*, vol. 12, nos. 2–3, pp. 3–26

——(1981c) 'School and the Myth of Objectivity: Stalking the Politics of the Hidden Curriculum', *McGill Journal of Education*, vol. 17, pp. 282–304

——(1983) *Theory and Resistance in Education: A Pedagogy for the Opposition* (South Hadley, Mass.: Bergin and Harvey)

Goffman, E. (1959) *The Presentation of Self in Everyday Life* (Harmondsworth: Penguin)

Goldschmidt, E. P. (1943) *Medieval Texts and their First Appearance in Print* (Oxford: Oxford University Press)

Goodwin, A. (1986) 'Editorial', *Media, Culture and Society*, vol. VIII, no. 3, pp. 259–61

Goody, J. and Watt, I. (1963) 'The Consequences of Literacy', *Comparative Studies in Society and History*, vol. V, pp. 304–45

Gough, K. (1968) 'Implications of Literacy in Traditional China and India', in Goody, J. (ed.), *Literacy in Traditional Societies* (Cambridge: Cambridge University Press), pp. 69–84

Gramsci, A. (1971) *Selections from the Prison Notebooks* (trs and eds Quintin Hoare and Geoffrey Nowell-Smith) (London: Lawrence and Wishart)

Hallowell, A. I. (1937) 'Temporal Orientations in Western Civilization and in a Pre-literate Society', *American Anthropologist*, vol. 39, pp. 647–70

Hanson, N. R. (1965) *Patterns of Discovery* (Cambridge: Cambridge University Press)

Harrison, F. Ll. (1963) 'American Musicology and the European Tradition', in Harrison, F. Ll., Hood, M. and Palisca, C. V., *Musicology* (Englewood Cliffs, N.J.: Prentice-Hall), pp. 1–85

Haughton, H. (1983) 'Social and Cultural Reproduction in the Music Curriculum Guideline Process in Ontario Education: "Ethnic Minorities" and Cultural Exclusion', D. Ed. thesis, Department of Sociology in Education, Ontario Institute for Education, Toronto

Hebdige, D. (1979) *Subculture: The Meaning of Style* (London: Methuen)

Hughes, A. (1955) 'The Birth of Polyphony', in Hughes, A. (ed.), *The New Oxford History of Music*, vol. II (Oxford: Oxford University Press), pp. 270–86

Jarocinski, S. (1976) *Debussy: Impressionism and Symbolism* (tr. Rollo Myers) (London: Eulenburg Books)

Jones, B. (1974) 'The Politics of Popular Culture', in *Working Papers on Cultural Studies*, no. 6, pp. 25–9

Kanter, R. (1977) *Men and Women of the Corporation* (New York: Basic Books)

Keddie, N. (1973) *Tinker, Tailor ... The Myth of Cultural Deprivation* (Harmondsworth: Penguin)

Keil, C. M. (1966) 'Motion and Feeling through Music', *Journal of Aesthetics and Art Criticism*, vol. XXIV, pp. 337–49

——(1979) *Tiv Song* (Chicago: Chicago University Press)

Kerman, J. (1965) 'A Profile for American Musicology', *Journal of the American Musicological Society*, vol. XVIII, pp. 61–9

——(1985) *Contemplating Music: Challenges to Musicology* (Cambridge, Mass.: Harvard University Press)

Langer, S. (1942) *Philosophy in a New Key* (Cambridge, Mass.: Harvard University Press)

Lawton, D. (1975) *Class, Culture and Curriculum* (London: Routledge and Kegan Paul)

Leach, E. R. (1954) 'Primitive Time-Reckoning', in Singer, C., Holmyard, E. J. and Hall, A. R. (eds), *A History of Technology*, vol. I (Oxford: The Clarendon Press), pp. 110–27

Leavis, F. R. (1948) *Education and the University* (London: Chatto and Windus)

Lee, D. (1970) 'Lineal and Non-Lineal Codifications of Reality', in Carpenter and McLuhan (1970b), pp. 136–54

Leppert, R. and McClary, S. (1987a) 'Introduction', in Leppert and McClary (1987b), pp. xi–xix

——(1987b) *Music and Society: The Politics of Composition, Performance and Reception* (Cambridge: Cambridge University Press)

Lévi-Strauss, C. (1968) *Structural Anthropology* (trs Jacobson, C. and Schoepf, B. G.) (Harmondsworth: Penguin)

Lord, A. B. (1964) *The Singer of Tales* (Cambridge, Mass.: Harvard University Press)

Lovell, T. (1972) 'Sociology of Aesthetic Structures and Contextualism', in McQuail, D. (ed.), *Sociology of Mass Communications* (Harmondsworth: Penguin), pp. 329–49

Lowe, D. (1982) *History of Bourgeois Perception* (Chicago: Chicago University Press)

Mâche, F.-B. (1973) 'Musical Composition Today', *Cultures*, vol. I, no. 1, pp. 101–11

McLuhan, M. (1962) *The Gutenberg Galaxy* (Toronto: Toronto University Press)

——(1964) *Understanding Media* (Toronto: The New American Library of Canada)

——(1970) 'The Effect of the Printed Book on Language in the Sixteenth Century', in Carpenter and McLuhan (1970b), pp. 125–35

McNeil, L. (1981) 'On the Possibility of Teachers as the Source of an Emancipatory Pedagogy – A Response to Henry Giroux', *Curriculum Inquiry*, vol. 11, pp. 205–10

McRobbie, A. (1980) 'Settling Accounts with Subcultures: A Feminist Critique', *Screen Education*, no. 34, pp. 37–49

Mellers, W. (1946) *Music and Society* (London: Denis Dobson)

——(1964) *Music in a New Found Land* (London: Barrie and Rockliff)

——(1968) *Caliban Reborn* (London: Victor Gollancz)

——(1973) *Twilight of the Gods: The Beatles in Retrospect* (London: Faber and Faber)

Mendel, A. (1962) 'Evidence and Explanation', in *Report of the Eighth Congress of the International Musicological Society* (Cassel, London and New York: Barenreiter), pp. 3–18

Merriam, A. P. (1964) *The Anthropology of Music* (Evanston: Northwestern University Press)

Meyer, L. B. (1956) *Emotion and Meaning in Music* (Chicago: Chicago University Press)

——(1959) 'Some Remarks on Value and Greatness in Music', *Journal of Aesthetics and Art Criticism*, vol. XVII, pp. 486–500

——(1973) *Explaining Music* (Los Angeles: University of California Press)

Middleton, R. (1984) 'Popular Music in Music Departments', oral presentation at a one-day colloquium, 'Popular Music in Higher Education', Department of Music, Dartington College of Arts, UK

Nef, J. V. (1958) *Cultural Foundations of Industrial Civilization* (Cambridge: Cambridge University Press)

Nutch, F. (1981) 'Emergence and Creativity', *Human Affairs*, vol. 1, pp. 14–27

Oliver, P. (1969) *The Story of the Blues* (London: Barrie and Jenkins)

Ong, W. J. (1967) *The Presence of the Word* (New Haven: Yale University Press)

——(1969) 'World as View and World as Event', *American Anthropologist*, vol. LXXI, pp. 634–47

Palisca, C. (1963) 'American Scholarship in Western Music', in Harrison, F. Ll., Hood, M. and Palisca, C., *Musicology* (Englewood Cliffs, N.J.: Prentice-Hall), pp. 89–213

Palmer, T. (1970) *Born under a Bad Sign* (London: William Kimber)

Papagiannis, G. J. et al. (1982) 'Toward a Political Economy of Educational Innovation', *Review of Educational Research*, vol. 52, no. 2, pp. 245–90

Pelinski, R. (1984) 'Perspectives méthodoliques pour l'analyse du tango', paper presented at the Annual Meeting of the Canadian Branch of the International

Association for the Study of Popular Music, Départment de musique, l'Université du Québec à Montréal

Pleasants, H. (1969) *Serious Music and All That Jazz* (London: Victor Gollancz)

Poulet, G. (1956) *Studies in Human Time* (tr. Coleman, E.) (Baltimore: Johns Hopkins University Press)

Pring, R. (1972) 'Knowledge out of Control', *Education for Teaching*, no. 89, pp. 19–28

Reese, G. (1940) *Music in the Middle Ages* (New York: W. W. Norton)

Reti, R. (1958) *Tonality, Atonality, Pantonality* (London: Rockcliff)

Riesman, D. (1970) 'The Oral and Written Traditions', in Carpenter and McLuhan (1970b), pp. 109–16

Rinehart, J. (1975) *The Tyranny of Work* (Toronto: Academic Press of Canada)

Routh, F. (1972) *Contemporary British Music* (London: Macdonald)

Schools Council (1971) *Music and the Young School-Leaver* (London: Schools Council Publications)

Schuller, G. (1968) *Early Jazz* (Oxford: Oxford University Press)

Shepherd, J. (1982) 'R. D. Laing and the Social Construction of Self: A Theoretical Speculation', *Human Affairs*, vol. 2, no. 1, pp. 1–17

——(1983) 'Conflict in Patterns of Socialization: The Role of the Classroom Music Teacher', *Canadian Review of Sociology and Anthropology*, vol. 20, no. 1, pp. 22–43

——(1984a) 'Music Education: A Sociological Perspective', in Runfola, M. (ed.), *Proceedings of the Research Symposium on the Male Adolescent Voice* (Buffalo: State University of New York), pp. 112–30

——(1984b) 'Music Education and the Male Adolescent', in Runfola, M. (ed.), *Proceedings of the Research Symposium on the Male Adolescent Voice* (Buffalo: State University of New York), pp. 131–54

——(1985) 'Definition as Mystification: A Consideration of Labels as a Hindrance to Understanding Significance in Music', *Popular Music Perspectives*, vol. 2 (Gothenburg, Exeter, Ottawa and Reggio Emilia: The International Association for the Study of Popular Music), pp. 84–98

——(1986) 'Music Consumption and Cultural Self-Identities: Some Theoretical and Methodological Reflections', *Media, Culture and Society*, vol. 8, no. 3, pp. 305–30

Shepherd, J. and Vulliamy, G. (1983) 'A Comparative Sociology of School Knowledge', *British Journal of Sociology of Education*, vol. 4, no. 1, pp. 3–18

Silbermann, A. (1963) *The Sociology of Music* (London: Routledge and Kegan Paul)

Spellman, A. B. (1970) *Black Music: Four Lives* (Oxford: Oxford University Press)

Spiess, L. B. (1957) 'Introduction to the Pre-History of Polyphony', in *Essays in Honour of Archibald Thompson Davison* (Cambridge: Cambridge University Press), pp. 11–15

Stearns, M. W. (1956) *The Story of Jazz* (Oxford: Oxford University Press)

Stevens, D. (1960) 'Ars Antiqua', in Robertson, A. and Stevens, D. (eds), *The Pelican History of Music*, vol. I (Harmondsworth: Penguin), pp. 211–58

Subotnik, R. (1982) 'Musicology and Criticism', in Holoman, D. K. and Palisca, C. (eds), *Musicology in the 1980s* (New York: Da Capo), pp. 145–60

Swanwick, K. (1979) *A Basis for Music Education* (Slough: NFER)

——(1984a) 'Problems of a Sociological Approach to Pop Music in Schools', *British Journal of Sociology of Education*, vol. 5, no. 1, pp. 49–56

——(1984b) 'A Further Note on Sociology of Music Education', *British Journal of Sociology of Education*, vol. 5, no. 3, pp. 303–7

Taylor, J. and Laing, D. (1979) 'Disco-Pleasure-Discourse: On "Rock and Sexuality"', *Screen Education*, no. 31, pp. 43–8

Thompson, E. P. (1967) 'Time, Work Discipline and Industrial Capitalism', *Past and Present*, no. 38, pp. 60–71

Virden, P. (1977) 'Some Observations on the Social Stratification of 20th Century Music', in Shepherd, J. et al., *Whose Music? A Sociology of Musical Languages* (London: Latimer New Dimensions), pp. 155–65

Vulliamy, G. (1972) 'Music Education in Secondary Schools: Some Sociological Observations', M.Sc. dissertation, University of London Institute of Education

——(1975) 'Music Education: Some Critical Comments', *Journal of Curriculum Studies*, vol. 7, pp. 18–25

——(1976a) 'What Counts as School Music?', in Whitty, G. and Young, M. F. D. (eds), *Explorations in the Politics of School Knowledge* (Driffield: Nafferton), pp. 19–34

——(1976b) 'Definitions of Serious Music', in Vulliamy, G. and Lee, E. (1976), pp. 33–48

——(1976c) 'Pupil-Centred Music Teaching', in Vulliamy and Lee (1976), pp. 49–61

——(1977a) 'Music and the Mass Culture Debate', in Shepherd, J. et al., *Whose Music? A Sociology of Musical Languages* (London: Latimer New Dimensions), pp. 179–200

——(1977b) 'Music as a Case Study in the New Sociology of Education', in Shepherd, J. et al., *Whose Music? A Sociology of Musical Languages* (London: Latimer New Dimensions), pp. 201–32

——(1978) 'Culture Clash and School Music: A Sociological Analysis', in Barton, L. and Meighan, R. (eds), *Sociological Interpretations of Schooling and Classrooms: A Reappraisal* (Driffield: Nafferton), pp. 115–27

——(1980) 'Music Education and Musical Languages', *Australian Journal of Music Education*, vol. 26, pp. 25–8

——(1984) 'A Sociological View of Music Education', *Canadian University Music Review*, no. 5, pp. 17–37

Vulliamy, G. and Lee, E. (1976) *Pop Music in School* (Cambridge: Cambridge University Press)

——(1982a) *Pop, Rock and Ethnic Music in School* (Cambridge: Cambridge University Press)

——(1982b) *Popular Music: A Teacher's Guide* (London: Routledge and Kegan Paul)

Vulliamy, G. and Shepherd, J. (1984a) 'Sociology and Music Education: A

Response to Swanwick', *British Journal of Sociology of Education*, vol. 5, no. 1, pp. 57–76

——(1984b) 'The Application of A Critical Sociology to Music Education', *British Journal of Music Education*, vol. 1, pp. 247–66

——(1985) 'Sociology and Music Education: A Further Response to Swanwick', *British Journal of Sociology of Education*, vol. 6, no. 2, pp. 225–9

Wallis, R. and Malm, K. (1984) *Big Sounds from Small Peoples* (New York: Pendragon)

Werner, E. (1948) 'The Origins of the Eight Modes of Music', *Hebrew College Annual*, vol. 21, pp. 211–55

Westrup, J. (1955) 'Medieval Song', in Hughes, A. (ed.), *The New Oxford History of Music*, vol. II (Oxford: Oxford University Press), pp. 220–69

Wexler, P. (1982) 'Structure, Text and Subject: A Critical Sociology of School Knowledge', in Apple (1982b), pp. 275–305

Whorf, B. L. (1971) *Language, Thought and Reality* (Boston: MIT Press)

Williams, R. (1961) *Culture and Society 1780–1950* (Harmondsworth: Penguin Books)

——(1965) *The Long Revolution* (Harmondsworth: Penguin Books)

——(1973) 'Base and Superstructure in Marxist Cultural Theory', *New Left Review*, no. 82, pp. 3–16

Willis, P. (1975) 'Symbolism and Practice: A Theory for the Social Meaning of Pop Music', *Occasional Paper* (Birmingham: Centre for Contemporary Cultural Studies)

——(1977) *Learning to Labour* (London: Saxon House)

——(1978) *Profane Culture* (London: Routledge and Kegan Paul)

Wishart, T. (1977a) 'Musical Speaking, Musical Writing', in Shepherd, J. et al., *Whose Music? A Sociology of Musical Languages* (London: Latimer New Dimensions), pp. 125–53

——(1977b) 'Some Observations on the Social Stratification of 20th Century Music: The Blues – An Ideal-Typical Example', in Shepherd, J. et al., *Whose Music? A Sociology of Musical Languages* (London: Latimer New Dimensions), pp. 166–77

Woods, P. and Hammersley, M. (1977) *School Experience* (London: Croom Helm)

Yasser, J. (1932) *A Theory of Evolving Tonality* (New York: American Library of Musicology)

——(1937) 'Medieval Quartal Harmony', *Musical Quarterly*, vol. XXIII, pp. 170–97, and vol. XXIV, pp. 351–85

Young, M. F. D. (1971) *Knowledge and Control: New Directions for the Sociology of Education* (London: Collier Macmillan)

Zuckerkandl, V. (1956) *Sound and Symbol: Music and the External World* (tr. Trask, W. R.) (London: Routledge and Kegan Paul)

Index

Index by Ann Barrett